T0263844

Budget Constraints and Optimization in Sponsored Search Auctions

Intelligent Systems Series

Editor-in-Chief

Fei-Yue Wang
Chinese Academy of Sciences
Contact information: feiyue@ieee.org

Editorial Board Members

Jim Hendler: Rensselaer Polytechnic Institute
William T Scherer: University of Virginia
Hsinchun Chen: University of Arizona
Kathleen Carley: Carnegie Mellon University
Ruwei Dai: Chinese Academy of Sciences
Youxian Sun: Zhejiang University
Chelsea (Chip) C White: Georgia Tech
Petros Ioannou: University of Southern California
Frank Lewis: University of Texas at Arlington
Bruno Sicilianos: Università degli Studi di Napoli Federico II
Wendy Hall: University of Southampton

Budget Constraints and Optimization in Sponsored Search Auctions

Yanwu Yang
Fei-Yue Wang

ZHEJIANG UNIVERSITY PRESS
浙江大学出版社

AMSTERDAM • BOSTON • HEIDELBERG • LONDON
NEW YORK • OXFORD • PARIS • SAN DIEGO
SAN FRANCISCO • SINGAPORE • SYDNEY • TOKYO
Academic Press is an imprint of Elsevier

Academic Press is an imprint of Elsevier
525 B Street, Suite 1800, San Diego, CA 92101-4495, USA
32 Jamestown Road, London NW1 7BY, UK
225 Wyman Street, Waltham, MA 02451, USA

Copyright © 2014 Zhejiang University Press Co. Ltd, Published by Elsevier Inc. All rights reserved.

No part of this publication may be reproduced, stored in a retrieval system, or transmitted in any form or by any means electronic, mechanical, photocopying, recording or otherwise without the prior written permission of the publisher.

Permissions may be sought directly from Elsevier's Science & Technology Rights, Department in Oxford, UK: phone (+44) (0) 1865 843830; fax (+44) (0) 1865 853333; email: permissions@elsevier.com. Alternatively, visit the Science and Technology Books website at www.elsevierdirect.com/rights for further information.

Notice
No responsibility is assumed by the publisher for any injury and/or damage to persons, or property as a matter of products liability, negligence or otherwise, or from any use or, operation of any methods, products, instructions or ideas contained in the material herein. Because of rapid advances in the medical sciences, in particular, independent verification of diagnoses and drug dosages should be made.

British Library Cataloguing-in-Publication Data
A catalogue record for this book is available from the British Library

Library of Congress Cataloging-in-Publication Data
A catalog record for this book is available from the Library of Congress

ISBN: 978-0-12-411457-9

For information on all Academic Press publications
visit our website at elsevierdirect.com

Working together
to grow libraries in
developing countries

www.elsevier.com • www.bookaid.org

Contents

Preface

Nowadays, more and more people use search engines as their main entrance to the Web and this offers fertile soil for sponsored search auctions to evolve into one of the most prominent online advertising channels. Search advertisements have also become the primary revenue source for search engines. The growing prosperity of search advertising markets is vastly driven by the influx of millions of advertisers. The search advertisers, especially those from small corporations, usually face budget constraints due to their financial conditions. On the one hand, budget constraints significantly influence advertisers' strategies in sponsored search auctions. On the other hand, one of the most difficult tasks for advertisers is how to effectively determine and allocate the optimum level of advertising budget, in order to survive in fierce competition and maximize profits.

The budget is an endogenous factor in sponsored search auctions that heavily influences other advertising strategies. There have been some research efforts regarding budget-related decisions in sponsored search auctions. Most either take the budget as the constraint for other advertising strategies, or allocate the budget to keywords. However, these works are not directly and operationally suitable for practical paradigms because they ignore the search advertising structure, game rules, and functionality provided by major search engines. As observed by some empirical studies, improving the profit by better allocation strategies is much more effective than improving the overall budget.

There are many challenges associated with budget decision-making in sponsored search auctions. First, the complex structure of search auction mechanisms (e.g. GSP) together with a high volume of search demands leads to continual dynamics in auction processes, which offers serious challenges to various decision-making activities in sponsored search auctions. Secondly, large uncertainties exist in the mapping from the search advertising budget to the expected profit. Thirdly, the budget is structured in the entire lifecycle of search advertising activities, rather than a simple constraint as in traditional economic phenomena. This makes budget decisions in sponsored search auctions a structured set of optimization problems. Thus, a great concern of advertisers in sponsored search auctions is not only to obtain local optimizations but a global optimal outcome with structured budget constraints.

Budget-related decisions in sponsored search auctions are recognized as an essentially structured decision problem, rather than a simple constraint. With consideration of the entire lifecycle of advertising campaigns in sponsored search auctions, budget decisions in sponsored search auctions occur at three levels: allocation across search markets, temporal distribution over a series of slots (e.g. day), and adjustment of the remaining budget (e.g. the daily budget). Therefore, we argue that it is of necessity to propose a novel framework for budget optimization in sponsored search auctions, taking into account the entire lifecycle of advertising campaigns. In this book we take the initiative to develop a hierarchical budget optimization framework (BOF) with consideration of the entire lifecycle of advertising campaigns in sponsored search auctions. The BOF framework could support a set of close-loop strategies across different levels of abstractions (e.g. system, campaign, and keyword), thus providing an environment/testbed for various budget strategies. Following the BOF framework and identified principles, we explore a spectrum of budget decisions at different levels of abstraction, and in different temporal granularities. Finally we shed some light on some interesting but challenging research prospects in budget-related issues in sponsored search auctions, and the joint optimization of advertising strategies.

We would like to thank our colleagues and graduate students in the ISEC research group (Internet Sciences and Economic Computing), and the State Key Laboratory of Management and Control for Complex Systems for their great assistance in the completion of this book. We also thank Prof. Yanqing Gao and Jiaying Xu for their support, and Ms. Juanjuan Li and Rui Qin for their hard work and great patience with the editing process. The publication of this book is partially supported by the National Natural Science Foundation of China (Nos. 71071152, 71272236, 60921061).

Yanwu Yang

Fei-Yue Wang

Chinese Academy of Sciences

Beijing, China

CHAPTER 1

Search Engine Meets Economics

1.1 The Web and Search Engines

1.1.1 The Web

The World Wide Web (WWW) is a repository of interlinked hypertext documents, and known as the information superhighway. With a Web browser, people can access various kinds of Web pages containing text, images, videos, and other multimedia, and navigate following hyperlinks. The advent of the Web has changed the way that people communicate with each other, perceive and interact with the environment. The information can be disseminated faster and faster around the globe. The goal at the initial stage is that a human user can seamlessly surf the existing World Wide Web and the emerging Web services, and easily compose and invoke Web services on the fly without being a software engineer (Agarwa, 2003). With the development of the Web, surfing the Web has been realized. A substantial amount of information has been provided which, to some degree, enables Web users to comprehensively and quickly grab accurate information and knowledge on the Web.

The Internet and the Web have been transforming our modern society, and search engines play an important role in this process (Lawrence and Giles, 1999). Web search behavior involves not only determination of terms, but also the construction of queries and selection of information entries using search engines (Eastman and Jansen, 2003). Also, how people search and interact with the Web and what they are searching for, "the why" of user search behavior, is actually essential to understand a user's information needs (Rose and Levinson, 2004). Most search engines design processes and algorithms to provide search results to satisfy users' information. The Web user's information needs can be classified into different states, namely informational, navigational, and transactional (Broder, 2002). Rose and Levinson (2004) described a framework for understanding the underlying goals of user search behavior, and found that navigational searches are less prevalent than generally believed, while a previously unexplored resource seeking goal may account for a large fraction of Web

Yang and Wang: Budget Constraints and Optimization in Sponsored Search Auctions. http://dx.doi.org/10.1016/B978-0-12-411457-9.00001-X
© 2014 Elsevier Inc. All rights reserved.

searches. This encompasses the requirement for novel ways of online searching, information retrieval and filtering, and user interfaces.

By taking users' interests and preferences into account, Web personalization explores the explicit and implicit needs of users to provide customized services to an individual (or group) Web user (Yang, 2005, 2007; Yang et al., 2010). Statistics collected by search engines and systems on the Web show that spatial information is pervasive on the Web, and that many queries contain implicit spatial factors. However, it is not straightforward to process location-aware (or location-driven) queries, especially when they are essentially context-aware (Boll et al., 2008). Yang et al. (2012a) introduced an integrated framework leveraging spatial knowledge and semantic considerations concerning the target places that users plan to visit. This framework can support user preference elicitation and a spectrum of personalized search strategies applied to spatial information retrieval on the Web (Yang, 2006).

1.1.2 Search Engines

Search engines are designed to help Web users search for useful and relevant information on the Web. Web users should be capable of distinguishing useful information. When a Web user queries a certain keyword, search engines will return organic search results through information retrieval and database techniques. The search results are presented as a list on the page referred to as search engine results pages (SERPs). The search results usually consist of Web pages, images, and other types of files. Some search engines can extract information and knowledge available in deep-Web databases and open directories. Unlike Web directories that are maintained mainly by human editors, search engines collect, store, process and maintain real-time information through various algorithms.

According to *Chitika*, major search engines (including Google, Yahoo, Bing, and Baidu) occupy 98.5% of the search engine market. In particular, Google takes first place in the search engine market, and its leading advantage will be kept in the future.

Search engines make information access more convenient, and more and more Web users take search engines as the main entrance to the Web. A recent Pew Internet study found that search engines are used by 92% of Internet users. "Search" has been the most important behavior of Internet users. According to *Forrester Research*, the number of global search users increases at a rate of 10% a year, which is higher than the 8% rise in the number of new Internet users. It also pointed out that whatever the language that search users use, they would like only to click on the first 10 results, and up to 99% of search users will not view more than 30 results.

The main purpose of search users is to quickly grab targeted information. Thus search engines have to estimate the user's requirements to provide the right results at the right moment accordingly. Users' behavioral trails can be exploited to analyze their requirements and then determine the targeted results. Google claimed that it will improve its search function to make it more intelligent. This is expected to help understand search users better, and to provide more direct answers, in order to improve efficiency and effectiveness.

The usefulness of a search engine depends on the relevance of the results returned to search users. There are plenty of Web pages that include a particular word or phrase; among them some pages are more relevant, popular, and authoritative than others. How a search engine determines which pages are the better matches, and by which order these results should be presented, varies widely in different search engines.

When search engines start to use hyperlink analysis, Web-positioning companies manipulate hyperlinks to boost the ranking of their clients' pages. This hinders the ability of search engines to return high-quality results to search users. In order to alleviate this problem, major search engines have put considerable effort into developing more sophisticated techniques that are kept as business secrets (Henzinger, 2001). Moreover, ranking algorithms are changed and optimized with endless effort over time.

Besides these generic search engines, specialized search engines are useful for Web users with special needs, such as commercial business, music and video. Also, mobile search has been developed to enable search users to look for information through mobile devices anywhere, anytime. With the development of social networks, the social search engine emerges as a new type of search engine. Horowitz and Kamvar (2010) declared that in traditional search engines people use keywords to search and the knowledge base is created by a small number of content publishers before the questions are asked; thus the trust is based on the authority, while in a social search engine people use natural languages to ask questions, answers can be generated in real-time by anyone in the community, and then the trust is based on intimacy.

1.2 Internet and Search Economics, Search Engine Marketing

1.2.1 Internet and Search Economics

The Internet has greatly changed the way that people perceive and interact with society, as with the economy. The Internet can never be separated from the economy, and its evolution goes along with economic innovations. Firstly, the Internet and related technologies have made the costs of many kinds of market interactions plummet (Borenstein and Saloner, 2001). Secondly, the Internet has facilitated the creation of new markets characterized by improved measurement, increased customization, rapid innovation, and more conscious market design (Levin, 2011). In summary, the Internet not only encourages the development of traditional businesses, but also shapes a new type of economy, which is termed the "Internet economy."

The Internet economy manages business through markets on the Internet or the Web. The Internet economy differs from the traditional economy in several aspects, including communication, market segmentation (Jansen et al., 2011), distribution, cost, and price. Electronic commerce is a typical Internet economic form, which refers to the buying and selling of products or services through electronic systems such as the Internet and other computer networks. Electronic commerce combines traditional business with the Internet to create more value while consuming less resources, since the Internet, e.g. social networks, enables e-commerce to participate actively in online word-of-mouth communication (Zhang et al., 2011; Jansen et al., 2009).

Internet economics can be considered as the study of the markets for various Internet services (McKnight and Bailey, 1997). With some advanced information and communication technologies to make the Internet work, economic and policy issues must be addressed to sustain growth and to expand the scope of the Internet. This has led to the emergence of the field of Internet economics as a subject of both academic and industry research.

Some principles of Internet economics have been developed by collaborative efforts among economists, engineers, and those from other fields. McKnight and Bailey (1997) believed that there are at least five areas where new solutions to Internet economic problems might be explored.

1. New empirical work, especially with respect to user behavior (Xu et al., 2010).
2. Congestion control protocols and user feedbacks in concert with one another.
3. Pricing as a congestion control method (or as part of an interconnection settlements process) in concert with enhancements to the TCP/IP protocol suite.
4. Increased data collection across Internet service providers to provide an understanding about the growth of the Internet and a rich dataset to develop economic models and increase the understanding of the subtle interaction between Internet engineering, economics, and cultural practices.
5. Further research on the development of technologies and policies for information security for electronic commerce and privacy protection.

Most current research on Internet economics tends to analyze usage-sensitive pricing models in online services. MacKie-Mason and Varian (1995, 1993) thought that usage-sensitive pricing was the most promising mechanism for accomplishing prioritization and socially efficient congestion control. They also described a possible smart-market mechanism for pricing congestion on the Internet.

With the prosperity of search engines, the search economy, as a special Internet economy, has attracted a lot of attention, both from academic and industrial fields. The search economy is mainly referred to as various economic activities associated with search engine marketing. It implies that the search economy is a relevant activity whereby search engines help websites to improve awareness and then product and service exchanges. Search economics studies the implications of frictions in individual behavior and market performance, due to imperfect information about exchange possibilities. The key implication of these frictions is that individuals are prepared to spend time and other resources to exchange information, and they search before buying or selling (Pissarides, 2001). A large number of search users provide a good platform for the enterprises to promote their products or services. It is termed search engine marketing (SEM).

1.2.2 Search Engine Marketing

Search engine marketing can be defined as a form of Internet marketing that involves the promotion of websites, products, and services, by increasing their visibility on search engine result pages (SERPs) through optimization (both on-page and off-page) and advertising (paid placements, contextual advertising, and paid inclusions). In other words, search engine marketing includes two main forms, namely search engine optimization (SEO) and sponsored search auctions (SSA).

Search engine optimization is the process of improving the visibility of a website in the list of search engines' organic or unpaid search results. As a search engine marketing strategy, search engine optimization concerns how search engines embody, rank, and classify websites, how people search, and what keyword can attract more targeted users. Search engine optimization experts organize a given website and arrange relevant keywords according to their understanding of ranking mechanisms (Li et al., 2012) of search engines under consideration. Search engine optimization helps websites rank better and thus get more traffic with low costs. However, it cannot exert the function in a short time. In this sense, search engine optimization is not an appropriate strategy for every website, depending on the website operator's goals. Most online sellers, however, do not invest in search engine optimization to get higher search-results rankings for their listings. Instead they prefer paid placements (Sen, 2005). This is termed sponsored search auctions.

In paid placements, sellers can pay the search engine for placement of their advertisement in the sponsored section of the search-results pages. This is a quick way to obtain visibility. Nonetheless, it takes up to 120 days to become visible, after a search engine optimization campaign (Hansell, 2001). The typical paid placement is a sponsored search auction which can improve the popularity of websites very quickly. In sponsored search auctions, the owner of a website should pay the search engine to gain the chance to show itself in paid listings, which are in different areas from organic listings on the search engine's results pages. However, some search engine users do not readily distinguish between these two.

1.3 A First Glimpse of Sponsored Search Auctions

Sponsored search auctions (SSA), also known as keyword auctions, are an indispensable part of the business model for modern Web hosts (Morpheus, 2012). Sponsored search auctions have been acknowledged as one of the most effective marketing vehicles available on the Web

(Jansen and Mullen, 2008), and the leading online category of display-related advertising (*IAB and PwC US*). In 2011, the market scale of sponsored search auctions in China reached 18.78 billion, accounting for 36.7%.

Compared with traditional advertisements, sponsored search auctions have some advantages. First, in sponsored search auctions, an advertiser bids for some keywords, and his/her advertisements will be displayed on the search engine result pages. Only if the advertisements are clicked by search users, will he/she be charged a certain amount of the budget according to the generalized second price auction mechanism or its derivations (Varian, 2007). Secondly, when the advertisements are clicked by search users, this might attract a potential customer or instant sales. In this sense, sponsored search auctions can exert an advertising effort more swiftly. Thirdly, sponsored search auctions, as a targeting advertising form, allow advertisers to target the appropriate users and manage advertising risks.

Advertisers choose some keywords relevant to their advertisements, then determine bids for these keywords for the chance to display their advertisements on search engine result pages. Most search engines now provide only 8–10 slots in the sponsored list. Consequently, many advertisers have to compete for opportunities to display their advertisements in a scheduling horizon (Amiri and Menon, 2006). Currently, search engines apply the generalized second price (GSP) auction mechanism to sell their advertising slots. Once a search user submits a query, a search auction process is triggered. Search engines retrieve advertisements relevant to the query, and rank them according to bids on the keyword and advertiser's quality score. According to Google Adwords, the quality score takes into account a variety of factors to measure the relevance among advertisers' keywords, ad copies, and users' search queries. A higher quality score for an advertiser will lead to the advertiser gaining from a lower cost and a better position. A good position can attract more attention and clicks from search users. When a search engine user clicks the advertisement on the search engine result pages, the advertiser needs to pay for it. However, not all clicks are valid, only those that are intentional and have a realistic probability of generating value once the visitor arrives at the website can be judged as valid clicks (Jansen, 2008). Nowadays, how to protect advertisers from damage from invalid clicks (especially click fraud and malicious clicks) is a big challenge, both for search engines and advertisers (Li et al., 2011).

1.4 Understanding the Budget in Sponsored Search Auctions

In finance, the budget is defined as a financial plan or a list of all planned expenses and revenues. It is a plan for saving, borrowing, and spending (Sullivan and Sheffrin, 2003). The budget is an important concept in microeconomics, which uses a budget line to illustrate the trade-offs between two or more goods. The term "budget constraint" is taken from the micro-theory of the household. In agreement with Clower (1965), budget constraint is a rational planning postulate. Two important properties of budget constraints must be underlined. First, the budget constraint refers to a behavioral characteristic of the decision maker: he is used to covering his expenses from income generated by selling his output and/or by earning return on his assets. Secondly, the budget constraint is a constraint on ex-ante variables and first of all on demands. It is based on expectations concerning his future financial situation when the actual expenditure will occur (Kornai, 1986). When there is budget constraint, budget planning and management is necessary in economic activities for the purpose of gaining maximum revenues.

The economic activities in search engine marketing are inevitably related to the budget, especially in the sponsored search auctions. Most search advertisers come from small and medium enterprises, and thus face serious budget constraints. In sponsored search auctions, the budget is referred to as the resource with which advertisers compete for advertising slots. If an advertiser has a bigger budget, he/she can bid higher for keywords to win more chances to display his/her advertisements. If the advertiser has less budget, he/she may bid lower or use up the budget too quickly, which will lead to the loss of some effective clicks. However, good budget decisions can bring in more revenues for the advertiser than by simply increasing the total budget. Thus, advertisers should carefully make their budget decisions, especially in the case of serious budget constraints.

In sponsored search auctions, most advertisers face hard budget constraints (Chakrabarty et al., 2007), which implies that they cannot borrow money to reach the optimal total budget. In practice, small and medium size enterprises always have difficulties in raising funds, for the reason that fund providers doubt their ability to pay the debt and there is no complete and feasible policy to support them to overcome the problem. If advertisers can break through the hard budget constraints and get funds from the bank or other financial institutions, it will be much easier for them to make budget decisions and gain more revenues. Soft budget constraints empower advertisers to borrow money moderately to satisfy the current financial requirements of search advertisements and pay back in the future with the achieved revenues. Hard budget constraints also affect the auction properties. For example, the VCG mechanism is not realistic when there are tough budgets (Borgs et al., 2005). However, in many cases, the budget constraints do not appear to be tough as bidders frequently adjust them. A bidder can also "expand" their budget simply by lowering their bid and paying less per click (Lahaie et al., 2007).

The budget is an endogenous factor in sponsored search auctions, which heavily influences other advertising strategies. Moreover, budget-related decisions in sponsored search auctions are recognized as a structured decision problem, rather than a simple constraint (Yang et al., 2012a, 2013). A budget decision is coupled with other strategies, such as bidding strategies, keyword strategies, and so on. What search auction system the advertiser chooses, how to choose keywords, and how much he/she should bid for each keyword is all done based on the budget decisions, and adversely the keyword strategy (Yang, 2012) and bidding strategy also create a great influence on budget decisions. That is, advertisers need to do joint optimization of all these strategies to gain optimal performance. Good budgeting strategies will influence other advertising strategies positively and, inversely, those strategies will create favorable feedback to budget strategies.

A budgetary decision is not a simple decision for advertisers in sponsored search auctions. First, budget decisions are related to a lot of factors and processes, including auction mechanism, rank algorithm, environment parameters (queries, clicks, and bid), campaign performance, and competitions. It makes the budget decisions too complicated and beyond the advertiser's ability. Secondly, with consideration of the entire lifecycle of search advertising, budget-related decisions exist on three levels (Yang et al., 2012a): allocation across search markets, temporal distribution over a series of promotional slots (e.g. days), and adjustment of the remaining budget (e.g. the daily budget). In this sense, budget optimization in sponsored search auctions is essentially a structured decision problem. Consequently, it demands a systematic approach and framework supporting a spectrum of budget decisions at different levels of abstraction, and in different temporal granularities.

1.5 How this Book is Organized

This book is organized in five parts. Part I starts with a state-of-the-art survey on budget constraints and optimization in the context from auctions to sponsored search auctions, and then discusses budget decision problems. It finally presents an integrated framework for budget optimization (BOF) in sponsored search auctions. Part II explores budget decision problems at the system level of our BOF framework, from two orthographic views: budget allocation across search markets, and budget competition among advertisers. Part III discusses budget decision problems at the campaign level of our BOF framework, taking into account uncertainties in search marketing environments and coupled relationships between campaigns in sponsored search auctions. Part IV deals with budget adjustment problems at the keyword level of our BOF framework, and Part V provides some valuable insights into budget decisions in sponsored search auctions.

1.5.1 Part I

This part includes three chapters. Chapter 2 explores budget constraints and optimizations, and presents a literature review of budget-constrained mechanisms and bidding strategies in sponsored search auctions. Chapter 3 discusses budget decisions during the entire life-cycle of advertising campaigns in sponsored search auctions. Chapter 4 presents the budget optimization framework (BOF) for search advertisements to manipulate budgeting problems during the entire lifecycle of advertising campaigns. The BOF framework consists of three levels, corresponding to these three budget decision scenarios: the system level, the campaign level, and the keyword level. Then, we make a mathematical analysis of desirable properties, a simple but illustrative framework instantiation and an effective solution algorithm.

1.5.2 Part II

This part includes four chapters. Chapter 5 studies the first step in allocating the budget across search advertising markets, which is defined as a knapsack problem. Two budget allocation models are developed for two different application scenarios: budget initialization prior to the SSA promotion and budget adjustment during the SSA promotion. In order to capture marketing dynamics, Chapter 6 formulates the budget allocation problem across several search markets as an optimal control process under a finite time horizon. A novel optimal budget allocation model is established with consideration of distinctive features of advertising campaigns in sponsored search auctions. Chapters 7 and 8 employ the game theory approach to study the budget allocation in competitive search advertising environments. Chapter 7 studies the static version of the budget competition problem with game-theory approaches. Chapter 8 explores the dynamic version of the budget competition problem, and proposes a novel budget model based on a differential game, by extending the advertising response function with dynamic advertising effort u and quality score q to fit search advertising scenarios.

1.5.3 Part III

This part includes four chapters. Chapter 9 presents some preliminary efforts to deal with uncertainties in search marketing environments, following principles of a hierarchical budget optimization framework (BOF). It proposes a stochastic, risk-constrained budget strategy, considering a random factor of clicks per unit cost to capture a kind of uncertainty at the campaign level. Uncertainties of random factors at the campaign level lead to risk at the market/system level. Chapter 10 studies sequential distribution of the budget in search advertisements, and proposes a stochastic model for budget distribution, by considering the optimal budget for temporal slots as a random variable. Chapter 11 proposes a two-stage fuzzy budget allocation model for the budget allocation over a series of sequential temporal slots, considering the optimal budgets as fuzzy variables. Chapter 12 explores the budget planning problem for coupled campaigns in sponsored search auctions. A multi-campaign budget planning approach is proposed using optimal control techniques, with consideration of the substitute relationship between advertising campaigns.

1.5.4 Part IV

This part includes two chapters. Chapters 13 and 14 explore dynamic budget adjustment problems in sponsored search auctions. In Chapter 13, we probe the budget adjustment problem according to the change in the effective click-through rate. Chapter 14 formulates the budget adjustment problem as a state-action decision process in the reinforcement learning (RL) framework. Considering dynamics of marketing environments and some distinctive features of sponsored search auctions, continuous reinforcement learning is extended to fit the budget decision scenarios. The market utility is defined as discounted total clicks to obtain during the remaining period of an advertising schedule.

1.5.5 Part V

This part includes one chapter. Chapter 15 analyzes some interesting and challenging budget-related research prospectives, and provides insights into joint optimization of advertising strategies in sponsored search auctions.

References

Agarwal, S., S. Handschuh, S. Staab. 2003. Surfing the service web, ISWC, LNCS 2870, Springer-Verlag, Berlin Heidelberg, 211–226.

Amiri A., S. Menon. 2006. Scheduling web banner advertisements with multiple display frequencies, IEEE Transactions on Systems Man and Cybernetics-Part A, 36(2):245–251.

Boll, S., C. Jones, E. Kansa, P. Kishor, M. Naaman, R. Purves, A. Scharl, E. Wilde. 2008. Location and the web, WWW 2008, 1261–1262.

Borenstein, S., G. Saloner. 2001. Economics and electronic commerce, The Journal of Economic Perspectives, 15(1):3–12.

Borgs, C., J. Chayes, N. Immorlica, M. Mahdian, A. Saberi. 2005. Multi-unit auctions with budget-constrained bidders, In Proceedings of the 6th ACM conference on Electronic commerce (EC '05). ACM, New York, NY, USA, 44–51.

Broder, A. 2002. A Taxonomy of Web search, SIGIR Forum, 36(2):3–10.

Chakrabarty D., Y. Zhou, R. Lukose. 2007. Budget constrained bidding in keyword auctions and online knapsack problems, In Proceedings of the 16th International World Wide Web Conference.

Clower, R. W. 1965. The Keynesian counter-revolution: a theoretical appraisal, The Theory of Interest Rates. London: Macmillan.

Eastman, C., B. Jansen. 2003. Coverage, relevance, and ranking: the impact of query operators on web search engine results, ACM Transactions on Information Systems, 21(4):383–411.

Hansell, S. 2001. Paid placement is catching on in Web searches. New York Times, June 4, 2001.

Henzinger, M. R. 2001. Hyperlink analysis for the web, IEEE Internet Computing, 5(1):45–50.

Horowitz, D., S. D. Kamvar. 2010. The anatomy of a large-scale social search engine, WWW 2010, April 26–30, 2010, Raleigh, North Carolina, USA.

Jansen, B. J., T. Mullen. 2008. Sponsored search: an overview of the concept, history, and technology, International Journal of Electronic Business, 6(2):114–131.

Jansen, B. J. 2008. Click fraud, IEEE Computer, 40(7):85–86.

Jansen, B. J., M. Zhang, K. Sobel, A. Chowdhury. 2009. Twitter power: tweets as electronic word of mouth, Journal of the American Society for Information Sciences and Technology, 60(11):2169–2188.

Jansen, B. J., K. Sobel, G. Cook. 2011. Classifying ecommerce information sharing behavior by youths on social networking sites, Journal of Information Science, 37(2):120–136.

Kornai, J. 1986. The soft budget constraint, KYKLOS, 39(1):3–30.

Lahaie, S., D. Pennock, A. Saberi, R. Vohra. 2007. Sponsored search auctions. In Nisan, Roughgarden, Tardos, Vazirani, editors, Algorithmic Game Theory. Cambridge, UK:Cambridge University Press.

Lawrence, S., C. L. Giles. 1999. Accessibility of information on the Web, Nature, 400:107–109.

Levin, J. 2011. The economics of Internet markets, Discussion paper, National Bureau of Economic Research.

Li, X., D. Zeng, Y. Liu, Y. Yang. 2011. Click fraud and the adverse effects of competition, IEEE Intelligent Systems, 26(6):31–39.

Li, K., E. C. Idemudia, Z. Lin, Y. Yu. 2012. A framework for intermediated online targeted advertising with banner ranking mechanism, Information Systems and E-Business Management, 10(2):183–200.

MacKie-Mason, J. K., H. R. Varian. 1995. Some economics of the internet, In Werner Sichel, editor, Networks, Infrastructure and the New Task for Regulation. University of Michigan Press.

MacKie-Mason, J. K., H. R. Varian. 1993. Pricing the internet, In the Conference of Public Access to the Internet, May 26–27, 1993.

McKnight, L. W., J. P. Bailey. 1997. An introduction to Internet economics, Internet Economics. Cambridge, MA: MIT Press.

Morpheus, I. K. 2012. Sponsored search auction, Utilpublishing.

Pissarides, C. A. 2001. The economics of search. In: Encyclopedia of the Social and Behavioral Sciences. Amsterdam: Elsevier, pp. 13760–13768.

Rose, D. E., D. Levinson. 2004. Understanding user goals in web search, WWW 2004, 13–19, May 17–22, New York, USA.

Sen, R. 2005. Optimal search engine marketing strategy, International Journal of Electronic Commerce, 10(1):9–25.

Sullivan, A., S. M. Sheffrin. 2003. Economics: principles in action. Upper Saddle River, New Jersey 07458:Pearson Prentice Hall.

Varian, H. 2007. Position auctions, International Journal of Industrial Organization, 25(6):1163–1178.

Xu, B., Z. Lin, B. Shao. 2010. Factors affecting consumer behaviors in online buy-it-now auctions, Internet Research, 20(5):509–526.

Yang, Y., C. Claramunt. 2005. A hybrid approach for spatial web personalisation, Springer, Lecture Notes in Computer Science 3833, December, 206–221.

Yang, Y. 2006, Towards Spatial Web Personalization, PhD Thesis.

Yang, Y., M. Aufaure, C. Claramunt. 2007. Towards a DL-based semantic user model for web personalization, In Proceedings of the Third international Conference on Autonomic and Autonomous Systems (June 19–25, 2007). ICAS. IEEE Computer Society, Washington, DC.

Yang, Y., C. Claramunt, M.-A. Aufaure. 2010. User-centric similarity and proximity measures for spatial personalization, International Journal of Data Warehousing and Mining, 6(2):59–78.

Yang, Y. 2012. Personalized search strategy for spatial information on the Web, IEEE Intelligent Systems, 27(1):12–20.

Yang, Y., J. Zhang, R. Qin, J. Li, F. Wang, Q. Wei. 2012a. A budget optimization framework for search advertisements across markets, IEEE Transactions on Systems, Man, and Cybernetics, Part A, 42(5):1141–1151.

Yang, Y., J. Zhang, R. Qin, J. Li. 2012b. Keyword research: a practical framework for optimization in search auctions, Working Paper.

Yang, Y., J. Zhang, R. Qin, J. Li, B. Liu, Z. Liu. 2013. Budget strategies in uncertain environments of search auctions: a preliminary investigation, IEEE Transactions on Services Computing, 6(2):168–176.

Zhang, M., B. J. Jansen, A. Chowdhury. 2011. Business engagement on twitter: a path analysis, Electronic Markets: The International Journal on Networked Business, 21(3):161–175.

CHAPTER 2

Budget Constraints in Sponsored Search Auctions

2.1 Introduction

The budget is an essential concept in microeconomics, where a budget line is used to illustrate the trade-off between two or more goods. When referring to budget constraints in microeconomics, it usually applies to hard budget constraints which strictly confine the decision space (e.g. procurement) of the business. A hard budget constraint means that even if the organization tries to cut its losses, the environment will not tolerate a protracted deficit (Kornai, 1986). Since the soft budget constraint was introduced by Kornai (1979, 1986), typically it has been applied to transition economics. The theory of soft budget constraint can be used to explain the reform of state-owned enterprises, financial crises, corporate governance, and so on. Literally, "soft" in the context of the budget means that while encountering the financial difficulty, an organization can gain financial help from outside strengths such as soft credit, soft subsidies, soft taxation, and soft administrative prices.

The budget can be considered as an organizational plan stated in monetary terms with two purposes (Sullivan and Sheffrin, 2002). On the one hand, it provides the prediction of revenues and expenditures, namely how the business might perform financially under the necessary condition pertaining to certain situations, events, and strategies. On the other hand, it enables the actual financial operation and outcome, measured against the prediction. From the budget point of view, the limited resource capacity significantly influences perceptions of the environment and thus the marketing performance of small businesses, because marketing exercises and expenses tend to have less priority over other elements (Fam and Yang, 2006). For small businesses, budget constraints and lack of time and expertise may lead to limited and often ad hoc or irrational promotional decisions.

The theory of auctions and mechanisms has been successfully employed to tackle a wide variety of economic issues, as a powerful means to distribute goods and services, especially in the privatization of state-owned property, since the pioneer research work of Vickrey (1961).

Yang and Wang: Budget Constraints and Optimization in Sponsored Search Auctions. http://dx.doi.org/10.1016/B978-0-12-411457-9.00002-1
© 2014 Elsevier Inc. All rights reserved.

In practice, budget constraints are a crucial feature of various kinds of auctions. The budget in auctions is of great significance to both auctioneers and bidders, in that it directly defines the bidders' feasible strategy set (Kotowski, 2010), then affects the equilibrium and revenues attained by auctioneers (Pitchik and Schotter, 1988; Kotowski, 2010; Laan and Yang, 2008).

When economics and auctions come together in a search (Jansen and Spink, 2007), sponsored search auctions have emerged and have proved to be a successful way to assign sponsored slots on the search engine result pages (SERPs) to display advertisements. Nowadays, it has already become the dominating revenue resource of major search engine companies such as Google and Yahoo!. For example, Google reported total revenue of 37.9 billion dollars in 2011, with the revenue from sponsored search auctions comprising about 96.

In sponsored search auctions, search engines provide a limited number of advertising slots for advertisers to display their advertisements along with organic search results on SERPs. Advertisers participate in keyword auctions through selecting a set of keywords that are relevant to their products or services, and entering a bid for each keyword. When a search user submits a query, an auction happens among advertisers who bid on those keywords matching the query. Advertisers will pay only when their advertisements are clicked by search users. The budget of an advertiser is also not infinite in sponsored search auctions. An advertiser can no longer be involved in the auction process if his/her budget is used up before the end of the advertising schedule. Thus the advertisement cannot show up either (Ghose and Yang, 2009).

Similarly, budget constraints significantly influence both auctioneers' revenues and advertisers' strategies in sponsored search auctions. Specifically, on the one hand, the limited budget forces advertisers to seek for more effective strategies to allocate and adjust their budget, to select keywords, to determine bids, and to cautiously predict the advertising performance, in order to maximize the total revenues (e.g. clicks and return on investment, etc.). Also, the distortion of budget constraints can affect advertisers even if the constraint does not bind the advertiser (Thomas, 2002); on the other hand, budget constraints add difficulties in designing a rational, stable searching auction mechanism. Moreover, the mutual effects in the game between search auctioneers and advertisers make the situation complex. In other words, budget-constrained auction mechanisms make it more complicated for advertisers to find optimal advertising strategies and, inversely, budget-constrained strategies place more burdens on the auction procedure, which are sharpened by the fact that online auctions require real-time, efficient reactions while facing a high volume of search demands.

Although plenty of research efforts were invested in studying budget constraints and optimal strategies for budget allocation and adjustment in modern economics and auctions, there is still a shortage of exploration of sponsored search auctions. With the rapid development of sponsored search auctions, budget constraints and optimal strategies are of great significance to instruct advertising operations. Encouragingly, we have witnessed a small research surge of budget-constrained sponsored search auctions in recent years, as noticed in this chapter.

A reasonable reason for this phenomenon might be the beginning of the realization of the advertising budget's role in sponsored search auctions. To the best of our knowledge, this chapter makes the first attempt at a systematic survey on budget constraints and optimal strategies with the focus on sponsored search auctions.

Sponsored search auctions can be characterized in terms of four basic elements, namely auction mechanism, bid, keyword, and budget, correspondingly leading to four interwoven advertising processes including auction mechanisms, bidding strategies, keywords strategies, budget allocation, and adjustment (Yang et al., 2012). This chapter starts with the state-of-art of the first three elements with budget constraints, covering budget-constrained auctions and sponsored search auctions. This chapter opens a wide scope of interesting and challenging issues on budget constraints and optimization strategies in sponsored search auctions.

The objective of this chapter is to give a systematic view of budget constraints and optimization in sponsored search auctions, and hopefully to arouse peer attention and then lead to more fruitful and thorough study in this area. Note that we also go through some literature on budget-constrained auctions, in order to give a more solid context for sponsored search auctions, due to the sparsity of study on the latter topic. This survey covers more than 80 papers concerning budget constraints and optimal strategies. We do not intend to make a complete survey of budget-constrained auctions, but discuss and elicit the role of the budget in the context of search advertisements. The contributions to this chapter make a systematic survey of budget constraints and optimization in sponsored search auctions.

The rest of this chapter is organized as follows. Section 2.2 reviews existing studies related to budget constraints covering auctions to sponsored search auctions, in terms of auction mechanisms in Section 2.2.2 and bidding strategies in Section 2.2.3. A summary of budget-constrained sponsored search auctions is given in Section 2.3.

2.2 Budget-Constrained Sponsored Search Auctions

2.2.1 Budget-Centered Views

In traditional works on auction mechanisms and bidding strategies, researchers usually neglected conditions such as constraints on the budget, so one can bid aggressively as long as there is a positive space for the marginal profit. A sufficient budget guarantees a large strategy space and possible opportunities available for advertisers in sponsored search auctions. However, obviously such assumptions about an infinite supply of resources contradict reality! Also, more than the optimal budget might lead to lower advertising performance such as revenue for investment (ROI). Therefore, it's practical and necessary to understand the effect of budget constraints in sponsored search auctions.

Search engine and advertiser are the two primary players in the game of sponsored search auctions, so-called auctioneer and bidder, respectively. Correspondingly, there are two major components in the entire bio-system of sponsored search auctions, namely the auction mechanism and the advertising strategy (Figure 2.1). Currently, sponsored search auctions are carried out on the basis of the advertisers bidding for keywords and are driven by the generalized second price auction mechanism (Krishna, 2002; Maille et al., 2010). Budget constraints represent advertisers' bidding abilities and decision space, which directly influence their choices of advertising strategies, including bidding strategy, keywords strategy, budget allocation and adjustment. The advertising budget allows neither too many keywords with high competition, nor bidding too high to get good positions. Then advertisers have to judge and cautiously make a balance between decision issues like the selection of keywords and the determination of bids. With millions of available keywords and a highly uncertain click-through rate associated with each keyword, identifying the most profitable set of keywords under the budget constraint becomes a challenging issue (Rusmevichientong and Williamson, 2006). From the view of search engines, it's necessary to design more effective

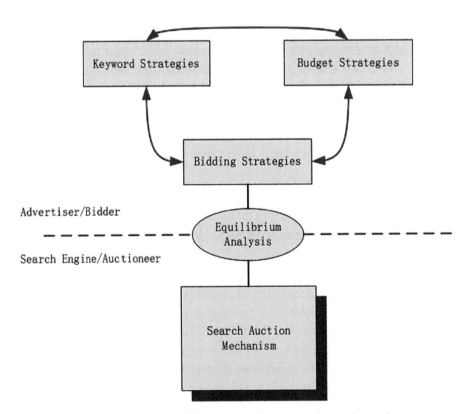

Figure 2.1   The entire bio-system of sponsored search auctions.

auction mechanisms which can encourage the advertisers to truthfully report their bids, and in the meantime to ensure optimal equilibrium outcomes.

2.2.2 Budget-Constrained Mechanisms

The budget is an endogenous factor in auctions (Benoit and Krishna, 2001). The budget constraints can be expressed in two forms, hard budget constraints and soft budget constraints. In the case of hard budget constraints in auctions (Borgs et al., 2005; Abrams, 2006; Hafalir et al., 2009; Kotowski, 2010), a bidder is strictly constrained by his/her ability to pay for items, beyond the willingness to pay (Kempe et al., 2009). That is, facing hard budget constraints, the bidders cannot spend more than the budget ceilings. However, in the case where the bidder has access to credit (Che and Gale, 1995), so-called soft budget constraints (Maskin, 2000), he/she can pay a bit more than the constrained budget. In other words, under soft or flexible budget constraints, the bidders can exceed the limited budget by some amount in certain circumstances, such as when bank credit is available.

Budget constraints don't affect a bidder's valuation of items, but directly constrain the ability to bid (Pái and Vohra, 2009), depressing bids as bidders hit spending limits and encouraging more aggressive bidding by bidders with bigger budgets (Kotowski, 2010), which definitely affect the optimal mechanism design and identified equilibrium properties. The normal situation, such as constraints on the budget, adds significant difficulties for existing techniques to analyze games in various auctions.

In this section we discuss budget constraints and impacts from auctions to sponsored search auctions.

2.2.2.1 Budget-Constrained Auction Mechanisms

Many researchers have studied optimal auctions with budget constraints in the setting where the valuation and budget are private to bidders (Laan and Yang, 2008; Bhattacharya et al., 2010; Abrams, 2006; Fang and Parreiras, 2002). The principal problem in a budget-constrained auction is how to design a reliable mechanism (Mehrabin, 2009; Pái and Vohra, 2009) to ensure the revenue of auctioneers.

Budget constraints make bidders either unwilling or incapable of paying up to the valuation of objects, thus affecting the bidding price and, indirectly, the revenues yielded to auctioneers. Moreover, budget-constrained equilibrium outcomes may also be neither efficient or social surplus optimal, since bidders cannot reach the optimal bidding strategies (Kempe et al., 2009). The possibility of a binding budget constraint changes the optimal sales mechanism qualitatively. Therefore, an optimal auction mechanism with budget constraints is more difficult to design on behalf of auctioneers. There is no truthful, incentive compatible, and

Pareto-optimal mechanism if the budget constraints are private, as justified by Dobzinski et al. (2012). In the setting where both the ability-to-pay (budget) and willingness-to-pay (valuation) are private, Che and Gale (1996, 2000) proved that all-pay auctions generate higher expected revenue than first-price sealed-bid auctions when buyers face budget constraints, and characterized an optimal selling mechanism involving non-trivial price discriminations. Inspired by Goldberg et al.'s (2001, 2003) works, Borgs et al. (2005) studied a multi-unit auction with multiple budget-constrained agents with private valuation and budget, and proved that it is impossible to design a non-trivial truthful auction allocating all items. Bhattacharya et al. (2010) designed an incentive-compatible, multi-unit auction and, a step further, Hafalir et al. (2009) presented a Pareto-optimal and semi-truthful mechanism for multi-unit auctions. Hafalir et al. (2012) introduced a mechanism in the spirit of the Vickrey auction to allocate a divisible good to a set of bidders with budget constraints, and showed that ex-post Nash equilibrium of the mechanism is near the Pareto-optimal in the sense that all full winners' values are above all full losers' values.

With a bit of relaxation of the conditions, the budget is public and the valuation is private. Dobzinski et al. (2012) proposed an adaptive clinching auction which proved to be incentive-compatible and Pareto-optimal. Focusing on a special setting where there are two bidders, the valuation is private, and one of the two bidders' budgets is public. Malakhov and Vohra (2008) derived an incentive-compatible auction with the revenue maximizing a subsidy free dominant strategy. Laffont and Robert (1996) characterized the optimal auction when bidders have financial constraints that are common knowledge. The optimal auction can be implemented by an all-pay auction with the proper reserve price: the highest bidder wins and all participants forfeit their bids. Bhattacharya et al. (2009) presented the first approximation algorithm for the problem of designing revenue optimal Bayesian incentive-compatible auctions when there are multiple (heterogeneous) items and bidders have arbitrary demand and publicly known budget constraints (and additive valuations).

Besides constraining a bidder's actions, budget constraints focus on the economic trade-offs in bidding decisions (Kotowski, 2010). In other words, limited budgets constrained the optimal allocation (Dobzinski et al., 2012), then affected the revenue of auctioneers (Garg et al., 2001). When a bidder cannot pay for his/her valuation, the valuation function may not be an additive function, which adds difficulties in finding optimal allocations and the equilibrium price (Andelman and Mansour, 2004). Focusing on whether an envy-free price can support optimal allocations with budget constraints, Kempe et al. (2009) provided two polynomial-time algorithms to find a maximum and a minimum envy-free price. The revenue outcome of auction mechanisms depends on various settings. When bidders faced absolute budget constraints, first-price auctions yielded higher than expected revenue and social surplus than second-price auctions (Che and Gale, 1995). In the setting where items have a common value to all bidders and budget constraints are public, sequential auctions yield more revenue than simultaneous and ascending auctions, either if the discrepancy among valuations is large or if there are significant complementaries; however, if the discrepancy among valuations is small, simultaneous auctions are superior (Benoit and Krishna, 2001). Multiple price auctions obtained more revenue than single-price auctions, in the setting where bidders have private information of budget constraints and valuations (Abrams, 2006). Krishna (2002) explored how the presence of financial constraints affects equilibrium behavior in first- and second-price auctions and what effect they have on the revenue from these auctions. He found that budget constraints are "softer" in first-price auctions than in second-price auctions. That is, when bidders are subject to budget constraints, the first and second-price auctions need not yield the same expected revenue. This conclusion proved the viewpoint of Klemperer (1999) that an important reason why revenue equivalence may fail in practice is that bidders face budget constraints.

Equilibrium existence and stability are crucial features for an optimal auction mechanism, especially for budget-constrained auctions (Pitchik and Schotter, 1988; Kotowski, 2010; Laan and Yang, 2008). Considering a set of indivisible heterogeneous items and a group of bidders with private budget constraints and valuations, Laan and Yang (2008) presented an ascending auction with a rationed equilibrium in a finite number of steps. Kotowski (2010) provided conditions for the equilibrium existence resulting from (Reny, 2009) for monotone strategies in a budget-constrained first-price, sealed-bid auction with private information. Chen et al. (2010) presented a strongly polynomial-time algorithm to tell whether or not a competitive equilibrium exists in the classic Shapley-Shubik assignment model with indivisible goods and unit-demand buyers, with budget constraints. They found that the single discontinuity introduced by the budget constraint fundamentally changes the properties of equilibria. It means that, with budget constraints, a competitive equilibrium does not always exist.

2.2.2.2 Budget-Constrained Search Auction Mechanisms

For major search engines, a significant part of their revenues is obtained from sponsored search ads displayed with algorithmic search results. To maximize revenue, it is essential to choose a good slate of ads for each query (Shaparenko et al., 2009), which is the preliminary work of sponsored search auction mechanism design. Most works on sponsored search auction mechanisms (Aggarwal et al., 2006, 2009; Edelman et al., 2007; Varian, 2007) neglected budget constraints and impacts. In practical advertising campaigns, search advertisers have either hard or soft budget constraints. A search engine must choose how to allocate its advertising inventory in response to changing search queries and advertiser's budgets (Bergemann and Said, 2011). Recently, it was acknowledged that budget constraints have significant impact on the mechanism design and equilibrium outcome of sponsored search auctions (Ashlagi et al., 2010; Feldman et al., 2008; Borgs et al., 2007). From an optimization viewpoint, there are plenty of efforts to design algorithms for various settings regarding budget-constrained bidders. Taking budget constraints into account, Abrams et al. (2007, 2008) dealt with the allocation of advertisers to queries to maximize the revenue.

Feldman et al. (2008) gave a truthful mechanism for offline ad slot scheduling where advertisers specify a budget constraint. In online advertisement auctions, the dynamics of the auction system make existing mechanisms incapable of converging, as budget-constrained advertisers try to optimize their utility by equalizing their return-on-investment across all keywords (Borgs et al., 2007). Then they proposed a modified mechanism with random perturbations, which provably converges in the first-price auction and experimentally converges in the second-price auction. A search engine needs to decide what ads to display with each query so as to maximize its revenue while respecting the daily budgets of the bidders, which turns out to be a generalization of the online bipartite matching problem. Mehta et al. (2005) introduced the notion of a trade-off revealing LP to derive two optimal algorithms achieving competitive ratios of $1 - 1/e$ for this problem. Deng et al. (2012) studied multiple item auctions in a setting similar to the position auction for sponsored search auctions where buyers are subject to budget constraints. They designed a 2-approximate truthful mechanism for the case where buyers are budget-constrained. Gonen and Pavlov (2007) presented an online sponsored search auction mechanism that motivates advertisers to report their true budget, arrival time, departure time, and value per click. The mechanism is based on a modified Multi-Armed Bandit mechanism that allows for advertisers to arrive and depart in an online fashion, with a value per click and budget constraints.

Equilibrium analysis is an important part of mechanism design. From some careful modifications of the Generalized English Auction, Edelman et al. (2007) and Ashlagi et al. (2010) designed a generalized position auction for advertisers with private values and budgets. They also proved that the ex-post equilibrium outcome of the auction is Pareto-efficient and envy-free. Colini-Baldeschi et al. (2012) studied multiple keyword sponsored search auctions with budgets. They presented an incentive compatible in expectation, individually rational in expectation, and a Pareto-optimal mechanism for the situation where click-through rates differ among slots, and a deterministic, incentive-compatible, individually rational, and Pareto-optimal mechanism for identical click-through rates for all slots. Motivated by sponsored search auctions, Hafalir et al. (2011) studied multi-unit auctions with budget constraints and proposed a Short-Cut mechanism, which achieves good incentive, revenue, and efficiency. Assuming that the optimal budget strategy can be made independently of the choice of bid for a specific keyword, it can be shown that it is a dominant strategy to report the optimal budget with one's bid. Then, Lahaie (2006) thought of the alternative slot auction design problem as an issue to ascertain that bids and budgets can indeed be optimized separately, or to find a plausible model in which both equilibrium bids and budgets can be derived.

In summary, budget constraints not only constrained the advertisers' abilities to bid, but also affected the competitive status of searching markets, which are indispensable factors for auction mechanism design and equilibrium analysis. Budget-constrained mechanisms in sponsored search auctions in turn determine both the revenues of search engines and bidding strategies taken by advertisers. Although there are plenty of studies paying attention to budget-constrained mechanism design and equilibrium analysis in auctions, the corresponding issues in sponsored search auctions are still at an early stage.

2.2.3 Budget-Constrained Bidding Strategies

How to choose the best bidding strategy is a crucial issue faced by the advertisers in sponsored search auctions. Different auction mechanisms might lead to different bidding strategies, in order to maximize the advertising performance. In other words, a certain bidding strategy may suit a given type of mechanism but not others. Therefore, an advertiser participating in two or more advertising auction systems with different mechanisms might have to adopt different bidding strategies. Moreover, current auction mechanisms employed by major search engines (e.g. the GSP mechanism) are not incentive compatible (Edelman et al., 2007), which complicates the task of designing optimal bidding strategies. In this section we go through bidding strategies from auctions to sponsored search auctions.

2.2.3.1 Budget-Constrained Bidding Strategies in Auctions

The bidder's choice of strategy can be constrained by the upper limit on the exposure times, an upper limit on the expected expenditures, or a lower limit on the expected profits. Engelbrecht-Wiggans (1987) proved that constraining the bidder only by an appropriate upper limit on the expected expenditures can in effect limit him to choose the expected profit maximizing strategies; in many examples, the expected profit maximizing strategies cannot be induced by solely limiting the bidder's exposure. According to Brandt and Wei (2001), in a dynamic setting with second pricing, the bidder is more likely to bid higher than his/her true value in order to exhaust the competitors' budgets for future negotiations. Bidders with budget constraints may demand one or a bundle of items by bidding in simultaneous or sequential auctions. In multiple simultaneous second-price auctions with goods that are perfect substitutes, Dash et al. (2008) considered optimal procedures for bidders with financial constraints, and concluded that in the case of two auctions, when the financial constraint is equal or less than a bidder's valuation, it is typically optimal to participate in a single auction. In sequential auctions with multiple heterogeneous common value objects, Fatima (2009) studied bidding strategies in each round of auctions for bidders with budget constraints and unit demands. They proved that strategic bidding behavior depends on the auction agenda: when the agenda is changed, the equilibrium bids also consequently change. Supposing the agenda is given, they also proposed equilibrium bidding strategies for each individual round in a series, under both first- and second-price rules in an incomplete information setting where the bidders are uncertain about the budget constraints. In sequential auctions, a firm might bid in a predatory manner, driving early prices unreasonably high to eliminate its budget-constrained rivals from the later bidding (Pitchik and Schotter, 1988).

In realistic multi-unit auctions, bidders have budget constraints and demand more than one item. To deal with bundle problems in auctions, Airiau and Sen (2003) proposed a strategic bidding agent that utilized a valuation function for different quantities of an item, and the knowledge of valuations of other bidders' in future auctions. Sometimes auctions have a reserve price to ensure the basic revenue for auctioneers. Supposing the attitude of bidders need not be risk-neutral, and they have uncertainty about the value of items, Vetsikas and Jennings (2010) derived equilibrium strategies for the mth price auction, and the dominant equilibrium strategy for the $(m + 1)$th price auction. Bidders can use these strategies to maximize their utility. In the meantime an auctioneer can improve his/her revenue by selecting the optimal reserve price. Bundle demands also occur in combinatorial auctions. Schwind et al. (2007) studied agents' bidding strategies in a combinatorial auction for two types of bidders with budget constraints: a quantity maximizing bidder with a low preference for fast bid acceptance and an impatient bidder who draws a big advantage from fast allocation of the requested resources. They also proved that for the quantity maximizing bidder it is profitable to be patient and to start with low bids, whereas the impatient bidder should avoid "overbidding" in his tendency to accelerate the resource procurement process. Besides bidding individually, coalitions also provide a very important bidding pattern, especially when bidders are budget constrained since coalitions can pool bidders' budgets. Following these observations, Cho et al. (2002) provided a coalitional bidding model where coalitions form endogenously and compete with each other, and analyzed the equilibrium coalition structure and the resulting bids. When the budget constraint is very severe, the equilibrium coalition structure consists of two coalitions with one slightly larger than the other. Goodman and Baurmeister (1976) considered a multi-contract bidding situation where the contracts are interrelated because of the limited productive facilities and budget. A dynamic programming model and its computational algorithm were presented to derive a bidding strategy to maximize the total expected return from all contracts. The proposed model and its computational algorithm are efficient in terms of the required storage capacity and computation time.

2.2.3.2 Budget-Constrained Bidding Strategies in Sponsored Search Auctions

Optimal bidding strategies are not independent of auction mechanisms. A sponsored search auction is not an exceptional case. Currently, major search engines adopt generalized second price auctions to sell advertising slots. The nature of the generalized second-price auction suggests that a better understanding of the competitors' keyword selection and bidding strategies can help the advertiser win in the auction (Wang et al., 2009). Thus, advertisers with severe budget constraints must solve a complex optimization problem to decide how to place bids for keywords, in order to maximize advertising performance.

Feldman et al. (2007) modeled the entire auction process and proposed a two-bid uniform bidding strategy that bids equally on all the keywords, by which advertisers can obtain at least

$1 - 1/e$ fraction of the maximum clicks possible. The distribution of future queries that cannot be known in advance, to a large degree influences the determination of optimal bidding strategies. Based on natural probabilistic models of distribution over future queries, Muthukrishnan et al. (2010) formulated three stochastic budget optimization models with budget constraints, and proved that simple prefix strategies that bid on all cheap keywords up to some level were either optimal or good approximations in many cases. Zhou et al. (2008) modeled the budget-constrained bidding optimization problem as an online (multiple-choice) knapsack problem, and designed deterministic and randomized algorithms that can achieve a provably optimal competitive ratio. Gummadi et al. (2011) considered the bidder's competitive problem when he has a limited budget in the second-price sponsored search auctions. They formulated the problem as a discounted Markov decision process, and provided explicit solutions when the bidder is involved in a large number of auctions. Hosanagar and Cherepanov (2008) studied optimal bidding strategies for advertisers in budget-constrained multi-item multi-slot auctions. They presented an analytical model to characterize the optimal bidding strategy and validated it using real-world data. Ghosh et al. (2009) studied the problem of acquiring a given number of impressions from displayed advertising under budget constraint by bidding against an unknown distribution. Their approach consisted of learning the distribution in the exploration phase and bidding according to the empirical distribution of observations from the exploration. Drosos et al. (2010) proposed a strategy for repetitive bidding for a single keyword auction based on dynamic programming. The objective is to help bidders to avoid overspending the budget. Moreover, sponsored search auctions enable advertisers to adjust their bids and rankings dynamically, and the payoffs are realized in real time. Zhang and Feng (2011) captured this unique feature with a dynamic model and identified an equilibrium bidding strategy. They pointed out that richer strategic bidding patterns can also be studied if they explicitly consider issues that arise only in dynamic games, such as discount factors, budget constraints, menu costs, entry and exit, learning and heuristics.

In sponsored search auctions, there are many advertisers bidding for the same keyword simultaneously and the equilibrium of bidding strategies is an inspired state. Optimal bidding strategies should be stable in equilibrium such as locally envy-free equilibrium (Edelman et al., 2007). With consideration of the stability property, Chaitanya and Narahari (2010) proposed two bidding strategies: the OPT strategy and the MAX strategy on the behalf of advertisers, and proved that if all bidders use the proposed bid strategy (either OPT or MAX), the bid profile converges to a locally envy-free equilibrium in the asynchronous model and in the restricted synchronous model. However, the bid profile may not converge to equilibrium in the general synchronous model, where the MAX bidding strategy achieves better advantages for advertisers than other strategies such as OPT. From the dynamic perspective of auctions, Borgs et al. (2007) proposed a bidding heuristic strategy for budget-limited advertisers by equalizing the return-on-investment (ROI) across keywords. Ravi et al. (2009) considered a weakly dominant bidding strategy, where all bidders with budget constraints are led to state their true budget rather than understate their own valuations. Since the budget of each advertiser is limited, strategic bidding behavior plays a crucial role in sponsored search auctions. From an advertiser's perspective, a good strategy can not only prevent him from overbidding for the preferred position but also guarantees that the favorite position beats the competitors. Liang and Qi (2007) analyzed the economic stability and dynamic manipulation of vindictive strategies in conjunction with forward-looking cooperative bidders. They showed that the Nash equilibrium is vulnerable even if there is one malicious vindictive bidder; there always exists an output truthful Nash equilibrium under conservative vindictive bidding strategy; a selective vindictive strategy always results in a unique truthful Nash equilibrium.

In summary, there is some progress on budget-constrained bidding strategies in sponsored search auctions. However, it still needs further exploration, as current studies usually take sponsored search auctions as static and one-shot games with a small number of advertisers, and millions of keywords available to searchers and advertisers.

2.3 Summary

We categorize these works on budget-constrained mechanism and bidding strategies either in auctions or in sponsored search auctions in Table 2.1.

From Table 2.1 we can get the following:

- There are more research efforts on auctions than on sponsored search auctions, with attention to budget constraints. This might be explained in that sponsored search auctions are a novel form of auction and researchers are just starting to realize the role of budget constraints within them.
- The above phenomenon is more obvious in terms of the auction mechanism. We can say that bidders are keener to get effective bidding strategies, than auctioneers are to get an optimal mechanism, because auctioneers have greater superiority than bidders, such as possessing professional knowledge and information.
- The earliest efforts on budget constraints in sponsored search auctions mainly started in 2005, then increased slowly.

In addition, we argue that budget constraints are also crucial factors in keyword strategies. Budget constraints force advertisers to select non-obvious but relevant keywords (Joshi and Motwani, 2006), and cautiously organize the keyword portfolio. However, to the best of our knowledge, there are few, if any, studies in this area.

Table 2.1 The effort distributions of auctions and sponsored search auctions in the literature.

	Auction	Sponsored Search Auctions
Auction mechanisms	Pitchik and Schotter (1988) Che and Gale (1995) Laffont and Robert (1996) Maskin (2000) Garg et al. (2001) Garg et al. (2001) Benoit and Krishna (2001) Fang and Parreiras (2002) Andelman and Mansour (2004) Borgs et al. (2005) Abrams (2006) Laan and Yang (2008) Brusco and Lopomo (2008) Malakhov and Vohra (2008) Brusco and Lopomo (2009) Pitchik (2009) Pái and Vohra (2009) Mehrabin (2009) Benoit and Krishna (2008) Hafalir et al. (2009) Pái and Vohra (2009) Hafalir et al. (2009) Kempe et al. (2009) Kotowski (2010) Bhattacharya et al. (2010) Chen et al. (2010) Dobzinski et al. (2011) Hafalir et al. (2012)	Mehta et al. (2005) Abrams et al. (2007) Borgs et al. (2007) Gonen and Pavlov (2007) Abrams et al. (2008) Feldman et al. (2008) Ashlagi et al. (2010) Hafalir et al. (2011) Deng et al. (2012) Colini-Baldeschi et al. (2012)
Bidding strategies	Goodman and Baurmeister (1976) Engelbrecht-Wiggans (1987) Cho et al. (2002) Airiau and Sen (2003) Schwind et al. (2007) Dash et al. (2008) Fatima (2009) Vetsikas and Jennings (2010)	Feldman et al. (2007) Borgs et al. (2007) Liang and Qi (2007) Zhou et al. (2008) Hosanagar and Cherepanov (2008) Ravi et al. (2009) Ghosh et al. (2009) Chaitanya and Narahari (2010) Muthukrishnan et al. (2010) Drosos et al. (2010) Gummadi et al. (2011) Zhang and Feng (2011)

References

Abrams, Z. 2006. Revenue maximization when bidders have budgets, In Proceedings of the 17th Annual ACM-SIAM Symposium on Discrete Algorithms.

Abrams, Z., O. Mendelevitch, J. A. Tomlin. 2007. Optimal delivery of sponsored search advertisements subject to budget constraints, EC'07, June 11–15, 2007. San Diego, California, USA.

Abrams, Z., S. S. Keerthi, O. Mendelevitch, J. A. Tomlin. 2008. Ad delivery with budgeted advertisers: A comprehensive LP approach, Journal of Electronic Commerce Research, 9:16–32.

Aggarwal, G., A. Goel, R. Motwani. 2006. Truthful auctions for pricing search keywords, In ACM Conference on Electronic Commerce, 1–7.

Aggarwal, G., S. Muthukrishnan, D. Pál, M. Pál. 2009. General auction mechanism for search advertising, WWW 2009, April 20–24, 2009, Madrid, Spain.

Airiau, S., S. Sen. 2003. Strategic bidding for multiple units in simultaneous and sequential auctions, Group Decision and Negotiation, 12(5):397–413.

Andelman, N., Y. Mansour. 2004. Auctions with budget constraints, In Ninth Scandinavian Workshop on Algorithm Theory (SWAT).

Ashlagi, I., M. Braverman, A. Hassidim, R. Lavi, M. Tennenholtz. 2010. Position auctions with budgets: Existence and uniqueness, The BE Journal of Theoretical Economics, 10(1).

Benoit, J. P., V. Krishna. 2001. Multiple-object auctions with budget constrained bidders, Review of Economic Studies, 68(1):155–179.

Benoit, J., V. Krishna. 2008. Multiple-object auctions with budget constrained bidders, Annual IEEE Symposium on Foundations of Computer Science, pp. 260–269.

Bergemann, D., M. Said. 2011. Dynamic Auctions: A Survey, Wiley Encyclopedia of Operations Research and Management Science.

Bhattacharya, S., G. Goel, S. Gollapudi, K. Munagala. 2009. Budget constrained auctions with heterogeneous items, In STOC 2009.

Bhattacharya, S., V. Conitzer, K. Munagala, L.R. Xia. 2010. Incentive compatible budget elicitation in multi-unit auctions, In Proceedings of SODA 2010, 554–572.

Borgs, C., J. Chayes, N. Immorlica, M. Mahdian, A. Saberi. 2005. Multi-unit auctions with budget-constrained bidders, In Proceedings of the Sixth ACM Conference on Electronic Commerce (EC'05). New York, NY, USA:ACM, 44–51.

Borgs, C., J. Chayes, O. Etesami, N. Immorlica, K. Jain, M. Mahdian. 2007. Dynamics of bid optimization in online advertisement auctions, Proc. WWW, 531–540.

Brandt, F., G. Wei. 2001. Antisocial agents and Vickrey auctions. Intelligent Agents VIII, Lecture Notes in Artificial Intelligence, Vol. 2333. Springer Verlag, 2001.

Brusco, S., G. Lopomo. 2008. Budget constraints and demand reduction in simultaneous ascending-bid auctions, The Journal of Industrial Economics, 56(1):113–142.

Brusco, S., G. Lopomo. 2009. Simultaneous ascending auctions with complementarities and known budget constraints, Economic Theory, 38:105–124.

Chaitanya, N., Y. Narahari. 2010. Optimal equilibrium bidding strategies for budget constrained bidders in sponsored search auctions, Operational Research. An International Journal.

Che, Y. K., I. Gale. 1995. Standard auctions with financially constrained bidders, Review of Economic Studies, 65:1–21, Cramton.

Che, Y. K., I. Gale. 1996. Expected revenue of the all-pay auctions and first-price sealed-bid auctions with budget constraints, Economics Letters, 50:373–380.

Che, Y. K., I. Gale. 2000. The optimal mechanism for selling to a budget-constrained buyer, Journal of Economic Theory, 92:198–233.

Chen, N., X. Deng, A. Ghosh. 2010. Competitive equilibria in matching markets with budgets, CoRR.

Cho, I. K., K. Jewell, R. Vohra. 2002. A simple model of coalitional bidding, Economic Theory, 19(3):435–457.

Colini-Baldeschi, R., M. Henzinger, S. Leonardi, M. Starnberger. 2012. On multiple keyword sponsored search auctions with budgets, In ICALP'12 Proceedings of the 39th International Colloquium Conference on Automata, Languages, and Programming - Volume Part II, 1–12.

Dash, R. K., E. H. Gerding, N. R. Jennings. 2008. Optimal financially constrained bidding in multiple simultaneous auctions, Lecture Notes in Business Information Processing, Negotiation, Auctions, and Market Engineering, 2:190–199, 2008.

Deng, X., P. Goldberg, B. Tang, J. Zhang. 2012. Multi-unit bayesian auction with demand or budget constraints, ACM EC 2012 Workshop on Incentives and Trust in E-Commerce.

Dobzinski, S., R. Lavi, N. Nisan. 2012. Multi-unit auctions with budget limits, Games and Economic Behavior, 74(2):486–503.

Drosos, D., E. Markakis, G. D. Stamoulis. 2010. Budget constrained bidding in sponsored search auctions, Working Paper.

Edelman, B., M. Ostrovsky, M. Schwarz. 2007. Internet advertising and the generalized second price auction: Selling billions of dollars worth of keywords, American Economic Review, 97(1):242–259.

Engelbrecht-Wiggans, R. 1987. Optimal constrained bidding, International Journal of Game Theory, 16(2):115–121.

Fam, K., Z. Yang. 2006. Primary influences of environmental uncertainty on promotions budget allocation and performance: A cross-country study of retail advertisers, Journal of Business Research, 59(2):259–267.

Fang, H., S. Parreiras. 2002. Equilibrium of affiliated value second price auctions with financially constrained bidders: The two-bidder case, Games and Economic Behavior, 39:215–236.

Fatima, S. 2009. Sequential auctions for common value objects with budget constrained bidders, Studies in Computational Intelligence, Advances in Agent-Based Complex Automated Negotiations, 233:21–37.

Feldman J., S. Muthukrishnan, M. Pál, C. Stein. 2007. Budget optimization in search-based advertising auctions, In Proceedings of the Eighth ACM Conference on Electronic Commerce, San Diego, California, USA, June 11–15, 2007.

Feldman, J., S. Muthukrishnan, E. Nikolova, M. Pál. 2008. A truthful mechanism for offline ad slot scheduling, In 1st International Symposium on Algorithmic Game Theory, Lecture Notes in Computer Science, 4997:182–193.

Garg, R., V. Kumar, V. Pandit. 2001. Approximation algorithms for budget-constrained auctions, Lecture Notes in Computer Science, vol. 2129 archive.

Ghose, A., S. Yang. 2009. An empirical analysis of search engine advertising: sponsored search in electronic markets, Management Science, 55(10):1605–1622.

Ghosh, A., B. I. P. Rubinstein, S. Vassilvitskii, M. Zinkevich. 2009. Adaptive bidding for displayed advertising, WWW2009, April 20–24, 2009, Spain.

Goldberg, A., J. Hartline, A. Wright. 2001. Competitive auctions and digital goods, In Proceedings of the 12th Annual ACM-SIAM Symposium on Discrete Algorithms, 735–744.

Goldberg, A., J. Hartline, A. Karlin, A. Wright, and M. Saks. Competitive auctions, preprint.

Gonen, R., E. Pavlov. 2007. An adaptive sponsored search mechanism delta-gain truthful in valuation, time, and budget, In Proceedings of the Workshop on Internet and Network Economics.

Goodman, D., H. Baurmeister. 1976. A computational algorithm for multi-contract bidding under constraints, Management Science, 22(7):788–798.

Gummadi, R., P. B. Key, A. Proutiere. 2011. Optimal bidding strategies in dynamic auctions with budget constraints, In 49th Annual Allerton Conference on Communication, Control, and Computing, 588.

Hafalir, I. E., R. Ravi, A. Sayedi. 2009. Sort-cut: A pareto-optimal and semi-truthful mechanism for multi-unit auctions with budget-constrained bidders, CoRR, abs/0903.1450.

Hafalir, I. E., R. Ravi, A. Sayedi. 2011. Multi-unit auctions with budget constraints, Working Paper.

Hafalir, I. E., R. Ravi, A. Sayedi. 2012. A near Pareto optimal auction with budget constraints, Games and Economic Behavior, 74:699–708.

Hosanagar, K., V. Cherepanov. 2008. Optimal bidding in stochastic budget constrained slot auctions, In Proceedings of ACM Conference on Electronic Commerce, July 8–12, 2008, Chicago, America.

Jansen, B. J., A. Spink. 2007. Sponsored search: Is money a motivator for providing relevant results? IEEE Computer, 40(8):50–55.

Joshi, A., R. Motwani. 2006. Keyword generation for search engine advertising, In Proceedings of the Sixth IEEE International Conference on Data Mining - Workshops.

Kempe, D., A. Mualem, M. Salek. 2009. Envy-free allocations for budgeted bidders, Lecture Notes in Computer Science. vol. 5929 archive.

Klemperer, P. 1999. Auction theory: a guide to the literature, Journal of Economic Surveys, 13(3):227–286.

Kornai, J. 1979. Resource-constrained versus demand-constrained system, Econometrica, 47:801–819.

Kornai, J. 1986. The soft budget constraint, Kyklos, Blackwell Publishing, 39(1):3–30.

Kotowski, M. H. 2010. First-price auctions with budget constraints, Working Paper, 2010.

Krishna, V. 2002. Auction Theory. Academic Press.

Laan, G. V. D., Z. F. Yang. 2008. An ascending multi-item auction with financially constrained bidders, Tinbergen Institute Discussion Paper.

Laffont, J. -J., J. Robert. 1996. Optimal auction with financially constrained buyers, Economics Letters, 52(1996):181–186.

Lahaie, S. 2006. An analysis of alternative slot auction designs for sponsored search, In Proceedings of the Seventh ACM Conference on Electronic Commerce, Ann Arbor, MI.

Liang, L., Q. Qi. 2007. Cooperative or vindictive: bidding strategies in sponsored search auction, In WINE 2007, 167–178.

Maille, P., E. Markakis, M. Naldi, G. D. Stamoulis, B. Tuffin. 2010. Sponsored search auctions: an overview of research with emphasis on game theoretic aspects, Working Paper.

Malakhov, A., R. V. Vohra. 2008. Optimal auctions for asymmetrically budget constrained bidders, Review of Economic Design, 12(4):245–257.

Maskin, E.S. 2000. Auctions, development and privatization: Efficient auctions with liquidity-constrained buyers, European Economic Review, 44:667–681.

Mehrabin, A. 2009. Budget constraints impact on multi unit auctions, 2009. http://www.cs.ubc.ca/~kevinlb/teaching/cs532l%20-%202008-9/projects/Amirhossein-project.pdf.

Mehta, A., A. Saberi, U. Vazirani, V. Vazirani. 2005. Adwords and generalized online matching, In Symposium on Foundations of Computer Science (FOCS).

Muthukrishnan, S., M. Pál, Z. Svitkina. 2010. Stochastic models for budget optimization in search-based advertising, Algorithmica, 58:1022–1044.

Pái, M. M., R. Vohra. 2009. Optimal auctions with financially constrained bidders, Working Paper.

Pitchik, C. 2009. Budget-constrained sequential auctions with incomplete information, Games and Economic Behavior, 66(2):928–949.

Pitchik, C., A. Schotter. 1988. Perfect equilibria in budget-constrained sequential auctions: An experimental study, RAND Journal of Economics, 19(3):363–388.

Ravi, R., I. Hafalir, A. Sayedi. 2009. Sort-cut: A pareto-optimal and semi-truthful mechanism for multi-unit auctions with budget-constrained bidders, In Fifth Workshop on Ad Auctions, July 6, 2009.

Reny, P. J. 2009. On the existence of monotone pure strategy equilibria in Bayesian games, Working Paper, University of Chicago, 2009.

Rusmevichientong, P., D. P. Williamson. 2006. An adaptive algorithm for selecting profitable keywords for search-based advertising services, In Proceedings of the Seventh ACM Conference on Electronic Commerce, ACM, New York, 260–269.

Schwind, M., T. Stockheim, O. Gujo. 2007. Agents' bidding strategies in a combinatorial auction controlled grid environment, Lecture Notes in Computer Science, Vol. 4452, Agent-Mediated Electronic Commerce. Automated Negotiation and Strategy Design for Electronic Markets, 149–163.

Shaparenko, B., O. Cetin, R. Iyer. 2009. Data-driven text features for sponsored search click prediction, In ADKDD '09 Proceedings of the Third International Workshop on Data Mining and Audience Intelligence for Advertising, 46–54.

Sullivan, O., S. M. Sheffrin. 2002. Economics: Principles in Action. Pearson Prentice Hall.

Thomas, L. 2002. Non-linear pricing with budget constraint, Economics Letters, 75(2002):257–263.

Varian, H. 2007. Position auctions, International Journal of Industrial Organization, 25(6):1163–1178.

Vetsikas, I. A., N. R. Jennings. 2010. Bidding strategies for realistic multi-unit sealed-bid auctions, Autonomous Agents and Multi-Agent Systems, 21(2):265–291.

Vickrey, W. 1961. Counterspeculation, auctions, and competitive sealed tenders, Journal of Finance, 16(1):8–37.

Wang, G., J. Hu, Y. Zhu, H. Li, Z. Chen. 2009. Competitive analysis from click-through log, In WWW '09 Proceedings of the 18th International Conference on World Wide Web, 1051–1052.

Yang, Y., J. Zhang, R. Qin, J. Li, F. Wang, Q. Wei. 2012. A budget optimization framework for search advertisements across markets, IEEE Transactions on Systems, Man, and Cybernetics, Part A, 42(5):1141–1151.

Zhang, X., J. Feng. 2011. Cyclical bid adjustments in search-engine advertising, Management Science, 57(9):1703–1719.

Zhou, Y., D. Chakrabarty, R. Lukose. 2008. Budget constrained bidding in keyword auctions and online knapsack problems, In Proceeding of the 17th International Conference on World Wide Web, Beijing, China, ACM.

CHAPTER 3

Budget Optimization in Sponsored Search Auctions

3.1 Introduction

In this chapter we provide a two-dimensional (temporal granularity and advertising objects) taxonomy of budget optimization specified in sponsored search auctions, with consideration of the entire lifecycle of advertising activities, and then categorize existing works. Then, based on empirical discussions about current works, we provide some preliminary conclusions on the research vacuum left in the taxonomy of budget optimization.

3.2 Budget Decision Scenarios

A budget decision is a critical issue for an advertiser participating in sponsored search auctions. Since most advertisers face serious financial constraints, they may be incapable of paying up to their valuation of objects on the Internet, which has a significant impact on the bidding price and thus the yield from the revenues. Budget decisions in sponsored search auctions cannot be once and forever. Advertisers should consider all the budget decision scenarios to make sure that a limited budget can exert the greatest effect.

Advertisers must make good use of limited budgets to maximize total revenues. This is especially critical in the case of flat or declining marketing budgets (Low and Mohr, 2000; Sriram and Kalwani, 2007). Then, brand managers must make trade-offs in deciding how to best allocate scarce marketing communication resources. In sponsored search auctions, a bid is triggered once an information request is submitted. A high volume of search demands makes the bidding a continuous, infinite process. The ranking results and prices will be different when any advertiser changes the keywords or bid at any time, such that an efficient advertising strategy, e.g. for budget allocation, should be capable of dynamically allocating and adjusting the advertising budget on the fly, according to the state of the marketing environment. In the entire lifecycle of advertising campaigns in sponsored search auctions, there are mainly three different scenarios where an advertiser has to make decisions about the advertising budget, as shown in Figure 3.1.

Yang and Wang: Budget Constraints and Optimization in Sponsored Search Auctions. http://dx.doi.org/10.1016/B978-0-12-411457-9.00003-3
© 2014 Elsevier Inc. All rights reserved.

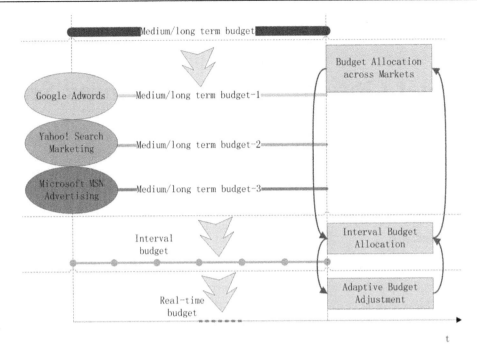

Figure 3.1   A multi-level budget optimization framework for search advertisement.

During the entire lifecycle of advertising campaigns in sponsored search auctions, there mainly exist three different budget decision scenarios, as shown in Figure 3.1.

First, an advertiser has to allocate the search advertising budget across several markets, supposing the overall budget for sponsored search auctions is determined.

Secondly, an advertiser has to distribute the advertising budget for a campaign over a series of temporal slots (e.g. daily budgets) during a certain promotion period, supposing the budget allocated in a search market is determined. If necessary, the advertiser should coarsely tune budget constraints for the coming slots, according to the advertising performance in historical slots.

Thirdly, in an ongoing slot of advertising campaigns, advertisers have to dynamically adjust the remaining budget, in order to avoid either too quickly wasting their budget or missing golden opportunities in the future, according to real-time advertising performance. For instance, when search demands are relatively higher than usual but lead to a lot of invalid clicks being detected, carefully keeping the remaining budget lower is a reasonable strategy.

Budget strategies at these three scenarios/levels complement each other, thus forming an integrated chain of budget optimization for the entire lifecycle of advertising campaigns in sponsored search auctions. That is, results of higher level constrain activities at lower levels, and conversely, operational results at lower levels create feedback to activities at higher levels.

Moreover, budget operations at these three levels interact with both various advertising strategies and outside environments, which result in great uncertainties, from advertising resources to marketing performance.

Correspondingly, it is necessary to explore an integrated framework for budget optimization with consideration of the entire lifecycle of search advertising campaigns, which can be capable of dealing with such structured budget problems in sponsored search auctions.

3.3 The Necessity of Budget Optimization

The budget is an endogenous factor in sponsored search auctions. In sponsored search auctions, when a search query is submitted, advertisers who bid on relevant keywords have chances to display their advertisements and one advertisement can only compete for one slot. Only if the advertisement is clicked, do advertisers need to pay for it. Advertisers cannot be involved in the auction process any longer if their budget is used up before the end of the advertising schedule, and thus the advertisement cannot be displayed either.

In general, advertisers, especially those from small corporations, usually face budget constraints due to their financial conditions, which significantly influence advertisers' strategies in sponsored search auctions. The limited budget forces advertisers to seek more effective strategies to allocate and adjust their budget, to select keywords, to determine bids, and to cautiously predict the advertising performance, in order to maximize the total revenues (e.g. clicks and return on investment, etc.). It demands that advertisers should appropriately allocate their limited budget in order to obtain the best response. Thus, how to rationally allocate the limited budget is a significant issue, which serves as a key input to other advertising strategies such as the keywords portfolio and bidding determination.

With consideration of budget decisions across these three levels in the entire lifecycle of search advertising, it's necessary to take the budget as an endogenous factor in a structured way, rather than a simple constraint on various advertising decisions. Thus, how to rationally allocate the limited budget is a fundamental marketing decision in sponsored search auctions, which serves as a key input to other advertising strategies such as the keywords portfolio and bidding determination. This falls under the broader umbrella term of budget optimization.

Budget optimization is a crucial issue faced by advertisers, but the factors, which include the diversity of the mechanisms in a sponsored search auction, unprecedented complexity and dynamics of the bidding processes, strong-coupling and unpredictability of markets under conditions of imperfect information, mean advertisers face tremendous difficulties and challenges in making decisions. First, advertisers should take their competitors' strategies into consideration when allocating their budgets. Secondly, limited advertising budgets should be wisely allocated at several levels of abstraction in sponsored search auctions, and at different time granularities, ideally in real-time. Thirdly, budget allocation and adjustment strategies heavily rely on other advertising strategies relevant to the keyword portfolio, bidding, and target audiences. Fourthly, consumer attention is by no means inexhaustible, in the sense that higher advertising pressure negatively affects the appraisal of individual advertisements and thus creates irritation (Pruyn and Riezebos, 2001).

The determination of advertising expenditures is not a new challenge. Several criteria that are widely used to determine spending levels in practice include: percent of sales (e.g. both one's own or a competitors'), objective and task (e.g. equating shares of equal value to a targeted share of the market), and advertising intensiveness curves (Sethi, 1977a; Feichtinger et al., 1994; Danaher and Rust, 1996; Miller and Pazgal, 2007). In early literature related to advertisements, the decision about advertising levels was incorporated with advertising/sale response functions to parsimoniously capture the relationship between advertising expenditure and unit sales (Sasieni, 1971; Rao and Rao, 1983). The pioneering work of Vidale and Wolfe (1957) took the initiative to define the concept of advertising effectiveness and equations of advertising/sales response dynamics, and provided a solution for optimal allocation with limited budgets. Another important concept is advertising goodwill introduced by Nerlove and Arrow (1962), which can be considered as the current aggregated advertisement effectiveness that can influence the budget allocation later on. Based on this concept, a dynamic adjustment framework was proposed for optimal advertising strategies and price policies in their work, which was further generalized by Sethi (1977b) in the case of limited budgets. Krishnan and Jain (2006) investigated the optimal advertising policy for new products under the influence of the diffusion phenomenon, and concluded that optimal advertising strategies are determined by advertising effectiveness, discount rate, and the ratio of advertisements to profits.

Sales and profit are more sensitive to the way the budget is allocated than to its overall level (Low and Mohr, 2000). Building effective budget strategies amidst so many parameters is quite a challenge. Thus, turning to pursue the best response became a feasible issue, that is to find the best strategies while fixing other competitors' (Yang et al., 2011). Dynamic competition to gain market share is a kernel concept for all kinds of business activities. In other words, advertising strategies of both a given advertiser and his/her competitors determine the market share. The best response can be abstracted as stochastic budget optimization problems: how to spread a given budget over keywords to maximize the expected profits (Feldman et al., 2007), which can be depicted as Markov decision processes (Du et al., 2007; Archak et al., 2010). Three stochastic versions of the budget model (including proportional, independent, and scenario) were presented in DasGupta and Muthukrishnan (2013) and Muthukrishnan et al. (2010), where some special cases identified were solvable in polynomial time or with improved approximative ratios, and approximation and complexity results showed that simple prefix strategies that bid on all cheap keywords up to some level were either optimal or a good approximation in many cases (Muthukrishnan et al., 2007, 2010). Archak et al. (2010) formulated the budget allocation as a constrained optimal control problem for a Markov Decision Process (MDP). Their main result showed that with the reasonable assumption that online advertising has positive carryover effects on the propensity and the form of user interactions with the same advertiser in the future, there exists a simple greedy algorithm for the budget allocation with the worst-case running time cubic in the number of model states (e.g. keywords). The budget optimization problem can also be cast as an online (multiple-choice) knapsack problem to achieve a provably optimal competitive ratio for advertisers (Babaioff et al., 2007; Chakrabarty et al., 2007). In a competitive environment, when advertisers have limited information and budget, they tend to participate in sponsored search auctions with a fixed probability that depends on their valuations: high-valuation advertisers often tend to bid less than those with low-valuation, because they win more auctions and use up their budget faster (Maille and Tuffin, 2011). Amin et al. (2012) considered the budget optimization problem faced by an advertiser participating in repeated sponsored search auctions, seeking to maximize the number of clicks attained under budget constraints. They cast the budget optimization problem under budget constraints as a Markov Decision Process (MDP) with censored observations, and proposed a learning algorithm based on the well-known Kaplan-Meier or product-limit estimator.

Due to the dynamic nature of SSA markets, various mathematical programming algorithms have been used to improve advertising strategies. Integer programming and nonlinear programming are effective in finding optimal solutions for budget allocation for keywords (Kitts and LeBlanc, 2004; Özlük and Cholette, 2007). The results from Özlük and Cholette (2007) showed that the price elasticities of the click-through rate and response functions are key factors for budget allocation decisions, and investing in more keywords under a certain threshold can help improve advertisers' profits. The search process for optimal budget allocation strategies can be modeled as an optimal control problem (Sethi, 1977a). Dynamic programming was used to derive the analytical solution to the optimal budget allocation problem among web portals (Fruchter and Dou, 2005), and their conclusions indicated that budget allocation strategies rely nonlinearly on the targeted audiences, average click-through rates and advertising effectiveness of websites. Thus, advertisers are advised to switch more budgets into specialized web portals, in order to maximize click volumes in the long term.

The budget optimization problem can also be cast as an online (multiple-choice) knapsack problem to achieve a provably optimal competitive ratio for advertisers (Babaioff et al., 2007; Chakrabarty et al., 2007). In the spirit of the Knapsack problem, DasGupta and Muthukrishnan (2013) proposed a "scenario" (stochastic) model framework for the budget allocation problem considering the probability distribution of scenarios of cost vs. click combinations. In this framework, each scenario may contain weekdays vs. weekend, different days of the week, or different months of the year.

3.4 A Budget Taxonomy in Sponsored Search Auctions

Budget optimization is a crucial issue faced by advertisers, and we should figure out how the budget is consumed by the campaigns of advertisers to achieve advertising effectiveness by making optimal budgeting decisions. A bid is triggered once an information request is submitted. The high volume of search demands makes the bidding a continuous, infinite process. The ranking results and prices will be different when any advertiser changes the keywords or the bid at any time. So an efficient advertising strategy, e.g. for budget allocation, should be capable of dynamically allocating and adjusting the advertising budget on the fly, according to the state of the marketing environment. In the entire lifecycle of advertising campaigns in sponsored search auctions, there are mainly three different scenarios where an advertiser has to make decisions about the advertising budget, as shown in Figure 3.1.

In this section, we propose a budget taxonomy in sponsored search auctions, which can be considered as a simple and robust conceptual framework for describing the context of budget decisions and classifying research efforts with two essential dimensions: domain and time (Figure 3.2). The domain dimension concerns the domain structure of sponsored search

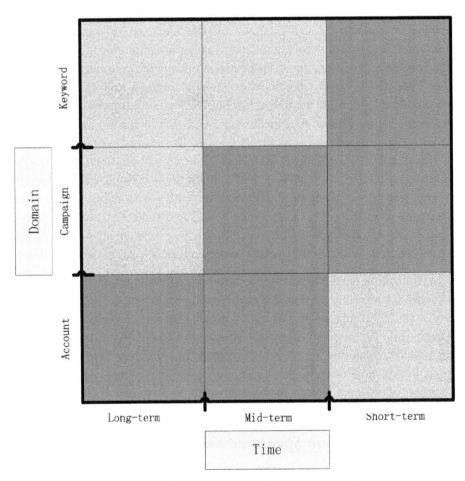

Figure 3.2 A taxonomy of budget optimization in sponsored search auctions.

auctions, namely basic objects and relationships defined by applications provided by major search engines. The time dimension concerns short-term, mid-term, and long-term. As shown in Figure 3.2, the product of these two dimensions constitutes 9 lattices. The green lattices denote possible zones in the context of budget decisions, while the shaded lattices denote non-existent or unnecessary points.

In the next chapter, we will provide a hierarchical framework for budget management with consideration of the entire lifecycle of advertising campaigns in sponsored search auctions in Figure 3.1. This budget framework consists of three levels, corresponding to these three budget management scenarios, with attention to the advertising system, campaign, and keywords, respectively. Specifically, the **system/account level** concerns budget allocation across several search advertising markets in the medium/long term (e.g. over half a year). The **campaign level** focuses on budget allocation over a series of temporal slots (e.g. day or month) during a promotion period. The **keyword level** aims to adaptively adjust the remaining budget during a temporal slot of advertising campaigns in order to keep valuable expenditure for potential clicks in the future. Budget strategies at these three levels complement each other, thus forming an integrated chain of budget optimization for the entire lifecycle of advertising campaigns in sponsored search auctions. That is, results of higher levels constrain activities at lower levels, and inversely, operational results at lower levels create feedback to activities at higher levels.

The taxonomy has immediate value in identifying and validating the budget roles of optimal advertising strategies in sponsored search auctions, helping to ensure that key viewpoints are not missed, and hence reducing the risk of instability and failure during development.

3.5 Discussions

The complexity of budget optimization in sponsored search auctions is amplified by the following facts. First, the complex structure of sponsored search auction mechanisms (e.g. GSP) together with a high volume of search demands leads to continual dynamics in auction processes, which offers serious challenges to various decision-making activities in sponsored search auctions. Secondly, large uncertainties exist in the mapping from the search advertising budget to expected profits. Thirdly, probably due to the previous two facts, it is difficult to predict some important factors such as queries, clicks, cost-per-click (CPC), and click-through rate (CTR). Fourthly, the budget is structured in the entire lifecycle of search advertising activities, rather than a simple constraint as in traditional economic phenomena. It makes budget decisions in sponsored search auctions a structured set of optimization problems. Thus, a great concern of advertisers in sponsored search auctions is not only to obtain local optimizations but a global optimal outcome with structured budget constraints. This demands an integrated framework and more practical budget optimization strategies, especially in cases where advertisers from small companies face serious budget constraints in sponsored search auctions.

The importance and difficulties of budget decisions for search advertisers encourage us to endeavor to study the problems in an integrated way. In the chapter that follows we will introduce a budget optimization framework aimed at helping advertisers make budget decisions during the lifecycle of sponsored search auctions. As mentioned before, the budget decision exists in three scenarios, including budget allocation across markets, interval budget allocation, and adaptive budget adjustment, and in this framework we will not only formulate these three budget decision problems, but also their relationships. And, in order to make an intensive study of budget decisions in the three scenarios, we will do detailed research on them in the budget optimization framework, and consider more ingredients of practical sponsored search auctions to make our research more applicable.

In practice, budget optimization should take a view of the entire lifecycle of search advertising activities. From the practical viewpoint, it is of tremendous importance to design a commonly used budget allocation framework for sponsored search auctions. Therefore, we argue that it is necessary to propose a novel framework for budget optimization in sponsored search auctions, taking into account the entire lifecycle of advertising campaigns. This framework should, in the meantime, provide an open environment for various research proposals relevant to budget allocation and adjustment, to validate and evaluate their performances, with flexible designs or combinations of complementary models, strategies, and algorithms. This intuition directly motivates our research of budget optimization. In a previous work (Yang et al., 2012), we took the initiative in providing a hierarchical framework for budget management with consideration of the entire lifecycle of advertising campaigns in sponsored search auctions (Figure 3.1). This budget framework consists of three levels, corresponding to these three budget management scenarios, paying attention to the advertising system, campaign, and keywords, respectively.

Following this consideration, we categorize current efforts on budget constraints and optimization in the state-of-the-art literature of sponsored search auctions, according to the taxonomy of budget optimization as described in Section 3.4. The populated taxonomy is illustrated in Table 3.1.

From Table 3.1, we can see that most of the current works on budget constraints and optimization are focused on budget allocations over keywords (e.g. DasGupta and Muthukrishnan, 2013; Feldman et al., 2007; Muthukrishnan et al., 2010). These works usually took keywords as first-class objects in distributing the budget. However, they do not directly fit into practical scenarios in sponsored search auctions, as provided currently by major search engine companies. We argue that such works at the keyword level should fall into the category of either keyword strategies or bidding strategies, with consideration of budget constraints. In Chaitanya and Narahari (2012), budget optimization was defined as selecting an optimal set of keywords to bid for, given a limited amount of budget. Muthukrishnan et al. (2010) regarded this problem as determining how to place bids on the keywords that are of interest to advertisers in order to maximize their return in a given budget. From the viewpoint of the

Table 3.1 The populated taxonomy of budget constraints and optimization in sponsored search auctions.

	System level	Campaign level	Keyword level
Long term	Fruchter and Dou (2005)	—	Borgs et al. (2005) Chaitanya and Narahari (2012) Muthukrishnan et al. (2010)
Medium term	—	—	Abrams (2007, 2008) Zhou et al. (2008) Ashlagi et al. (2010) DasGupta and Muthukrishnan (2013)
Short term	—	Archak et al. (2010) Amin et al. (2012)	Kitts and LeBlanc (2004) Krishnan and Jain (2006) Chakrabarty et al. (2007) Feldman et al. (2007) Du et al. (2007) Özlük and Cholette (2007) Feldman et al. (2008) Muthukrishnan et al. (2010)

entire lifecycle of sponsored search auctions, the first definition is actually keyword selection, and the second one is bid optimization. They only regarded the budget as a boundary condition, and considered the optimization problem at keyword level. Studies at the campaign level and system level are somewhat scarce, with the exception of Fruchter and Dou (2005) paying attention to the website level.

3.6 Conclusions

In this chapter, we provide a two-dimensional taxonomy of budget optimization in sponsored search auctions, which provides a reference frame to categorize current works and get valuable insights into perspectives. Our survey opens a wide spectrum of research perspectives relevant to budget constraints and optimization in sponsored search auctions.

References

Abrams, Z., O. Mendelevitch, J. A. Tomlin. 2007. Optimal Delivery of Sponsored Search Advertisements Subject to Budget Constraints, EC'07, June 11–15, 2007, San Diego, California, USA.

Abrams, Z., S. S. Keerthi, O. Mendelevitch, J. A. Tomlin. 2008. Ad delivery with budgeted advertisers: A comprehensive LP approach, Journal of Electronic Commerce Research 9:16–32.

Amin, K., M. Kearns, P. Key, A. Schwaighofe. 2012. Budget optimization for sponsored search: censored learning in MDPs, UAI 2012, 54–63.

Archak, N., V. S. Mirrokni, S. Muthukrishnan. 2010. Budget optimization for online advertising campaigns with carryover effects, In Proceedings of the Sixth Workshop on Ad Auctions (co-located with the Eleventh ACM SIGECOM International Conference on Electronic Commerce), June 8, Cambridge, Massachusetts.

Ashlagi, I., M. Braverman, A. Hassidim, R. Lavi, M. Tennenholtz. 2010. Position auctions with budgets: Existence and uniqueness, BE Journal of Theoretical Economics, 10(1).

Babaioff, M., N. Immorlica, D. Kempe, R. Kleinberg. 2007. A knapsack secretary problem with applications, Lecture Notes in Computer Science, 4627:16–28.

Borgs, C., J. Chayes, N. Immorlica, M. Mahdian, A. Saberi. 2005. Multi-unit auctions with budget-constrained bidders, In Proceedings of the 6th ACM Conference on Electronic Commerce (EC '05), ACM, New York, NY, USA, 44–51.

Chaitanya, N., Y. Narahari. 2012. Optimal equilibrium bidding strategies for budget constrained bidders in sponsored search auctions, Operational Research, 12(3):317–343.

Chakrabarty, D., Y. Zhou, R. Lukose. 2007. Budget constrained bidding in keyword auctions and online knapsack problems, In Proceedings of the 16th International World Wide Web Conference, May 8–12, Banff, Alberta, Canada.

Danaher, P. J., R. T. Rust. 1996. Determining the optimal return on investment for an advertising campaign, European Journal of Operations Research, 95, 511–521.

DasGupta, B., S. Muthukrishnan. 2013. Stochastic budget optimization in Internet advertising, Algorithmica, 65(3):634–661.

Du, R., Q. Hu, S. Ai. 2007. Stochastic optimal budget decision for advertising considering uncertain sales responses, European Journal of Operational Research, 183(3):1042–1054.

Feichtinger, G., R. F. Hartl, S. P. Sethi. 1994. Dynamic optimal control models in advertising: Recent developments, Management Science, 40(2):195–226.

Feldman J., S. Muthukrishnan, M. Pál, C. Stein. 2007. Budget optimization in search-based advertising auctions, In Proceedings of the Eighth ACM Conference on Electronic Commerce, USA, June 11–15, San Diego, California.

Feldman, J., S. Muthukrishnan, et al. 2008. A truthful mechanism for offline ad slot scheduling, 1st International Symposium on Algorithmic Game Theory, Lecture Notes in Computer Science, 4997:182–193.

Fruchter, G. E., W. Dou. 2005. Optimal budget allocation over time for portals, Journal of Optimization Theory and Applications, 124(1):157–174.

Kitts B., B. J. LeBlanc. 2004. A trading agent and simulator for keyword auctions, In Proceedings of the Third International Joint Conference on Autonomous Agents & Multi Agent Systems, New York, 228–235.

Krishnan, T. V., D. C. Jain. 2006. Optimal dynamic advertising policy for new products, Management Science, 52(12):1957.

Low, G. S., J. J. Mohr. 2000. Advertising vs sales promotion: a brand management perspective, Journal of Product & Brand Management, 9(6):389–414.

Maille, P., B. Tuffin. 2011. Adword auction bidding strategies of budget-limited advertisers on competing search engines, In Seventh International Conference on Network and Service Management, October 24–28, Paris, France.

Miller, N., A. Pazgal. 2007. Advertising budgets in competitive environments, Quantitative Marketing and Economics, 5(2):131–161.

Muthukrishnan, S., M. Pál, Z. Svitkina. 2007. Stochastic models for budget optimization in search-based advertising, Lecture Notes in Computer Science, 4858:131–142.

Muthukrishnan, S., M. Pál, Z. Svitkina. 2010. Stochastic models for budget optimization in search-based advertising, Algorithmica, 58:1022–1044.

Nerlove, M., K. J. Arrow. 1962. Optimal advertising policy under dynamic conditions, Economica, 29(114):129–142.

Özlük, Ö., S. Cholette. 2007. Allocating expenditures across keywords in search advertising, Journal of Revenue and Pricing Management, 6(4):347–356.

Pruyn, A., R. Riezebos. 2001. Effects of the awareness of social dilemmas on advertising budget-setting: A scenario study, Journal of Economic Psychology, 22(1):43–60.

Rao, A. G., M. R. Rao. 1983. Optimal budget allocation when response is S-shaped, Operations Research Letters, 2(5):225–230.

Sasieni, M. W. 1971. Optimal advertising expenditure, Management science, Application series, Part 2, Marketing Management Models, 18(4):64–72.

Sethi, S. P. 1977b. Optimal advertising for the Nerlove-Arrow model under a budget constraint, Operational Research Quarterly (1970–1977), 28(3):683–693.

Sriram, S., M. U. Kalwani. 2007 Optimal advertising and promotion budgets in dynamic markets with brand equity as a mediating variable, Management Science, 53:46–60.

Suresh P. Sethi. 1997a. Dynamic optimal control models in advertising: A survey, SIAM Review, 19(4):685–725.

Vidale, M. L., H. B. Wolfe. 1957. An operations research study of sales response to advertising, Operations Research, 5(3):370–381.

Yang, Y., J. Li, J. Zhang, D. Zeng. 2011. Budget allocation in competitive search advertisements, In 21st Workshop on Information Technologies and Systems, 219–220, December 3–4, 2011, Shanghai, China.

Yang, Y., J. Zhang, R. Qin, J. Li, F. Wang, Q. Wei. 2012. A budget optimization framework for search advertisements across markets, IEEE Transactions on Systems, Man, and Cybernetics, Part A, 42(5):1141–1151.

Zhou, Y., D. Chakrabarty, R. Lukose. 2008. Budget constrained bidding in keyword auctions and online knapsack problems, In Internet and Network Economics, Springer: Berlin Heidelberg, 566–576.

Budget Optimization in Space of Effective Agents

CHAPTER 4

A Budget Optimization Framework for Search Advertisements*

4.1 Introduction

Recent years have witnessed a booming growth in sponsored search auctions when "economics meets search" (Jansen and Spink, 2007). Specifically, there is an emerging tendency to increasingly integrate web information retrieval and online marketing techniques, leading to a targeted advertising form with some either explicit or implicit "long-tail" effects. Sponsored search auctions have now become a primary online advertising format being acknowledged as a promising business model. This is approved by the fact that it serves as the primary revenue source for major search engine companies. For example, Google reported a total revenue of $10.58 billion in the fourth quarter of 2011, with the revenue via sponsored search auctions comprising about 97% of the total. According to statistics from IAB, more than 47% of the US online advertising revenue came from search auctions in the first half of 2010, followed by the second largest format of display advertisements (36%).

The growing prosperity of search advertising markets is vastly driven by the influx of millions of advertisers. However, most search engine companies currently provide a limited number of advertising slots (e.g. 8–10) on their Search Engine Result Pages (SERPs). More and more advertisers have to advertise their products or services simultaneously across several search engines, in order to increase the coverage of their advertisements and expected profits, and to survive in the fierce competition. Consequently, many advertisements compete for space on SERP pages in any given scheduling horizon (Amiri and Menon, 2006). How to rationally allocate the limited advertising budget is a critical issue in sponsored search auctions, even before conducting advertising campaigns.

Sponsored search auctions fall into the category of complex systems capable of evolving with feeds from outside environments and intra-interactions (Wang, 2010), due to some factors including the diversity of sponsored search auction mechanisms (Aggarwal et al., 2009), the

---

* This chapter is a modified version of an article published in IEEE Transactions on Systems, Man, and Cybernetics, Part A, Volume 42, Number 5.

Yang and Wang: Budget Constraints and Optimization in Sponsored Search Auctions. http://dx.doi.org/10.1016/B978-0-12-411457-9.00004-5
© 2014 Elsevier Inc. All rights reserved.

unprecedented complexity and dynamics of bidding processes (Mahdian and Wang, 2009), and the strong-coupling and unpredictability of markets under conditions of imperfect information (Borgs et al., 2005). Moreover, there are plenty of uncertainties in the mapping from the budget into the advertising performance (Muthukrishnan et al., 2010). Thus, search advertisers face tremendous difficulties and challenges while making budget decisions. First, advertisers should take competitors' budget strategies into consideration in order to choose the best response. Secondly, limited advertising budgets should be wisely allocated at different levels of abstraction, in different time granularities, and ideally be adjusted in real-time. Thirdly, budget strategies heavily rely on other advertising strategies relevant to keyword portfolio, bids, and the prediction of advertising targets. Therefore, it is crucial to explore an integrated framework for optimal strategies of budget allocation and adjustment in sponsored search auctions. To the best of our knowledge, this is the first research effort in this direction.

This chapter proposes a novel hierarchical budget optimization framework (BOF) for advertisers to allocate and adjust their advertising budgets throughout the entire lifecycle of advertising campaigns in sponsored search auctions. Our BOF framework provides a basic infrastructure for various optimal budget strategies. We formulate our BOF framework and approve its theoretical soundness through mathematical analysis of relevant properties. Furthermore, we establish a simple but illustrative instantiation of our framework, and design some experiments to evaluate our framework and instantiated strategies, with field data from real-world search advertising campaigns. Experimental results show that our proposed BOF framework and instantiated strategies can effectively decrease the loss of effective clicks by comparing with two baseline budget strategies commonly used in real advertising campaigns.

The contributions of this chapter can be summarized as follows.

- We propose a novel hierarchical framework for budget optimization in search advertisements across several markets, with consideration of the entire lifecycle of advertising campaigns.
- We formulate our BOF framework, and study some desirable properties, then provide an effective solution algorithm. The proposed BOF framework can integrate different optimal algorithms for budget decisions in sponsored search auctions, without adding computational complexity.
- We also establish a simple but illustrative instantiation of our BOF framework, and design some experiments to validate its effectiveness with real-world data from search advertising campaigns.

The rest of this chapter is organized as follows. In Section 4.2, we first state the relevant problems related to budget decisions in search advertisements, and then present the concept of budget optimization. Section 4.3 introduces the budget optimization framework (BOF). Section 4.4 formulates the BOF framework, analyzes its properties, and presents a solution algorithm. Section 4.5 provides an instantiation of the BOF framework. Section 4.6 reports some experimental settings and results to validate the BOF framework and instantiated strategies. Section 4.7 provides some discussions and Section 4.8 concludes this chapter.

4.2 Challenges

4.2.1 Problem Statement

Bidding is triggered once an information request is submitted. A high volume of search demands makes the bidding a continuous, infinite process. The ranking results and prices will be different when any advertiser changes his/her keywords and/or bids at any time, such that an efficient advertising strategy, e.g. for budget allocation, should be capable of dynamically allocating and adjusting advertising budgets on the fly, according to the state of the marketing environment. In the entire lifecycle of advertising campaigns in sponsored search auctions, there mainly exist three different budget decision scenarios, as shown in Figure 3.1.

1. Budget allocation across search advertising markets.

   At the very beginning of a sponsored search auction, given the total budget, the advertiser should decide the budget allocated to each search engine considering the competition and market status.

2. Budget allocation over temporal slots.

   In order to reduce budget waste and improve budget usage efficiency, the advertiser needs to allocate the budget over a series of temporal slots (e.g. daily budget) during a certain promotion period of search advertising campaigns, supposing the budget allocated in a search market is determined. Also, coarse tuning should be made according to the previous performance (e.g. click-through rate and conversion rate of the last temporal slot).

3. Real-time budget adjustment.

   During a certain temporal slot, the advertiser should do real-time adjustment of the remaining budget according to search advertisement efficiency indexes (e.g. click-through rate or conversion rate) in order to avoid either too quickly wasting the budgets or missing golden opportunities in the future. For example, if the advertiser finds that the conversion rate of a certain keyword is high, and that the budget will be used up in a short time, he/she may try to add more budget.

During the entire lifecycle of sponsored search auctions, advertisers must take the promotional purpose and dynamic environment into account to decide the budget allocation across search engines to ensure optimal performance. Correspondingly, it is of necessity to explore an integrated framework for budget optimization with consideration of the entire lifecycle of search advertising campaigns. Such a framework should be capable of dealing with such structured budget problems in sponsored search auctions.

4.2.2 Definition

The following gives a definition for formally specific budget optimization problems in sponsored search auctions.

Definition 4.1 (Budget Optimization).

Input: Given an overall search advertising budget B for an advertiser, a set of search markets $SE, n_1 = |SE|$, a series of temporal slots in a promotion period $TS, n_2 = |TS|$, a series of real-time adjustments of the remaining budget in a temporal slot $RA, n_3 = |RA|$.

Output: A distribution structure for search advertising budgets $\mathcal{A} = (\mathcal{A}_1, \mathcal{A}_2, \mathcal{A}_3)$ with $\mathcal{A}_1$ over market-budget vectors $x \in \mathcal{R}^{n_1}$, $\mathcal{A}_2$ over interval-budget vectors $y \in \mathcal{R}^{n_2}$, $\mathcal{A}_3$ over realtime-budget vectors $z \in \mathcal{R}^{n_3}$, such that $expenditure(\mathcal{A}_1, \mathcal{A}_2, \mathcal{A}_3) \leq B$ and $loss(\mathcal{A}_1, \mathcal{A}_2, \mathcal{A}_3)$ is minimized.

4.3 A Budget Optimization Framework

This research provides a hierarchical budget optimization framework (BOF), with consideration of the entire lifecycle of advertising campaigns in sponsored search auctions (Figure 3.1). The BOF framework consists of three levels, corresponding to these three budget decision scenarios as discussed in Section 4.2.1, with attention to the advertising system, campaign, and keywords, respectively. Specifically, the **system/account level** concerns budget allocation across several search markets in the medium/long term (e.g. over half a year). The **campaign level** focuses on budget distribution over a series of temporal slots (e.g. day or month) during a promotion period. The **keyword level** aims to adaptively adjust the remaining budget during a temporal slot of advertising campaigns in order to keep valuable expenditure for potential clicks in the future. Budget strategies at these three levels complement each other, thus forming an integrated chain of budget optimization in sponsored search auctions. That is, results at higher levels constrain activities at lower levels and, inversely, operational results at lower levels create feedbacks to activities at higher levels.

The notations used in this chapter are listed in Table 4.1.

The System Level

Generally, budget decisions across several advertising markets comprise the first issue faced by an advertiser in sponsored search auctions. Let B^l denote the overall budget for search advertisements for an advertiser $l, l = 1, 2, \ldots, r$, across n_1 markets, then budget allocation at the system level can be given as:

$$\xi : B^l \rightarrow x_1^l, \ldots, x_i^l, \ldots, x_s^l, i \in \{1, 2, \ldots, n_1\},$$

Table 4.1 List of notations.

Notation	Definition
B	The overall budget for search advertisements
n_1	The number of search markets
n_2	The number of temporal slots during a promotion period
n_3	The number of real-time adjustments in each temporal slot in every search market
x_i	The budget allocated in the ith search market, $i = 1, 2, \ldots, n_1$
$y_{i,j}$	The budget allocated in the jth temporal slot in the ith search market, $j = 1, 2, \ldots, n_2$
$z_{i,j,k}$	The budget allocated for the kth real-time adjustment in the jth temporal slot in the ith search market, $k = 1, 2, \ldots, n_3$
$d_{i,j,k}$	The optimal budget for the kth real-time adjustment in the jth temporal slot in the ith search market
$c_{i,j,k}$	Clicks per unit cost of the kth real-time adjustment in the jth temporal slot in the ith search market
$p_{i,j,k}$	The effective CTR of the kth real-time adjustment in the jth temporal slot in the ith search market (below the optimal budget)
$p'_{i,j,k}$	The effective CTR of the kth real-time adjustment in the jth temporal slot in the ith search market (above the optimal budget)
$l^+_{i,j,k}$	The exceeded section (the allocated budget minus the optimal budget) of the kth real-time adjustment in the jth temporal slot in the ith search market
$l^-_{i,j,k}$	The insufficient section (the optimal budget minus the allocated budget) of the kth real-time adjustment in the jth temporal slot in the ith search market

where x^l_i denotes the budget allocated to a given search advertising market i. Advertising costs are positively proportional to the sum of budgets allocated to a search advertising market by all advertisers. That is, the higher the budget that is allocated to a market, the more competitive the bidding, and then the higher the advertising costs. For a given type of competitive advertiser (e.g. a group of advertisers with similar advertising targets), search demands from relevant keywords are finite. Therefore, from the point of view of marketing efficiency, the search advertising efficiency of a market is not a rigid, monotonically increasing function of the allocated budget. Although all advertisers have common knowledge that the budget allocated to a market should not exceed a certain amount in order to keep the marketing efficiency at a certain level, no advertiser knows their competitors' budget strategies exactly, e.g. the amount of these competitors' allocated budget, while manipulating their budget at the system level. In this sense, budget allocation across search advertising markets can be viewed as a game with incomplete information.

The Campaign Level

Budget decisions at the campaign level aim to distribute x^l_i over a series of temporal slots (e.g. a day) during an advertising period, which can be given as:

$$\tau : x^l_i \rightarrow y^l_{i,1}, \ldots, y^l_{i,j}, \ldots, y^l_{i,n_2}, \; j \in \{1, 2, \ldots, n_2\},$$

where $y^l_{i,j}$ represents the budget allocated to the jth slot during a period in a search advertising market i by an advertiser l, which acts as a constraint for relevant bidding strategies. Budget decisions at the campaign level should consider various performance indicators including the distribution of search demands, total clicks, ineffective clicks, cost-per-click, bids, the conversion rate, and revenue per click. At this level, advertisers are also supposed to make some coarse adjustment for budgets in future slots according to historical advertising effects (especially in the immediately previous temporal slot). The advertiser makes budget decisions at the campaign level with the outcome from the system level as constraint. Apparently the former will also provide valuable feedback to the latter.

The Keyword Level

Budget decisions at keyword level aim to dynamically adjust the remaining budget (with the initial value as $y^l_{i,j}$) for advertising campaigns, during a given temporal slot, which can be given as

$$\gamma : y^l_{i,j}(t) \rightarrow y^l_{i,j}(t+1),$$

where $y^l_{i,j}(t+1)$ represents the remaining budget (through some possible adjustments on $y^l_{i,j}(t)$) at time $t+1$ in the jth slot in the search advertising market i by advertiser l. Budget adjustment at the keyword level is made mainly according to some performance indicators of keywords, and bidding strategies as well. In the literature, most studies (DasGupta and Muthukrishnan 2013; Feldman et al., 2007; Muthukrishnan et al., 2010) were done at this level, focusing on the bidding determination but ignoring the adjustment of the remaining budget of a temporal slot. Again, the adjustment at this level takes the budget allocated to a temporal slot as a constraint. Meanwhile, the former provides valuable feedback to the latter.

4.4 Mathematics of the Budget Optimization Framework

4.4.1 Formulation

We formulate the BOF framework as a hierarchical programming model. In related literature various hierarchical optimization techniques were developed to model decentralized planning problems with multiple decision-makers in a hierarchical organization (Anandalingam and Friese, 1992; Lai, 1996). In this section, we establish a three-level programming model for budget optimization throughout the entire lifecycle of advertising campaigns in sponsored search auctions.

Model 1 (System Level Model).   *Let $h^{(1)} : \mathbb{R}^{n_1+p} \rightarrow \mathbb{R}$ be the loss function at the system level, $f^{(1)} : \mathbb{R}^{n_1} \rightarrow \mathbb{R}^{m_1}$ be budget constraints at the system level, $g^{(1)} : S_1 \rightarrow \mathbb{R}^p$ be the optimal loss function at the campaign level, $S_1 \subset \mathbb{R}^{n_1}$, then the budget optimization at the* system level can be modeled as,

$$
g^{(0)} := \min_{x} h^{(1)}(x, g^{(1)}(x))
$$
$$
s.t. f^{(1)}(x) \leq \mathbf{0}, \tag{4.1}
$$
$$
x \in X \subset \mathbb{R}^{n_1}.
$$

Model 2 (Campaign Level Model). *Let $h_i^{(2)} : \mathbb{R}^{n_2+q} \to \mathbb{R}$ be the loss function at the campaign level, $f_i^{(2)} : \mathbb{R}^{n_1+n_2} \to \mathbb{R}^{m_2}$ be budget constraints at the campaign level, $g_i^{(2)} : S_2 \to \mathbb{R}^q$ be the optimal loss function at the keyword level, where $i \in \{1, \ldots, p\}$, and $x \in S_1 = \{x \in X, f^{(1)}(x) \leq \mathbf{0}\}$, $S_2 \subset \mathbb{R}^{n_2}$, then the budget optimization at the campaign level can be modeled as,*

$$
g_i^{(1)}(x) := \bar{g}_i^{(1)}(x, g_i^{(2)}) = \min_{y_i} h_i^{(2)}(y_i, g_i^{(2)}(y_i))
$$
$$
s.t. f_i^{(2)}(x, y_i) \leq \mathbf{0}, \tag{4.2}
$$
$$
y_i \in Y \subset \mathbb{R}^{n_2}.
$$

Model 3 (Keyword Level Model). *Let $h_{ij}^{(3)} : \mathbb{R}^{n_3} \to \mathbb{R}$ be the loss function at the keyword level, $f_{ij}^{(3)} : \mathbb{R}^{n_2+n_3} \to \mathbb{R}^{m_3}$ be budget constraints at the keyword level, where $i \in \{1, \ldots, p\}$, $j \in \{1, \ldots, q\}$, and $y \in S_2 = \{y \in Y, f(x, y) \leq \mathbf{0} \text{ for } x \in S_1\}$, then the budget optimization at the keyword level can be modeled as,*

$$
g_{ij}^{(2)}(y) := \min_{z} h_{ij}^{(3)}(z_{ij})
$$
$$
s.t. f_{ij}^{(3)}(y, z_{ij}) \leq \mathbf{0}, \tag{4.3}
$$
$$
z_{ij} \in Z \subset \mathbb{R}^{n_3}.
$$

These three models consider budget decision problems at three interactive levels together in a hierarchical way, taking into account of the entire lifecycle of search advertising campaigns. **System Level Model**, **Campaign Level Model**, and **Keyword Level Model** form the overall formulated structure of our BOF framework, that is an integrated close-loop chain model of budget optimization in sponsored search auctions. Our BOF framework considers not only budget decision problems at each of the three levels, but also interactive relationships between these levels. Feasible regions of upper-models constrain lower-models. Conversely, solutions of lower-models also affect optimal solutions of upper-models. Furthermore, note that our framework will not degenerate even if considering more complicated situations in sponsored search auctions.

4.4.2 Properties

In the following, we discuss some convex properties of our BOF framework.

Theorem 4.1.   *If $h(z)$ and $f(y,z)$ are convex functions, $g(y) = \min_z\{h(z) : f(y,z) \le 0\}$, then $g(y)$ is also a convex function.*

Proof.   Let $S = \{(y,z)|f(y,z) \le 0\}$. Since $f(y,z)$ is a convex function, it can be deduced that S is a convex set.

Define $I_S(t)$ as

$$I_S(t) = \begin{cases} 0, & \text{if } t \in S \\ \infty, & \text{else.} \end{cases}$$

We can prove that $I_S(t)$ is a convex function.

Define $\hat{h}(y,z) = h(z) + I_S(y,z)$. Because $h(z)$ and $I_S(t)$ are convex functions, $\hat{h}(y,z)$ is also a convex function. Hence, we have $\min_z \hat{h}(y,z)$ convex and

$$\hat{h}(y,z) = \begin{cases} h(z), & \text{if } (y,z) \in S \\ \infty, & \text{otherwise.} \end{cases}$$

Thus, $min_z h(z) = \min_z \hat{h}(y,z)$ for $(y,z) \in S$. Therefore, $g(y)$ is convex.

Theorem 4.2.   *If $h(y,\hat{y}), g(y),$ and $f(x,y)$ are convex functions, $h(y,\hat{y})$ is non-decreasing on $\hat{y}$ and $\bar{g}(x) = \min_y\{h(y,g(y)) : f(x,y) \le 0\}$, then $\bar{g}(x)$ is also a convex function.*

Proof.   Let $S = \{(x,y)|f(x,y) \le 0\}$. Since $f(x,y)$ is a convex function, it can be deduced that S is a convex set, hence I_S is a convex function.

Define $\hat{h}(x,y) = h(y,g(y)) + I_S(x,y)$. Because $h(y,\hat{y})$ is convex and non-decreasing on $\hat{y}$, $\hat{h}(y,z)$ is also a convex function. Hence, we have $\min_y \hat{h}(x,y)$ convex and

$$\hat{h}(x,y) = \begin{cases} h(y,g(y)), & \text{if } (x,y) \in S \\ \infty, & \text{otherwise.} \end{cases}$$

Thus $min_y h(y,g(y)) = \min_y \hat{h}(x,y)$ for $(x,y) \in S$. Therefore, $\bar{g}(x)$ is convex.

From Theorem 4.1 and 4.2, we can obtain the following corollaries.

Corollary 4.1.   *If $h^{(3)}(z)$ and $f^{(3)}(y,z)$ are convex functions, then the optimization problem (4.3) is a convex programming problem.*

Corollary 4.2.   *If $h^{(3)}(z), f^{(3)}(y,z), h^{(2)}(y,\hat{y}),$ and $f^{(2)}(x,y)$ are convex functions, $h^{(2)}(y,\hat{y})$ is non-decreasing with $\hat{y}$, then the optimization problem (4.2) is a convex programming problem.*

Corollary 4.3.   *If $h^{(3)}(z), f^{(3)}(y,z), h^{(2)}(y,\hat{y}), f^{(2)}(x,y), h^{(1)}(x,\hat{x}),$ and $f^{(1)}(x)$ are convex functions, $h^{(2)}$ is non-decreasing with $\hat{y}$ and $h^{(1)}$ is non-decreasing with $\hat{x}$, then model (4.1) is a convex programming problem.*

4.4.3 The Solution

Here we provide a general solution process for our BOF framework, described as follows,

Step 1: Solve each **Keyword Level Model** and interpolate $g^{(2)}(y)$ (e.g. 1D interpolate for a piecewise linear objective function $h^{(3)}$), denoted by $\eta(y)$.

Step 2: Substitute $g^{(2)}(y)$ with $\eta(y)$, solve each **Campaign Level Model** and interpolate $g^{(1)}(x)$, denoted by $\phi(x)$.

Step 3: Substitute $g^{(1)}(x)$ with $\phi(x)$, minimize $h^{(1)}(x, \phi(x))$ under constraints from model (4.1).

Finally it comes to a solution for our framework, namely optimal budget decisions in sponsored search auctions.

4.5 The Framework Instantiation

4.5.1 Basis

In this section, we propose a simple but illustrative instantiation for our BOF framework. In sponsored search auctions, a click is an action initiating a visit to a website via a sponsored link, and if a click is an intentional click that has a realistic probability of generating values once the visitor arrives at the website, then it is a *valid click*, otherwise it is *invalid* (Jansen, 2008). In this chapter, we consider the generated value obtained through some kind of user behavior including purchase, registration, staying on the landing page for more than 5s, surfing more than 2 links, bookmarking and downloading relevant pages. Then we give a concept of effective click-through rate (CTR) as follows.

Definition 4.2 (Effective CTR). Effective CTR is the ratio of valid clicks and total clicks, i.e.

$$\text{Effective CTR} = \frac{\text{valid clicks}}{\text{total clicks}}.$$

In the objective function, we consider minimizing the loss in terms of effective clicks. In this research, we make the following assumptions.

- If the allocated budget is less than the optimal budget, the effective CTR is denoted by a constant $p_{i,j,k}$.
- If the allocated budget is larger than the optimal budget, the exceeded section (the allocated budget minus the optimal budget) will be used up.

The effective CTR of the exceeded section is denoted by a constant $p'_{i,j,k}$, which is smaller than $p_{i,j,k}$. This can be justified by the law of diminishing marginal utility (Mankiw, 1998). Specifically, when advertisers invest more and more budgets in a search market, the total effective clicks increase at high rates until the total budget arrives at a certain amount (e.g. the optimal budget); when it exceeds the certain amount, total effective clicks increase at comparatively lower rates.

For each i and j, $i = 1, 2, \ldots, n_1$, $j = 1, 2, \ldots, n_2$, the loss of the kth real-time adjustment contains the following three parts:

- If $I_{i,j,k}^+ = I_{i,j,k}^- = 0$, then the loss concerns ineffective clicks generated from $z_{i,j,k}$, that is,

$$c_{i,j,k} z_{i,j,k} (1 - p_{i,j,k}).$$

- If $I_{i,j,k}^+ > 0$, then the loss includes ineffective clicks generated from $z_{i,j,k} - I_{i,j,k}^+$ and from $I_{i,j,k}^+$, that is,

$$c_{i,j,k}(z_{i,j,k} - I_{i,j,k}^+)(1 - p_{i,j,k}) + c_{i,j,k} I_{i,j,k}^+ (1 - p'_{i,j,k}) - c_{i,j,k} I_{i,j,k}^+ p'_{i,j,k}$$
$$= c_{i,j,k} z_{i,j,k} (1 - p_{i,j,k}) + c_{i,j,k} I_{i,j,k}^+ (p_{i,j,k} - 2p'_{i,j,k}).$$

- If $I_{i,j,k}^- > 0$, then the loss is the ineffective clicks generated from $z_{i,j,k}$ and the lost effective clicks by $I_{i,j,k}^-$, that is,

$$c_{i,j,k} z_{i,j,k} (1 - p_{i,j,k}) + c_{i,j,k} I_{i,j,k}^- p_{i,j,k}.$$

4.5.2 The Model

We establish a model with the notations in Table 4.1 as follows.

The system level concerns minimizing the total loss in terms of effective clicks across n_1 search markets,

$$\min \sum_{i=1}^{n_1} g_i^{(1)}(x)$$

$$s.t. \sum_{i=1}^{n_1} x_i - B \leq 0 \tag{4.4}$$

$$x \geq 0,$$

where $g_i^{(1)}$ is the minimum of the loss in terms of effective clicks in the ith search market at the campaign level, given as,

$$g_i^{(1)}(x) := \min \sum_{j=1}^{n_2} g_{i,j}^{(2)}(y)$$

$$s.t. \sum_{j=1}^{n_2} y_{i,j} - x_i \leq 0 \tag{4.5}$$

$$y \geq 0,$$

where $g_{i,j}^{(2)}$ is the minimum of the loss in terms of effective clicks in the jth temporal slot in the ith search market at the keyword level, given as,

$$g_{i,j}^{(2)}(y) := \min \sum_{k=1}^{n_3} c_{i,j,k}[z_{i,j,k}(1 - p_{i,j,k}) + I_{i,j,k}^- p_{i,j,k} + I_{i,j,k}^+(p_{i,j,k} - 2p'_{i,j,k})]$$

$$s.t. \sum_{k=1}^{n_3} z_{i,j,k} - y_{i,j} \leq 0$$

$$I_{i,j,k}^+ = [z_{i,j,k} - d_{i,j,k}] \vee 0$$

$$I_{i,j,k}^- = [d_{i,j,k} - z_{i,j,k}] \vee 0$$

$$z_{i,j,k} \geq 0, k = 1, 2, \ldots, n_3.$$

(4.6)

4.6 Experiments and Validation

4.6.1 Data Description

We collected field reports and logs from practical search advertising campaigns by several enterprises and organizations in two search markets during the period from September 2008 to August 2010, and designed experiments to validate the proposed budget optimization framework and instantiated strategies. In addition, we also did some approximate treatments on the statistical data in order to support intelligible experimental settings. We made independent budget optimization experiments in different temporal granularities (year/month/week/day). This research reports experimental settings and some relevant results following the framework instantiation and solutions given in the previous section. We also compared optimal values with the performance of two baseline budget strategies commonly used in practical advertising campaigns.

4.6.2 Experimental Design

We conducted some preliminary computational evaluations of our approach. For comparison purposes, we implemented two baseline budget strategies that are commonly applied in practical search advertising campaigns. The first benchmark, called BASE1-Fixed, represents the budget strategy from a type of advertiser who sets a fixed daily budget according to experiential or survey knowledge, however without any adjustments to the remaining budget. The second benchmark is called BASE2-Heuristics with some necessary adjustments based on the fixed strategy. In other words, the middle-term (e.g. monthly) budget is equally distributed over a series of short-term temporal slots (e.g. daily), then the advertiser adjusts the daily budget through some heuristic rules: if the loss of effective clicks for the current day is less than the average loss computed from the historical data, then the daily budget for the next day is increased proportionally; if the loss for the current day is more than the average loss, then the daily budget for the next day is decreased proportionally; otherwise the daily budget is kept unchanged.

The evaluation focuses on a two-fold purpose. The first is to prove some properties of the BOF framework as analyzed in Section 4.4.2. The second is to evaluate the performance of the framework instantiation in the crisp case given in Section 4.5.2 and instantiated strategies given in Section 4.5. Below, we provide details about our experimental evaluation results.

The experimental scene is described as follows: an advertiser takes a advertising schedule of 8 hours (e.g. 9:00–17:00) to participate in sponsored search auctions each day; then he/she plans to adjust the remaining budget 4 times, e.g. once every 2 h. Clicks per unit cost and the effective CTR given in Table 4.2 and 4.3 are collected from field logs of practical advertising campaigns during 5 days, where $c_{i,j,1} = \cdots = c_{i,j,4}$ ($c_{i,j}$ for short) reflects that these four segments of real-time adjustment have the same clicks per unit cost in the jth day in the ith search market, and

$$\boldsymbol{p}_{i,j} = (p_{i,j,1}, p_{i,j,2}, p_{i,j,3}, p_{i,j,4}), \boldsymbol{p}'_{i,j} = (p'_{i,j,1}, p'_{i,j,2}, p'_{i,j,3}, p'_{i,j,4}).$$

Suppose that the overall budget during the 5 days is $B = \$500.000$. The optimal budget $d_{i,j,k}$ for every two hours can be obtained through statistical analysis from historical logs of advertising campaigns, $\boldsymbol{d}_{i,j} = (d_{i,j,1}, d_{i,j,2}, d_{i,j,3}, d_{i,j,4})$, as shown in Table 4.4. Notice that these optimal budgets somewhat reflect budget constraints in historical campaigns, which can be viewed as the reference for the optimal procedure of budget manipulation for advertising campaigns in the future, since they are independent of budget constraints in the coming days.

Table 4.2   Values of $c_{i,j}$ from promotion reports of an advertiser.

$c_{i,j}$	$j = 1$	$j = 2$	$j = 3$	$j = 4$	$j = 5$
$i = 1$	0.7	0.65	0.75	0.68	0.72
$i = 2$	0.68	0.62	0.78	0.72	0.80

Table 4.3   Values of $p_{i,j}$ and $p'_{i,j}$ from promotion reports of an advertiser.

	$p_{1,j}$	$p'_{1,j}$	$p_{2,j}$	$p'_{2,j}$
$j = 1$	(0.80,0.75,0.78,0.70)	(0.20,0.25,0.21,0.24)	(0.88,0.79,0.75,0.80)	(0.16,0.14,0.25,0.27)
$j = 2$	(0.82,0.84,0.80,0.78)	(0.26,0.18,0.24,0.26)	(0.76,0.84,0.68,0.61)	(0.24,0.13,0.24,0.18)
$j = 3$	(0.81,0.76,0.65,0.60)	(0.15,0.19,0.21,0.16)	(0.79,0.82,0.76,0.78)	(0.12,0.17,0.23,0.27)
$j = 4$	(0.79,0.82,0.80,0.78)	(0.25,0.23,0.18,0.12)	(0.85,0.79,0.82,0.75)	(0.19,0.22,0.26,0.17)
$j = 5$	(0.86,0.75,0.80,0.76)	(0.24,0.26,0.18,0.27)	(0.87,0.82,0.76,0.68)	(0.19,0.24,0.16,0.26)

Table 4.4 The optimal budget reference $d_{i,j}$ (unit: $).

	$d_{1,j}$	$d_{2,j}$
$j = 1$	(15.000,19.000,11.500,16.500)	(11.500,16.500,18.500,13.500)
$j = 2$	(18.500,11.500,17.000,16.000)	(10.000,12.500,17.000,22.000)
$j = 3$	(20.500,12.000,14.000,14.500)	(12.000,8.500,17.500,16.000)
$j = 4$	(16.500,13.000,11.000,9.000)	(12.000,9.500,8.000,14.000)
$j = 5$	(13.000,18.500,15.000,11.500)	(16.000,18.500,11.500,9.000)

4.6.3 Experimental Results

The optimal solutions are obtained through the BOF framework instantiation and solution proposed in Section 4.4.3. We employed the sequential least square quadratic programming method to solve the budget optimization model (as described in Section 4.5.2) embedded in our BOF framework. The main experimental results are described as follows:

1. At the system level, the optimal budget allocated to search market-1 is $247.000, and to search market-2 is $253.000.
2. At the campaign level, optimal budgets for each day in these two markets are shown in Table 4.5.
3. At the keyword level, optimal budgets for every two hours in each day in these two markets are shown in Table 4.6.
4. The overall optimal value (e.g. the cumulative loss of effective clicks) for this case by our BOF framework and instantiated strategies is 106.032.
5. As shown in Figures 4.1 and 4.2, budget decisions abstracted at all these three levels in our BOF framework are convex programming problems. Therefore, the overall budget optimization problem in the hierarchical BOF framework is convex.

In typical scenarios of budget manipulation with the BASE1-fixed strategy, most advertisers evenly divide the overall budget in the two search markets (i.e. $250.000 in each), keep budgets distributed in a series of temporal slots (e.g. 5 days) unchanged (i.e. $50.000 as daily budget), and ignore the necessity for real-time adjustments of (remaining) daily budgets but just allocate the same amount of budget for every two hours (i.e. $12.500). Some cautious advertisers would like to take chances to adjust the daily budget (e.g. either increase or decrease), but without consideration of real-time adjustments, probably due to the fact that the latter is time-consuming and sophisticatedly complex. The cumulative loss of effective clicks

Table 4.5 Optimal solutions at the campaign level (unit: $).

	$j = 1$	$j = 2$	$j = 3$	$j = 4$	$j = 5$
Search market-1	27.065	56.096	60.124	49.098	54.617
Search market-2	59.124	41.571	54.108	43.085	55.110

Table 4.6 Optimal solutions at the keyword level (unit: $).

Search market *i*, day *j*	*k* = 1	*k* = 2	*k* = 3	*k* = 4
		*k*th two-hour		
$i = 1, j = 1$	15.000	0.565	11.500	0.000
$i = 1, j = 2$	18.500	11.500	17.000	9.096
$i = 1, j = 3$	20.500	12.000	14.000	13.624
$i = 1, j = 4$	16.500	13.000	11.000	8.598
$i = 1, j = 5$	13.000	15.117	15.000	11.500
$i = 2, j = 1$	11.500	16.500	17.624	13.500
$i = 2, j = 2$	10.000	12.500	17.000	2.071
$i = 2, j = 3$	12.000	8.500	17.500	16.000
$i = 2, j = 4$	12.000	9.500	8.000	13.585
$i = 2, j = 5$	16.000	18.500	11.500	9.000

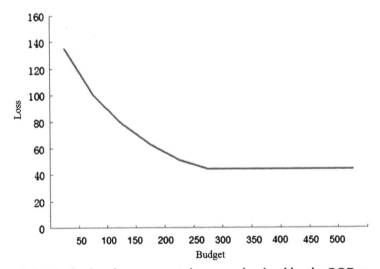

Figure 4.1 The budget-loss curve at the campaign level by the BOF strategy.

is 134.567 and 133.729 for the BASE1-Fixed strategy and the BASE2-Heuristics strategy, respectively. Figures 4.3 and 4.4 illustrate the budget distribution over time in these two search advertising markets, respectively. Figures 4.5 and 4.6 illustrate the loss of effective clicks over time in these two search advertising markets, respectively. Several interesting findings are given as follows:

1. From Figures 4.3 and 4.4, we note that the amplitude variation in budget adjustment by our BOF framework is larger than the other two baseline strategies. This indicates that our BOF framework is more sensitive to the dynamics of advertising markets.
2. We also notice that the budget allocated initially to the search market-1 by our BOF framework is much less than that of the other two baseline strategies; then the loss of

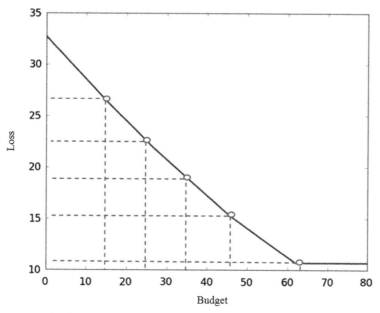

Figure 4.2　The budget-loss curve at the keyword level by the BOF strategy.

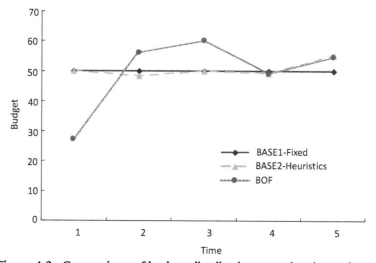

Figure 4.3　Comparison of budget distribution over time in market-1.

effective clicks is higher. The cumulative loss of effective clicks by our BOF framework gradually decreases, and then becomes less than that of the other two baseline strategies.

3. In the search market-2, we observe that our BOF framework always performs better than the other two baseline strategies in terms of the loss of effective clicks.

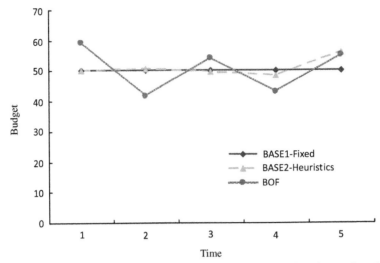

Figure 4.4 Comparison of budget distribution over time in market-2.

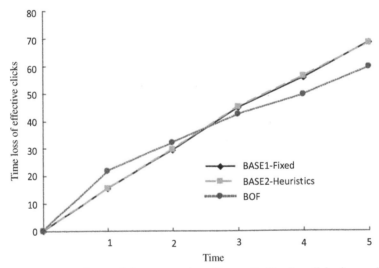

Figure 4.5 Comparison of the accumulated loss of effective clicks in market-1.

4. From Figures 4.5 and 4.6, we note that our BOF framework performs better than the other two baseline strategies in these two search markets, in terms of the cumulative loss of effective clicks. In detail, our BOF framework and instantiated strategies can effectively decrease the loss of effective clicks (about 21.21% and 20.71%, respectively) over the performance of the BASE1-Fixed strategy and the BASE2-Heuristics strategy in practical search advertising campaigns.

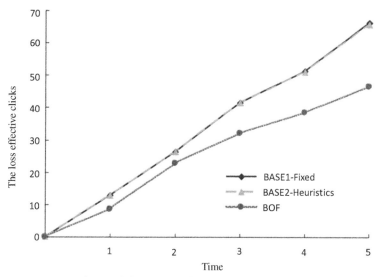

Figure 4.6   Comparison of the accumulated loss of effective clicks in market-2.

5. We also notice that the BASE2-Heuristic strategy outperforms the BASE1-Fixed strategy. The possible reason might be that it adapts to the dynamics of the advertising environment through considering the historical knowledge of advertising performance.

4.7 Discussions

From the budget point of view, limited resource capacity significantly influences perceptions of the environment and thus the marketing performance of small businesses, because marketing exercises and expenses tend to have lesser priority over other elements (Fam and Yang, 2006). For small businesses, budget constraints and lack of time and expertise may lead to limited and often ad hoc or irrational promotional decisions. On the one hand, budget constraints limit the feasible space of various optimal strategies (e.g. bidding strategies, keyword strategies), and thus complicate operational situations in different contexts (e.g. sponsored search auctions). On the other hand, budget constraints naturally lead to an important problem: how to allocate and adjust the limited budget in a rational way to maximize the expected profit.

The state-of-the-art budget-related work, in the context of sponsored search auctions, usually takes the budget as a constraint to determine bids over keywords (e.g. DasGupta and Muthukrishnan 2013; Feldman et al., 2007; Muthukrishnan et al., 2010). We categorize such work under the term of budget-constrained bidding strategies. To the best of our knowledge, there are few, if any, research efforts on budget optimization in an integrated way in sponsored search auctions. Moreover, we argue that the budget in sponsored search auctions is structured as we analyzed in Section 4.2.1. Our work is the first initiative to consider budget decision problems in various decision-making situations of sponsored search auctions as a whole, and the first to propose a novel integrated framework that could be viewed as an environment/testbed for various budget optimization strategies.

Our research provides key managerial insights for advertisers in sponsored search auctions. Advertisers usually take the budget as simple constraints, and put a lot of effort into finding more effective ways for possible operations as defined by various kinds of markets (e.g. sponsored search auctions). This work indicates that a simple strategy for budget allocation and adjustment can significantly minimize the loss in terms of effective clicks in sponsored search auctions. Note that we do not expect that our BOF framework is the only way to deal with budget-related problems in search auctions. We hope that our work could raise our peers' interest in budget decision problems at different levels, in different situations (e.g. goals, schedules), with different settings of various parameters (e.g. auction mechanisms, processes).

4.8 Conclusions

In this chapter we propose a novel hierarchical budget optimization framework with consideration of the entire lifecycle of advertising campaigns in sponsored search auctions. We formulate our BOF framework, make a mathematical analysis of some desirable properties, and present an effective solution algorithm. Furthermore, we provide a simple but illustrative instantiation of our BOF framework, and perform some experiments to validate our work with real-world data from advertising campaigns. Experimental results are quite promising, where our BOF framework and instantiated strategies perform better than two other typical budget strategies commonly used in practical search advertising campaigns.

This chapter reports some preliminary research on our BOF framework. It not only provides an open context for possible efforts on budget strategies, but also is valuable in helping advertisers in practical sponsored search auctions. In an ongoing work we extend the BOF framework to more complicated situations with uncertainties in sponsored search auctions. Another interesting but challenging perspective is to explore game-theoretical budget decisions at the system level, and to study optimal social efficiency. Thirdly, we also intend to extend our BOF framework in the direction of co-optimization with various advertising strategies (e.g. bidding strategies, keyword strategies), and thus facilitate advertising performance in an innovative way.

References

Aggarwal, G., S. Muthukrishnan, D. Pál, M. Pál. 2009. General auction mechanism for search advertising. In: Proceedings of the 18th International Conference on World Wide Web, April 20–24, Madrid, Spain, 2009.

Amiri A., S. Menon. 2006. Scheduling web banner advertisements with multiple display frequencies. IEEE Transactions on Systems, Man and Cybernetics-Part A, 36(2):245–251.

Anandalingam G., T. L. Friese. 1992. Hierarchical optimization: An introduction. Annals of Operations Research, 34(1):1–11.

Borgs C., J. Chayes, N. Immorlica, M. Mahdian, A. Saberi. 2005. Multi-unit auctions with budget-constrained bidders. In: Proceedings of the 6th ACM Conference on Electronic Commerce, June 5–8, Vancouver, BC, Canada, 2005.

DasGupta, B., S. Muthukrishnan. 2013. Stochastic budget optimization in Internet advertising, Algorithmica, 65(3):634–661.

Fam K., Z. Yang. 2006. Primary influences of environmental uncertainty on promotions budget allocation and performance: A cross-country study of retail advertisers. Journal of Business Research, 59(2):259–267.

Feldman J., S. Muthukrishnan, M. Pál, C. Stein. 2007. Budget optimization in search-based advertising auctions. In: Proceedings of the 8th ACM Conference on Electronic Commerce, June 11–15, San Diego, California, USA, 2007.

Jansen, B. J. 2008. Click fraud. IEEE Computer, 40(7):85–86.

Jansen, B. J., A. Spink. 2007. Sponsored search: Is money a motivator for providing relevant results?. IEEE Computer, 40(8):50–55.

Lai, Y. J. 1996. Hierarchical optimization: A satisfactory solution. Fuzzy Sets and Systems, 77(3):321–335.

Mahdian, M., G. Wang. 2009. Clustering-based bidding languages for sponsored search. In: Proceedings of the 17th Annual European Symposium on Algorithms, September 7–9, Copenhagen, Denmark, 2009.

Mankiw, N. G. 1998 Principles of economics. Fort Worth, TX.

Muthukrishnan S, M. Pál, Z. Svitkina. 2010. Stochastic models for budget optimization in search-based advertising. Algorithmica, 58(4):1022–1044.

Wang, F. Y. 2010. The emergence of intelligent enterprises: From CPS to CPSS. IEEE Intelligent Systems, 25(4):85–88.

CHAPTER 5

The First Step to Allocate Advertising Budget in Sponsored Search Auctions

5.1 Introduction

With the development of the Internet, more and more internet users take search engines as the entrance. In China, the search engine market scale has reached 18.78 billion, and the number of search users has reached more than 407 million, accounting for 79.4% of internet users by the end of 2011. On the one hand, search users are highly task-driven, which makes search advertising more targeted than other advertising forms. On the other hand, advertisers only need to pay when corresponding advertisements are clicked in sponsored search auctions. However, advertisers from middle or small enterprises usually have limited budgets, thus have to make budget decisions wisely in different search advertising markets, either to promote their brands or to enhance sales.

In sponsored search auctions (SSA) how to allocate a limited budget rationally is a critical issue that is also important to various other advertising strategies. Fruchter and Dou (2005) used dynamic programming techniques to get analytical solutions to optimal budgeting decisions between a generic market and a specialized market. They found that in the long run an advertiser should always spend more in the specialized market. The budget optimization problem can also be cast as an online (multiple-choice) knapsack problem (Babaioff et al., 2007; Chakrabarty et al., 2007; Zhou et al., 2008; Zhou and Naroditskiy, 2008) to achieve a provably optimal competitive ratio for the advertisers. Several stochastic models were established (Du et al., 2007; DasGupta and Muthukrishnan, 2012; Feldman et al., 2007; Muthukrishnan et al., 2007, 2010) to spread a given amount of advertising budget over a set of keywords of interest to maximize the expected number of clicks.

With consideration of the entire lifecycle of advertising campaigns in sponsored search auctions, there exist three budget allocation scenarios at different temporal granularities, including long-term allocation across search markets prior to SSA promotion, budget

Yang and Wang: Budget Constraints and Optimization in Sponsored Search Auctions. http://dx.doi.org/10.1016/B978-0-12-411457-9.00005-7
© 2014 Elsevier Inc. All rights reserved.

distribution over a series of temporal slots (e.g. daily budget constraints) for a specific SSA campaign, and real-time adjustment of the budget within given temporal slots (Yang et al., 2012). Budget allocation and adjustment strategies at these three stages construct a closed-loop, composite strategy for budget decisions in sponsored search auctions, via forms of constraints and feedbacks. This chapter aims to find an effective solution for budget allocation at the first stage.

We define the budget allocation problem as a knapsack problem, and propose feasible solutions for two different decision scenarios: budget initialization prior to SSA promotion and budget adjustment during SSA promotion. The number of clicks triggered from a specific set of keywords and average cost-per-click (CPC) serve as main inputs for budget allocation decisions. We use some keyword tools provided by Google and the sequential importance sampling (SIS) filter (Liu et al., 2001) to estimate parameters necessary for our budget allocation models, and employ dynamic programming to find the optimal solution. In order to validate our model, we design some computational experiments with the data collected from practical campaigns in sponsored search auctions. Experimental results show that our budget allocation models outperform the baseline that is widely used in practice.

The rest of the chapter is organized as follows. In Section 5.2 we state the first-stage budget allocation problem, and provide the allocation model for the budget decision prior to SSA promotion in Section 5.3, and the adjustment model for the budget decision during SSA promotion in Section 5.4. In Section 5.5, we conduct some experiments with the data from practical advertising campaigns to illustrate the effectiveness of our budget models. Section 5.6 concludes this chapter.

5.2 Problem Statement

Consider there are two search advertising markets, market-1 and market-2, for advertisers to promote their products or services. They need to rationally allocate their advertising budget across these two markets to maximize their revenue expected from promotional activities. The revenue is measured as the number of clicks generated by their SSA campaigns, and the payment for these clicks is taken as the cost. During the period T_j, $(j = 0, 1, 2, \ldots)$, given the total budget $B(T_j)$ is determined, the advertiser needs to decide the budget segment $B_1(T_j)$ for market-1 and the budget segment $B_2(T_j)$ for market-2.

The process of budget allocation across search advertising markets can be divided into two decision scenarios: prior to SSA promotion and during SSA promotion. Prior to SSA promotion, the advertiser can only rely on statistics from keyword research to guide the budget allocation; while during SSA promotion, the advertiser can adjust the budget allocation according to historical performance of his/her campaigns to maximize the expected revenue, and more reports about advertising performance will be obtained. How to use these reports to get more accurate parameters is a crucial issue. We use the particle filter to estimate

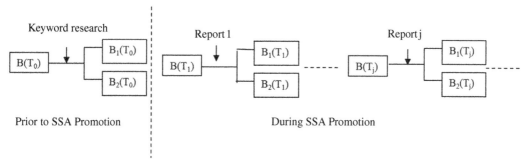

Figure 5.1 Two decision scenarios of budget allocation in sponsored search auctions.

Table 5.1   List of notations.

Notation	Definition
B	The budget for the decision scenario prior to SSA promotion
C_i	The initialized number of clicks generated in market i, $i = 1, 2$
P_i	The initialized cost-per-click (CPC) in market i, $i = 1, 2$
λ_j	The percentage of the number of potential clicks that can be obtained from market i, $i = 1, 2$
$v_i(T_j)$	The number of clicks generated in market i during period T_j
$m_i(T_j)$	The average CPC in market i during the period T_j
β_i	The changing proportion of clicks generated in market i during period T_j (e.g. different from period T_{j-1})

parameters necessary for our budget models. Each time a new report is received, the set of particles is updated by generating and weighting a new set of particles. A particle contains the current estimate of parameters as well as the estimate in the past period. The budget decision scenarios are illustrated in Figure 5.1.

During SSA promotion, the advertiser may delete some keywords or add some new ones. In this work we assume that the co-variance of the average CPC is close to zero, which means the average CPC is not distinctly different between keywords. Our current research considers the budget allocation problem across two search advertising markets. However, these models can be extended to three markets or more with some adaptations.

In the following two sections, we present budget models for these two decision scenarios, and correspondingly discuss feasible solution methods. The notations used in this chapter are shown in Table 5.1.

5.3 Budget Initialization

The budget for the decision scenario prior to SSA promotion is $B(T_0)$, B for short. At the beginning, advertisers should decide a rational proportion of the budget allocated to all the markets. This budget decision problem can be formulated as a knapsack problem. Through keyword researches, it is possible to know that, in market i the initialized number of clicks generated by a specific set of keywords is C_i, and the initialized CPC is P_i. Due to the budget constraint, we assume $B \leq \sum C_i P_i$.

The revenue is measured as the number of total potential clicks obtained from all the markets. Because of the limited budget, advertisers cannot get all potential clicks in a market. Let λ_i be the percentage of potential clicks that can be obtained from market i. Obviously, λ_i can be influenced by the budget allocation decision. If market i can get more advertising budgets, λ_i might increase. So the total revenue is given as $\sum \lambda_i C_i$.

Let B_i denote the budget allocated to market i. Thus we have

$$B_i = \lambda_i C_i P_i.$$

The budget allocation problem can be expressed as the following model

$$\max \sum \lambda_i C_i$$
$$\text{s.t. } \sum \lambda_i C_i P_i \leq B \tag{5.1}$$
$$0 \leq \lambda_i \leq 1.$$

Suppose there are two search markets (e.g. market-1 and market-2) for advertisers to promote their products and services, model (5.1) can be given as follows,

$$\max \lambda_1 C_1 + \lambda_2 C_2$$
$$\text{s.t. } \lambda_1 C_1 P_1 + \lambda_2 C_2 P_2 \leq B \tag{5.2}$$
$$0 \leq \lambda_1, \lambda_2 \leq 1.$$

This model can be solved by dynamic programming methods. Denoting the optimal value of model (5.2) by $g_2[B]$, we have

$$
\begin{aligned}
g_2[B] &= \max_{\substack{\lambda_1 C_1 \times P_1 + \lambda_2 C_2 P_2 \leq B \\ 0 \leq \lambda_1, \lambda_2 \leq 1}} \{\lambda_1 C_1 + \lambda_2 C_2\} \\
&= \max_{\substack{\lambda_1 C_1 \times P_1 \leq B - \lambda_2 C_2 P_2 \\ 0 \leq \lambda_1, \lambda_2 \leq 1}} \{\lambda_1 C_1 + [\lambda_2] C_2\} \\
&= \max_{\substack{B - \lambda_2 C_2 P_2 \geq 0 \\ 0 \leq \lambda_2 \leq 1}} \left\{ \lambda_2 C_2 + \max_{\substack{\lambda_1 C_1 \times P_1 \leq B - \lambda_2 C_2 \times P_2 \\ 0 \leq \lambda_1 \leq 1}} \lambda_1 C_1 \right\} \\
&= \max_{\substack{B - \lambda_2 C_2 P_2 \geq 0 \\ 0 \leq \lambda_2 \leq 1}} \{\lambda_2 C_2 + g_1[B - \lambda_2 C_2 \times P_2]\} \\
&= \max_{0 \leq \lambda_2 \leq \frac{B}{C_2 P_2}} \{\lambda_2 C_2 + g_1[B - \lambda_2 C_2 \times P_2]\}.
\end{aligned}
$$

The value of $g_1[B - \lambda_2 C_2 P_2]$ can also be calculated as follows,

$$g_1\left[B - \lambda_2 C_2 P_2\right] = \max_{\substack{\lambda_1 C_1 \times P_1 \leq B - \lambda_2 C_2 P_2 \\ 0 \leq \lambda_1 \leq 1}} \{\lambda_1 C_1\}$$

$$= \max_{0 \leq \lambda_1 \leq \frac{B - \lambda_2 C_2 P_2}{C_1 \times P_1}} \{\lambda_1 C_1\}.$$

Then we can get the value of $g_2[B]$.

5.4 Budget Adjustment

When the search advertising campaigns are executed, advertisers have to adjust their budget allocations in order to optimize their budget decision globally. During period T_j, advertisers can allocate and/or adjust the budget according to the advertising performance in the period T_{j-1}.

In this section, we propose a particle filtering approach to estimate some necessary parameters for our budget models, such as the number of clicks and the average CPC.

5.4.1 Parameters Estimation

First, we describe a particle filter (Nummiaro et al., 2002) for estimating the number of clicks, by using the sequential importance sampling (SIS) filter. Each particle c contains a current estimate for the number of clicks generated in both markets, as well as the estimate for past periods. We apply the particle filter from the very beginning of the period T_2, and the initial scale of particles is N. Each particle receives a weight $w_c = 1/N$. During the search promotional activities, a new report will be received at the beginning of the next period. It can be used to update the weight w_c to w'_c, then the new particles are sampled for each existing particle.

If the particle c has weight w_c, then the updated particle c' will receive a weight

$$w'_c = w_c \frac{\Pr\left(report \left| c'\right.\right) \Pr\left(c' \left| c\right.\right)}{\pi\left(c' \left| c, report\right.\right)},$$

where $\pi(c'|c, report)$ represents a distribution to sample new particles. It can be any kind of distribution. Typically, the proposal distribution is $\pi(c'|c, report) = \Pr(c'|c)$, which results in $w'_c = w_c \Pr(report|c')$. The typical proposal distribution is much easier to apply in practice. However, it has a serious flaw: $\Pr(report|c')$ may frequently be zero, because most particles may not receive a weight if they do not satisfy the state condition. The optimal proposal distribution can be applied although it may be difficult to sample.

The optimal proposal distribution is known as $\pi(c'|c, report) = \Pr(c'|c, report)$, thus the updated weight is $w'_c = w_c \Pr(report|c)$. Then the main problem is to compute $\Pr(report|c)$ and sample $\Pr(c'|c, report)$.

For a given set of current estimate of clicks, we define a_1, a_2 as the states where the volume of clicks generated in market-1 and market-2 is consistent with the budget allocated. That is, if the budget allocated to market-1 increases, the number of clicks generated by market-1 will increase; and due to the budget constraint, correspondingly, the budget allocated to market-2 will decrease; then the number of clicks generated in market-2 will decrease. Then $\Pr(report|c) = \Pr(a_1 \cap a_2|c)$. In other words, the probability of particle c from the previous period leading to an updated particle consistent with the report is equal to the probability that the volume of clicks generated in a market will not conflict with the budget allocated. Furthermore, $\Pr(a_1 \cap a_2|c) = \Pr(a_2|c, a_1) \Pr(a_1|c))$. If the probability mass function for clicks can be found, given the information in c, we can compute $\Pr(report|c)$ thus w'_c. Let $f_i, i = 1, 2$ be the probability mass functions for clicks generated in market i. In the next period, the probability mass functions are $f'_i, i = 1, 2$, and the corresponding cumulative distribution function is $F'_i, i = 1, 2$. It begins with $F'_0 = 0$.

$$\Pr(a_1 \cap a_2|c) = \Pr(a_2|c, a_1) \Pr(a_1|c)$$
$$= (1 - F'_1)f_2 \times (1 - F'_0)f_1.$$

Then, given a particle c and the report, we can sample a new particle c'. This involves generating the new volume of clicks v_i in market i, thus

$$\Pr(c'|c, report) = \Pr(v_1 \cap v_2|c, report)$$
$$= \Pr(v_1|c, report, v_2) \Pr(v_2|c, report).$$

In order to sample a new particle c', we first sample v_2 from f'_2 and then sample v_1 from f'_1. From the new particle c', we can get the important parameters (e.g. v_1 and v_2) to solve the optimal control problem.

Similarly, by using the SIS particle filter, we can also estimate the average CPC of the next period. We define each particle p contains current estimates of the average CPC in both markets, as well as the average CPC estimate in past periods. We use the particle filter from the very beginning of the period T_2, and the initial scale of particles is K. Each particle receives a weight $w_p = 1/K$. During the promotion, a new report will be received at the beginning of the next period, and it can be used to update the weight w_p to w'_p

$$w'_p = w_p \frac{\Pr(report|p') \Pr(p'|p)}{\pi(p'|p, report)}.$$

Then the new particles are sampled. With the optimal proposal distribution $\pi(p'|p, report) = \Pr(p'|p, report)$, we can get the updated weight $w'_p = w_p \Pr(report|p)$. We then need to compute $\Pr(report|p)$ and sample $\Pr(p'|p, report)$ to find a new particle.

For a given set of current average CPC estimates, we define b_1 b_2 as the states where the average CPC in market-1 and market-2 will follow the previous trend. That is, if the average CPC in market-1 is much higher than that in market-2 during the period T_{i-1}, we can believe that the average CPC in market-1 will continue to be higher than that in market-2 during period Ti. Thus

$$\Pr(report \,|\, p) = \Pr(b_1 \cap b_2 \,|\, p), \Pr(b_1 \cap b_2 \,|\, p) = \Pr(b_2 \,|\, p, b_1) \Pr(b_1 \,|\, p).$$

If the probability mass function for the average CPC can be found with the information in p, we can compute $\Pr(report|p)$ and then w'_p.

Let z_i be the probability mass function for the average CPC in market i. In the next period, the probability mass function is z'_j, and the corresponding cumulative distribution function is Z'_j. It begins with $Z'_0 = 0$.

$$\Pr(b_1 \cap b_2 \,|\, p) = \Pr(b_2 \,|\, p, b_1) \Pr(b_1 \,|\, p)$$
$$= (1 - Z'_1)z_2 \times (1 - Z'_0)z_1.$$

Then we need to sample a new particle p', given the particle p and the report. In the step of sampling, we also need to find the new average CPC m_1, m_2, then

$$\Pr(p' \,|\, p, report) = \Pr(m_1 \cap m_2 \,|\, p, report)$$
$$= \Pr(m_1 \,|\, p, report, m_2) \Pr(m_2 \,|\, p, report).$$

Through an iterative method, we can finally sample a new particle p'.

5.4.2 Model Formulation and Solution

The optimal control problem of budget allocation at the beginning of the period T_j can be given as

$$\max \sum (1 + \beta_i)v_i(T_j)$$
$$\text{s.t.} \sum (1 + \beta_i)v_i(T_j)m_i(T_j) \le B(T_j) \tag{5.3}$$
$$\beta_i \ge -1,$$

where $v_i(T_j)$ denotes the number of clicks generated in market i during period T_j, $m_i(T_j)$ is the average CPC in market i during the period T_j, and β_i represents the changing proportion of clicks generated in market i during period T_j. If the clicks increase, $\beta_i \ge 0$, otherwise $\beta_i \le 0$.

Suppose there are two search advertising markets, then model (5.3) can be given as follows,

$$\max (1 + \beta_1)v_1(T_j) + (1 + \beta_2)v_2(T_j)$$
$$\text{s.t.} (1 + \beta_1)v_1(T_j)m_1(T_j) + (1 + \beta_2)v_2(T_j)m_2(T_j) \le B(T_j) \tag{5.4}$$
$$\beta_1 \ge -1, \beta_2 \ge -1.$$

Through the SIS particle filter, we can sample new particles c' and p', and the parameters can be obtained as follows,

$$v_1(T_j) = v_1, \quad v_2(T_j) = v_2, \quad m_1(T_j) = m_1, \quad m_2(T_j) = m_2.$$

Thus, model (5.4) is equivalent to

$$\begin{aligned}
&\max (1 + \beta_1)v_1 + (1 + \beta_2)v_2 \\
&\text{s.t. } (1 + \beta_1)v_1 m_1 + (1 + \beta_2)v_2 m_2 \leq B(T_i) \\
&\beta_1 \geq -1, \beta_2 \geq -1.
\end{aligned} \tag{5.5}$$

In order to make the solution procedure more convenient, we simplify model (5.5) as follows

$$\begin{aligned}
&\max \beta_1 v_1 + \beta_2 v_2 \\
&\text{s.t. } \beta_1 v_1 m_1 + \beta_2 v_2 m_2 \leq B(T_i) - v_1 m_1 - v_2 m_2 \\
&\beta_1 \geq -1, \beta_2 \geq -1.
\end{aligned} \tag{5.6}$$

By using the dynamic programming method, we can get optimal values of model (5.6)

$$g_2 \left[B(T_i) - v_1 m_1 - v_2 m_2 \right]$$
$$= \max_{-1 \leq \beta_2 \leq \frac{B(T_i) - v_1 m_1}{v_2 \times m_2} - 1} \left\{ \beta_2 v_2 + g_1 \left[B(T_i) - v_1 m_1 - v_2 m_2 - \beta_2 v_2 m_2 \right] \right\},$$

$$g_1 \left[B(T_i) - v_1 m_1 - v_2 m_2 - \beta_2 v_2 m_2 \right] = \max_{0 \leq \beta_1 \leq \frac{B(T_i) - v_2 m_2 - \beta_2 v_2 \times m_2}{v_1 \times m_1} - 1} \left\{ \beta_1 v_1 \right\},$$

where $\dot{\beta}_1, \dot{\beta}_2$ are the optimal solution. As a result, the advertiser should invest $(1 + \dot{\beta}_1)v_1 m_1$ amount of budget to market-1 and $(1 + \dot{\beta}_2)v_2 m_2$ amount of budget to market-2, and then he/she can get $(1 + \dot{\beta}_1)v_1$ clicks from market-1 and $(1 + \dot{\beta}_2)v_2$ clicks from market-2.

5.5 Experimental Validation

5.5.1 Data Preparation

We conducted some computational experiments to illustrate the effectiveness of the models, with the data collected from practical advertising campaigns in two search markets in June 2009. The report is shown in Table 5.2.

Generally speaking, the number of clicks does not have severe fluctuations if the total budget is kept stable. We suppose that clicks generated in these two markets have the same distribution mass function, and in each period the number of clicks will increase or decrease by 10% with the probability of 0.5 in each market. At the very beginning of period T_j, we can obtain the operational report of the previous period.

Table 5.2 The report of advertising campaigns in June, 2009.

	Market-1	Market-2
Clicks	168	167
CPC	0.67	0.48
Budget	164.4	57.3

Similarly, if the total budget for both markets does not vary widely, the average CPC will not change too much. Through statistics, we found that the average CPC always fluctuates with the range ± 0.2. Here we only consider the extreme situation and suppose that the probability mass function is given as follows.

$$\begin{cases} \Pr\left(m(T_i) = m(T_{i-1}) + 0.2\right) = 1/3 \\ \Pr\left(m(T_i) = m(T_{i-1}) - 0.2\right) = 1/3 \\ \Pr\left(m(T_i) = m(T_{i-1})\right) = 1/3 \end{cases}$$

5.5.2 Experimental Results

From the operational reports, we can know the particle c with the following click volumes: $v_G = 167$, $v_B = 168$. First, let us determine $\Pr\left(report|c\right)$. From the assumption above, we know $f_G(183.7) = f_G(150.3) = 0.5$ and $f_G(184.8) = f_G(151.2) = 0.5$. For market-2, we have $\Pr\left(a_1|c\right) = 1$ and $f'_g = f_G$. For market-1, we have $\Pr\left(a_2|c, a_1\right) = 0.25$, and $f'_B(184.8) = 1$, because $1 - f'_G(151.2) = 0$, $1 - f'_G(184.8) = 0.5$. Then the new particle c' is sampled: $v_G = 150.3$, $v_B = 184.8$.

The particle p contains the estimate of the average CPC: $m_G = 0.48$, $m_B = 0.67$. First, we will compute $\Pr\left(report|p\right)$. From the assumption above, $z_G(0.48) = z_G(0.68) = z_G(0.28) = 1/3$, $z_G(0.47) = z_G(0.67) = z_G(0.87) = 1/3$ can be obtained. For market-2, we have $\Pr\left(b_1|p\right) = 1$, and $z'_G = z_G$. For market-1, we have $\Pr\left(b_2|p, b_1\right) = 2/3$, and $z'_B(0.67) = 2/9$, $z'_B(0.87) = 1/3$, $z'_B(0.47) = 1/9$, because $1 - z'_G(0.67) = 2/3$, $1 - z'_G(0.87) = 1$, $1 - z'_G(0.47) = 1/3$. The updated particle p' can be obtained by using an iterative method: $m_G = 0.41$, $m_B = 0.74$. Both m_G and m_B are expected values. So model (5.6) can be written as

$$\max 150.3\beta_G + 184.8\beta_B$$
$$\text{s.t. } 150.3 \times 0.41\beta_G + 184.8 \times 0.74\beta_B \leq 221.7 - 150.3 \times 0.41 - 184.8 \times 0.74 \quad (5.7)$$
$$\beta_G \geq 0, \beta_B \geq 0.$$

Here we assume that the total budget for each period is fixed. By using the dynamic programming method, we can obtain the optimal value of model (5.7)

$$g_2\left[B(T_i) - v_G m_G - v_B m_B\right] = g_2\left[23.33\right] = \max_{0 \le \beta_B \le 0.17}\left\{184.8\beta_B + g_1\left[23.33 - 136.75\beta_B\right]\right\}.$$

Suppose that $\beta_B = 0.1$ or $\beta_B = 0$, then

$$g_1\left[B(T_i) - m_G v_G - m_B v_B - \beta_B v_B \times m_B\right] = \left\{\begin{array}{ll} g_1\left[9.65\right], & if\,\beta_B = 0.1 \\ g_1\left[23.33\right], & if\,\beta_B = 0 \end{array}\right\}$$

and

$$g_1\left[9.65\right] = \max_{0 \le \beta_G \le 0.16}\left\{150.3\beta_G\right\}, g_1\left[23.33\right] = \max_{0 \le \beta_G \le 0.38}\left\{150.3\beta_G\right\}.$$

Similarly, suppose β_G can only takes the values: 0.3, 0.2, 0.1, or 0, then we have

$$g_1\left[9.65\right] = 150.3 \times 0.1 = 15.03, g_1\left[23.33\right] = 150.3 \times 0.3 = 45.09$$

Thus,

$$g_2\left[23.33\right] = \max\left\{18.48 + g_1\left[9.65\right], g_1\left[23.33\right]\right\}$$
$$= \max\{18.48 + 15.03, 45.09\}$$
$$= 45.09(\beta_G = 0.3, \beta_B = 0).$$

Thus the optimal value is 379.92. From the operational report, we know that the real volume of total clicks is 335. Therefore, experimental results prove that our budget allocation model is more effective.

5.6 Conclusions

In this chapter, we define the budget allocation problem at the first stage of budget decisions in sponsored search auctions (e.g. across search advertising markets) as a knapsack problem, and develop several allocation models for two different decision scenarios: budget initialization prior to SSA promotion and budget adjustment during SSA promotion. The number of clicks and the average Cost-Per-Click serve as main inputs, which can be estimated either from statistics by keyword tools provided by search engines, or through predictions by using the particle filter. We also design some computational experiments to illustrate the effectiveness of our models, and the results show that our approaches outperform the baseline approach.

In future research we will consider more complicated budget decision situations in sponsored search auctions, where the total budget of each period may vary widely, and every keyword might have a different CPC. Furthermore, the capacity of the search market can be saturated when the total budget reaches a certain amount. We also intend to study and analyze the equilibrium distribution where each advertiser takes his/her own budget allocation strategy to maximize the expected revenue from search advertising activities.

References

Babaioff, M., N. Immorlica, D. Kempe, R. Kleinberg. 2007. A knapsack secretary problem with applications, Lecture Notes in Computer Science, 4627:16–28.

Chakrabarty, D., Y. Zhou, R. Lukose. 2007. Budget constrained bidding in keyword auctions and online knapsack problems, Proceedings of the 16th International World Wide Web Conference, 2007.

DasGupta, B., S. Muthukrishnan. 2012. Stochastic budget optimization in Internet advertising, Algorithmica, DOI: 10.1007/s00453-012-9614-x.

Du, R., Q. Hu, S. Ai. 2007. Stochastic optimal budget decision for advertising considering uncertain sales responses, European Journal of Operational Research, 183:1042–1054.

Feldman, J., S. Muthukrishnan, M. Pál, C. Stein. 2007. Budget optimization in search-based advertising auctions, Proceedings of the 9th ACM Conference on Electronic Commerce, 2007.

Fruchter, G. E., W. Dou. 2005. Optimal budget allocation over time for keyword ads in web portals, Journal of Optimization Theory and Applications, 124(1):157–194.

Liu, J. S., R. Chen, T. Logvinenko. 2001. A theoretical framework for sequential importance sampling with resampling, in Sequential Monte Carlo Methods in Practice, Berlin: Springer Verlag.

Muthukrishnan, S., M. Pál, Z. Svitkina. 2007. Stochastic models for budget optimization in search-based advertising, Lecture Notes in Computer Science, 4858:131–142.

Muthukrishnan, S., M. Pál, Z. Svitkina. 2010. Stochastic models for budget optimization in search-based advertising, Algorithmica, 58:1022–1044.

Nummiaro, K., E. Koller-Meier, L. Van Gool. 2002. An adaptive color-based particle filter, Image and Vision Computing 1–12.

Yang, Y., J. Zhang, R. Qin, J. Li, F. Wang, Q. Wei. 2012. A budget optimization framework for search advertisements across markets, IEEE Transactions on Systems, Man, and Cybernetics, Part A, 42(5):1141–1151.

Zhou, Y., V. Naroditskiy. 2008. Algorithm for stochastic multiple-choice knapsack problem and application to keywords bidding, 17th International Conference on World Wide Web, Beijing, China, April 21–25, 2008:1175–1176.

Zhou, Y., D. Chakrabarty, R. Lukose. 2008. Budget constrained bidding in keyword auctions and online knapsack problems, Proceedings of the 17th International Conference on World Wide Web, Beijing, China, ACM.

CHAPTER 6

Optimal Budget Allocation Across Search Markets

6.1 Introduction

Nowadays, more and more people use search engines as their main entrance to the Web, and this offers a fertile soil for sponsored search auctions to evolve as a primary online advertising format. From the perspective of search engines, search advertisements have become a primary revenue source, e.g. Google gained 97% of its revenues from search auctions in 2011. The growing prosperity of search auctions markets is vastly driven by the influx of millions of advertisers. Advertisers, especially those from small and medium enterprises, usually have serious budget constraints, such that advertisers have to make advertising decisions wisely, in order to survive the fierce competition and maximize their profits.

With consideration of the entire lifecycle of search advertising campaigns, budget decisions in sponsored search auctions exist at three levels (Yang et al., 2012), as described in Chapter 4; allocation across search markets, temporal distribution over a series of slots (e.g. day), and adjustment of the remaining budget (e.g. the daily budget). This work aims to study and understand budget allocation problems across several search markets given that the total search advertising budget is determined. First, advertisers do not have sufficient knowledge to deal with budget decisions in search auctions because the underlying mechanism is complex and search engines usually refuse to provide more information with excuses about business secrets. Secondly, it is becoming increasingly difficult for an advertiser to manipulate the advertising budget simultaneously across several search markets. Thirdly, search markets are coupled in the sense that advertising efforts exerted in a market have some influence on advertising effects in another market (Shakun, 1965) because there are big overlaps in terms of search users among several search engines. Fourthly, there exists a saturation level of advertising expenditure in a search market, above which the marginal cost is larger than the marginal return. Therefore, it's not a straightforward task to allocate a limited advertising budget across markets in search auctions.

Yang and Wang: Budget Constraints and Optimization in Sponsored Search Auctions. http://dx.doi.org/10.1016/B978-0-12-411457-9.00006-9
© 2014 Elsevier Inc. All rights reserved.

In early literature related to advertisements, decisions on advertising levels were incorporated with advertising/sales response functions to parsimoniously capture the relationship between advertising spend and unit sales (Sasieni, 1971). However, there is no more difficult, complex, or controversial problem in marketing than measuring the influence of advertising on sales (Bass, 1969). The pioneering work of Vidale and Wolfe (1957) took the initiative to define the concept of advertising effectiveness and equations of advertising/sales response dynamics, and provided a solution for optimal allocation with limited budgets. Simon and Arndt (1980) found that studies of the response function linking the physical measures of sales impact to physical amounts of advertising consistently indicate diminishing returns to advertising over the range of investigations in test experiments and over the normal range of advertising budgets for operating firms. Feinberg (2001) formulated a flexible class of S-shaped response models for which it is demonstrated that, in contrast to findings in the literature on discretized advertising models, continuous periodic optima cannot be supported. Furthermore, a set of conditions for the advertising response function are derived, that contain and extend those suggested by Sasieni (1971). Fruchter and Dou (2005) employed dynamic programming to derive the analytical solution to the optimal budget allocation problem among web portals, and their conclusions indicated that advertisers should switch more budgets into specialized web portals, in order to maximize click volumes in the long term. These research efforts on optimal advertising budget/expenditures are less suitable to budget decision scenarios in search advertisements that have distinctive features such as the quality score and continuous operations.

In this chapter we formulate the budget allocation problem across several search markets as an optimal control process with a finite time horizon. This chapter develops a novel dynamic budget decision model that captures distinctive features of search advertisements. First, we extend the response function given by Prasad and Sethi (2004) to fit search advertising scenarios by introducing the dynamical advertising effort u and quality score q. Major search engines have adopted quality-based ranking and pricing mechanisms in recent years. Secondly, we relax the concavity assumption that the advertising effort is a concave function of the advertising budget (e.g. $u = b^{\alpha}$). The advertising elasticity α is fixed (e.g. about 1/2) empirically (Sethi, 1977) because traditional advertisers usually trust professional agencies to manipulate their advertisements. However, sponsored search auctions allow more flexible styles in terms of keyword selection, bids, budget decisions, and advertising schedules. These factors definitely affect the mapping from the advertising budget to the advertising effort. Thirdly, we provide a feasible solution to our model and study some desirable properties, and prove (a) Sasieni's assumption that the marginal return from increased advertising expenditure is non-increasing (Sasieni, 1971) is realistic and valuable; (b) the optimal budget solution satisfies the condition that the advertising effort u is positively proportional to the product of the change in accumulated revenue in a market ∂V, the change in market share $\partial \theta$, and the advertising elasticity α. We also conduct computational experiments to validate our model and identified properties. Experimental results show that the advertiser with increasing advertising elasticity is encouraged to invest more budget in the late stages, but the advertiser with decreasing advertising elasticity should invest more budget in the initial stage, in order to maximize net profits.

The remainder of this chapter is organized as follows. Section 6.2 gives the modeling elements in this chapter. Section 6.3 presents an optimal budget allocation model across search advertising markets and discusses some desirable properties and solution for our budgeting model. We then present a computational experimental study to illustrate the potential usefulness and practical value of our model in Section 6.4. Finally, we conclude this research and discuss future research directions in Section 6.5.

6.2 Modeling Elements

In this section, we propose an optimal decision model for budget allocation across search markets in a finite time horizon T. Suppose there is no advertisement differentiation. By advertisement differentiation, we mean that, for an advertiser, his/her advertising structure and content are the same (or similar) in several markets. Let B be the total advertising budget for search-based promotions, m the search demand, and c the click-through rate (CTR).

The notations used in this chapter are shown in Table 6.1.

6.2.1 The Advertising Effort

Advertisers invest in the budget with the intention of making a better advertising effort, but not all the budget works. In other words, the advertising effort represents the effective part of the advertising budget, and only this part can exert an effect. According to Little (1979), there is an exponential relationship between the budget b and the advertising effort u : $u = b^{\alpha}$, where α denotes the advertising elasticity, which is empirically fixed as a constant in traditional advertisements (Erickson, 1992; Prasad and Sethi, 2004). In Sethi (1983) and Prasad and Sethi

Table 6.1   List of notations.

Notation	Definition
u	The advertising effort
B	The total budget for an advertiser
$b_i(t)$	The budget allocated to search market i at time t
$\alpha_i(t)$	The advertising elasticity in search market i
$\theta_i(t)$	The advertiser's market share in search market i at time t
$v_i(t)$	The advertiser's value of a click in market i at time t
$m_i(t)$	The search demands in market i at time t
$c_i(t)$	The proportion of effective clicks in market i at time t
ρ_i	The response constant in search market i
q_i	The advertiser's quality score in search market i
e^{-rt}	The discount factor

(2004), the advertising effort u is given as $u = b^{1/2}$, where the advertising elasticity is assumed as $1/2$, which can be explained by the uniformity of professional activities by advertising agencies in traditional advertisements. However, sponsored search auctions allow more flexible styles in terms of keyword selection, bids, budget decisions, and advertising schedules that to a large extent affect the mapping from the advertising budget to the advertising efforts. Specifically, (1) an advertiser can make changes to his/ her advertising strategies at any time in search auctions, (2) most advertisers are not professional, and (3) data (e.g. the historical CPC, the effectiveness of clicks) needed for computing the optimal daily budget and bidding strategies are uncertain and difficult to obtain. In this sense, we argue that the relationship between b and u is time-varying: $u = b^{\alpha(t)}$, which also varies in different search advertising markets.

6.2.2 The Response Function for Search Advertisements

The advertising response function is introduced as a formula to show the cumulative advertising effect for an individual advertiser. In a non-competitive environment, Prasad and Sethi (2004) and Sethi (1977, 1983) gave the deterministic monopoly advertising response function, $d\theta = (\rho u \sqrt{1 - \theta} - \delta\theta)dt$, where u denotes the advertising effort, ρ is a response constant, and δ denotes a market share decay constant. We amend the advertising function to fit search advertising scenarios from three aspects. First, we take clicks as the form of profit for advertisers to maximize in search auctions. The advertiser pays once his/her advertisements are clicked, thus there is less decay. Therefore, we take $\delta = 0$ in search auction scenarios, i.e. $d\theta/dt = \rho u \sqrt{1 - \theta}$. Secondly, the search advertising elasticity α is time-varying as described previously. Thirdly, besides the advertising budget, an advertiser's quality score q can also have a significant influence on his/her capacity to gain market share. A higher quality score entitles an advertiser to pay less for each click, so the same amount of advertising budget can result in more market share than other advertisers with lower quality scores. Because an advertiser's click-through rate (CTR) is the core component for the quality score, we use the CTR to denote the quality score. Therefore, the advertising response function for search advertisements is given as

$$d\theta/dt = \rho q u \sqrt{1 - \theta}$$

with $u = b^{\alpha(t)}$.

6.3 Optimal Budget Allocation Across Search Markets

6.3.1 The Model

The objective of budget allocation across search markets is to maximize the net profit of the advertiser

$$\sum_i \int_0^T e^{-rt}(v_i(t)m_i(t)c_i(t)\theta_i(t) - b_i(t))dt,$$

where $\theta_i(t)$ denotes an advertiser's market share in search market i at time t, e^{-rt} is a discount factor, $v_i(t)$ denotes an advertiser's value of a click in market i at time t, $m_i(t)$ and $c_i(t)$ denote the number of clicks and the proportion of effective clicks in market i at time t, respectively. Closed-loop strategies are more valuable than open-loop strategies in dynamic advertising budget problems (Erickson, 1992), thus we will provide a closed-loop method to study the budget allocation problem. An advertiser can observe real-time clicks himself/ herself, and get the total clicks for a given market through a distribution of search demands and an average CTR that can be obtained from sponsored search auction providers. In this sense, an advertiser's real-time market share in terms of clicks can be accessed, which makes a closed-loop method feasible. Thus, we build an optimal control model for budget allocation across search markets as follows:

$$\max \sum_i \int_0^T e^{-rt}(v_i(t)m_i(t)c_i(t)\theta_i(t) - b_i(t))\mathrm{d}t$$

$$\text{s.t. } \mathrm{d}\theta_i/\mathrm{d}t = \rho_i q_i(t)(b_i(t))^{\alpha_i(t)}\sqrt{1 - \theta_i(t)}$$

$$\sum_i \int_0^T e^{-rt}b_i(t)\mathrm{d}t \leqslant B \tag{6.1}$$

$$b_i(t) \geqslant 0.$$

We will get optimal budget $b_i^*(t) = b_i^*(t, \theta_i(t))$ allocated to market i at time t through solving this model, and the final budget decision for an advertiser in market i is

$$\int_0^T e^{-rt}b_i^*(t)\mathrm{d}t.$$

6.3.2 Properties

In this section we will study some desirable properties and present a solution algorithm for model (6.1) in the case of two search markets.

The constraints

$$\sum_i \int_0^T e^{-rt}b_i(t)\mathrm{d}t \leqslant B$$

can be taken into account by introducing a Lagrange multiplier λ.

Starting at any pair of initial market shares $(y_1, y_2) \in [0, 1] \times [0, 1]$ at time t, we define the value function $V_\lambda(t, y_1, y_2)$ as the greatest payoff we can obtain during time interval $[t, T]$. In other words,

$$V_\lambda(t, y_1, y_2) := \sup_{b_1(\cdot)\geq 0, b_2(\cdot)\geq 0} \int_t^T e^{-rs}\{C_1(s)\theta_1(s) - b_1(s)$$
$$+ C_2(s)\theta_2(s) - b_2(s) - \lambda(b_1(s) + b_2(s))\}\mathrm{d}s.$$

Here we set $C_i(t) = v_i(t)m_i(t)c_i(t)$ for simplicity. Note that for all $(y_1, y_2) \in [0, 1] \times [0, 1]$, $V_\lambda(T, y_1, y_2) = 0$. Following the principle of dynamic programming, we have the Hamilton-Jacobi-Bellman equation:

$$0 = V_{\lambda,t} + \max_{b_1 \geq 0, b_2 \geq 0}\{\rho_1 q_1 (b_1)^{\alpha_1}\sqrt{1 - \theta_1} \cdot V_{\lambda,\theta_1}$$
$$+ \rho_2 q_2 (b_2)^{\alpha_2}\sqrt{1 - \theta_2} \cdot V_{\lambda,\theta_2} + e^{-rt}(C_1\theta_1 + C_2\theta_2 - (1 + \lambda)(b_1 + b_2))\}. \quad (6.2)$$

Differentiating (6.2), we obtain the optimal feedback advertising decisions:

$$b_1 = \left(\frac{(1 + \lambda)e^{-rt}}{\rho_1 q_1 \alpha_1 \sqrt{1 - \theta_1}V_{\lambda,\theta_1}}\right)^{\frac{1}{\alpha_1 - 1}}, \quad b_2 = \left(\frac{(1 + \lambda)e^{-rt}}{\rho_2 q_2 \alpha_2 \sqrt{1 - \theta_2}V_{\lambda,\theta_2}}\right)^{\frac{1}{\alpha_2 - 1}}. \quad (6.3)$$

Substituting (6.3) in (6.2), we obtain the Hamilton-Jacobi equation

$$V_{\lambda,t} + \left(\alpha_1^{\frac{\alpha_1}{1-\alpha_1}} - \alpha_1^{\frac{1}{1-\alpha_1}}\right)\left(e^{rt}\frac{1}{1+\lambda}\frac{1 - k_1 k_2}{1 + k_1}\right)^{\frac{\alpha_1}{1-\alpha_1}}\left(\rho_1 q_1\sqrt{1 - \theta_1}V_{\lambda,\theta_1}\right)^{\frac{1}{1-\alpha_1}}$$
$$+ \left(\alpha_2^{\frac{\alpha_2}{1-\alpha_2}} - \alpha_2^{\frac{1}{1-\alpha_2}}\right)\left(e^{rt}\frac{1}{1+\lambda}\frac{1 - k_1 k_2}{1 + k_2}\right)^{\frac{\alpha_2}{1-\alpha_2}}\left(\rho_2 q_2\sqrt{1 - \theta_2}V_{\lambda,\theta_2}\right)^{\frac{1}{1-\alpha_2}}$$
$$+ e^{-rt}(C_1\theta_1 + C_2\theta_2) = 0. \quad (6.4)$$

$$V_{\lambda,t} + \left(\alpha_1^{\frac{\alpha_1}{1-\alpha_1}} - \alpha_1^{\frac{1}{1-\alpha_1}}\right)\left(e^{rt}\frac{1}{1+\lambda}\right)^{\frac{\alpha_1}{1-\alpha_1}}\left(\rho_1 q_1\sqrt{1 - \theta_1}V_{\lambda,\theta_1}\right)^{\frac{1}{1-\alpha_1}}$$
$$+ \left(\alpha_2^{\frac{\alpha_2}{1-\alpha_2}} - \alpha_2^{\frac{1}{1-\alpha_2}}\right)\left(e^{rt}\frac{1}{1+\lambda}\right)^{\frac{\alpha_2}{1-\alpha_2}}\left(\rho_2 q_2\sqrt{1 - \theta_2}V_{\lambda,\theta_2}\right)^{\frac{1}{1-\alpha_2}}$$
$$+ e^{-rt}(C_1\theta_1 + C_2\theta_2) = 0.$$

i.e.

$$V_{\lambda,t} + (1 - \alpha_1)\left(e^{rt}\frac{\alpha_1}{1+\lambda}\right)^{\frac{\alpha_1}{1-\alpha_1}}\left(\rho_1 q_1\sqrt{1 - \theta_1}V_{\lambda,\theta_1}\right)^{\frac{1}{1-\alpha_1}}$$
$$+ (1 - \alpha_2)\left(e^{rt}\frac{\alpha_2}{1+\lambda}\right)^{\frac{\alpha_2}{1-\alpha_2}}\left(\rho_2 q_2\sqrt{1 - \theta_2}V_{\lambda,\theta_2}\right)^{\frac{1}{1-\alpha_2}}$$
$$+ e^{-rt}(C_1\theta_1 + C_2\theta_2) = 0. \quad (6.5)$$

Solve (6.5) with the terminal value condition $V_\lambda(T, \theta_1, \theta_2) = 0$ to get $V_\lambda(t, \theta_1, \theta_2)$. Substituting it into (6.3), we then obtain the optimal control $b^*_{\lambda,1}(t, \theta_1, \theta_2)$, $b^*_{\lambda,2}(t, \theta_1, \theta_2)$.

Now let us determine the constant λ. If

$$\int_0^T e^{-rt}(b^*_{0,1}(t, \theta_1, \theta_2) + b^*_{0,2}(t, \theta_1, \theta_2))dt \leq B,$$

then we set $\lambda = 0$. Note that this is the case when the budget is sufficient or unlimited, which is rarely possible in practice.

Then let us consider the case in which the budget is limited, i.e.

$$\int_0^T e^{-rt}(b_{0,1}^*(t, \theta_1, \theta_2) + b_{0,2}^*(t, \theta_1, \theta_2))dt > B,$$

we choose the minimal constant $\lambda > 0$ so that

$$\int_0^T e^{-rt}(b_{\lambda,1}^*(t, \theta_1, \theta_2) + b_{\lambda,2}^*(t, \theta_1, \theta_2))dt = B. \tag{6.6}$$

The choice of λ together with the correspondent $(b_{\lambda,1}^*(t, \theta_1, \theta_2), b_{\lambda,2}^*(t, \theta_1, \theta_2))$ gives the theoretical solution of model (6.1).

From the above analysis, we can get the following theorem and proposition,

Theorem 6.1. *If the total budget B is larger than $\int_0^T e^{-rt}(b_{\lambda,1}^* + b_{\lambda,2}^*)dt$, the optimal way is to invest $\int_0^T e^{-rt}(b_{\lambda,1}^* + b_{\lambda,2}^*)dt$ in these search advertising markets.*

This can also be justified by the fact that the marginal return of the optimal budget strategy is equal to 0, and the residual budget over $\int_0^T e^{-rt}(b_{\lambda,1}^* + b_{\lambda,2}^*)dt$ cannot yield revenues (e.g. $v_i(t)m_i(t)c_i(t)\theta_i(t) - b_i(t)$) any more. In this sense, this theorem implies that marginal returns are non-increasing as assumed in Sasieni (1971).

Proposition 6.1. *For all $t \in [0, T]$ and $i = 1, 2$, under the optimal control $b_i^*(t, \theta_i)$, function*

$$V_{\theta_i}\dot{\theta}_i\alpha_i/b_i^*$$

is constant with respect to different markets.

Proof. From (6.3), we always have the following equation

$$\rho_1 q_1 \alpha_1 (b_1^*)^{\alpha_1 - 1}\sqrt{1 - \theta_1^*}V_{\theta_1^*} = \rho_2 q_2 \alpha_2 (b_2^*)^{\alpha_2 - 1}\sqrt{1 - \theta_2^*}V_{\theta_2^*} = e^{-rt}(1 + \lambda).$$

Substituting into the dynamic system (6.1), we rewrite the above equation as

$$V_{\theta_1^*}\frac{d\theta_1^*}{dt}\frac{\alpha_1(t)}{b_1^*(t)} = V_{\theta_2^*}\frac{d\theta_2^*}{dt}\frac{\alpha_2(t)}{b_2^*(t)} = e^{-rt}(1 + \lambda),$$

which implies the above result. Note that this result is also valid in the case of more than two markets.

6.3.3 The Solution

Although the above method by using the Lagrange multiplier provides a result, we cannot apply it to the real-world computation. The reason is that, without the monotonicity of λ, the determination process of the Lagrange multiplier leads to the solution of an infinite number of fully nonlinear partial differential equations. Thus we have to find a computable method in practice.

We can get rid of the budget constraint to obtain a new optimal control problem through introducing a new state variable, which will be proved to be equivalent to the original problem (6.1).

Let $R(t)$ be the amount of the remaining advertising budget at the present value, i.e.

$$R(t) = \int_t^T e^{-rs}(b_1(s) + b_2(s))ds + R(T).$$

Then $dR/dt = -e^{-rt}(b_1(t) + b_2(t))$. Let us consider the new optimal control problem

$$\max \int_0^T e^{-rt}\{C_1(t)\theta_1(t) - b_1(t) + C_2(t)\theta_2(t) - b_2(t))\}dt$$

$$\text{s.t. } d\theta_1/dt = \rho_1 q_1(b_1)^{\alpha_1(t)}\sqrt{1 - \theta_1}$$

$$d\theta_2/dt = \rho_2 q_2(b_2)^{\alpha_2(t)}\sqrt{1 - \theta_2} \tag{6.7}$$

$$dR/dt = -e^{-rt}(b_1(t) + b_2(t))$$

$$b_i(t) \geqslant 0$$

$$R(0) = B, R(T) \geqslant 0.$$

We have the following theorem for computing purposes.

Theorem 6.2.   *The optimal control problem (6.7) is equivalent to the optimal control problem (6.1). The optimal control of model (6.1) is also the optimal control of model (6.7).*

Proof.   Let $(b_1^*(t), b_2^*(t))$ be the optimal solution of model (6.7). Hence,

$$\int_0^T e^{-rt}(b_1^*(t) + b_2^*(t))dt = R^*(0) - R^*(T) \leq B,$$

$$d\theta_1^*/dt = \rho_1 q_1(b_1^*)^{\alpha_1(t)}\sqrt{1 - \theta_1^*},$$

$$d\theta_2^*/dt = \rho_2 q_2(b_2^*)^{\alpha_2(t)}\sqrt{1 - \theta_2^*},$$

and $b_i^*(t) \geqslant 0$. Let $(\tilde{b}_1(t), \tilde{b}_2(t))$ be the optimal solution of model (6.1), $\tilde{\lambda}$ be the corresponding Lagrange multiplier. By the definition of "optimum," we have

$$\int_0^T e^{-rt}\{C_1(t)\tilde{\theta}_1(t) - \tilde{b}_1(t) + C_2(t)\tilde{\theta}_2(t) - \tilde{b}_2(t) - \tilde{\lambda}(\tilde{b}_1(t) + \tilde{b}_2(t))\}dt$$

$$\geq \int_0^T e^{-rt}\{C_1(t)\theta_1^*(t) - b_1^*(t) + C_2(t)\theta_2^*(t) - b_2^*(t) - \tilde{\lambda}(b_1^*(t) + b_2^*(t))\}dt \quad (6.8)$$

and

$$\int_0^T e^{-rt}\{C_1(t)\tilde{\theta}_1(t) - \tilde{b}_1(t) + C_2(t)\tilde{\theta}_2(t) - \tilde{b}_2(t)\}dt$$

$$\leq \int_0^T e^{-rt}\{C_1(t)\theta_1^*(t) - b_1^*(t) + C_2(t)\theta_2^*(t) - b_2^*(t)\}dt, \tag{6.9}$$

(i) On the one hand, comparing (6.8) with (6.9), we have

$$\tilde{\lambda}\int_0^T e^{-rt}(\tilde{b}_1(t) + \tilde{b}_2(t))\}dt \leq \tilde{\lambda}\int_0^T e^{-rt}(b_1^*(t) + b_2^*(t))\}dt \leq \tilde{\lambda}B. \tag{6.10}$$

If $\tilde{\lambda} = 0$, then

$$\int_0^T e^{-rt}\{C_1(t)\tilde{\theta}_1(t) - \tilde{b}_1(t) + C_2(t)\tilde{\theta}_2(t) - \tilde{b}_2(t)\}dt$$

$$= \int_0^T e^{-rt}\{C_1(t)\theta_1^*(t) - b_1^*(t) + C_2(t)\theta_2^*(t) - b_2^*(t)\}dt,$$

This proves that $(b_1^*(t), b_2^*(t))$ is the optimal solution of model (6.1).

If $\tilde{\lambda} \neq 0$, from (6.10), we get $\int_0^T e^{-rt}(\tilde{b}_1(t) + \tilde{b}_2(t))\}dt \leq B$. From the method of selecting λ in (6.6), $\tilde{\lambda} = 0$, which leads to a contradiction to $\tilde{\lambda} \neq 0$. So the optimal control of model (6.7) is the optimal control of model (6.1).

(ii) On the other hand, we can show that $(\tilde{b}_1(t), \tilde{b}_2(t))$ is the optimal solution of model (6.7) as well.

If $\tilde{\lambda} = 0$, then

$$\int_0^T e^{-rt}\{C_1(t)\tilde{\theta}_1(t) - \tilde{b}_1(t) + C_2(t)\tilde{\theta}_2(t) - \tilde{b}_2(t)\}dt$$

$$= \int_0^T e^{-rt}\{C_1(t)\theta_1^*(t) - b_1^*(t) + C_2(t)\theta_2^*(t) - b_2^*(t)\}dt.$$

Hence, $(\tilde{b}_1(t), \tilde{b}_2(t))$ is the optimal control of model (6.7).

If $\tilde{\lambda} > 0$, then

$$\int_0^T e^{-rt}(\tilde{b}_1(t) + \tilde{b}_2(t))\}dt = B.$$

$$-\tilde{\lambda}\int_0^T e^{-rt}(\tilde{b}_1(t) + \tilde{b}_2(t))\}dt \leq -\tilde{\lambda}\int_0^T e^{-rt}(b_1^*(t) + b_2^*(t))\}dt.$$

Using (6.8), we get

$$\int_0^T e^{-rt}\{C_1(t)\tilde{\theta}_1(t) - \tilde{b}_1(t) + C_2(t)\tilde{\theta}_2(t) - \tilde{b}_2(t)\}dt$$

$$\geq \int_0^T e^{-rt}\{C_1(t)\theta_1^*(t) - b_1^*(t) + C_2(t)\theta_2^*(t) - b_2^*(t)\}dt,$$

which implies $(\tilde{b}_1(t), \tilde{b}_2(t))$ is the optimal control of model (6.7).

Therefore, the optimal control problem (6.1) is equivalent to the optimal control problem (6.7).

Algorithm 1 (to solve the optimal control).

- Solve the partial differential equation

$$0 = W_t + \alpha_1^{\frac{1}{1-\alpha_1}}\left(\frac{1}{\alpha_1} - 1\right)\left((1 + W_R)e^{-rt}\right)^{-\frac{\alpha_1}{1-\alpha_1}}\left(W_{\theta_1}\rho_1 q_1\sqrt{1 - \theta_1}\right)^{\frac{1}{1-\alpha_1}}$$

$$+ \alpha_2^{\frac{1}{1-\alpha_2}}\left(\frac{1}{\alpha_2} - 1\right)\left((1 + W_R)e^{-rt}\right)^{-\frac{\alpha_2}{1-\alpha_2}}\left(W_{\theta_2}\rho_2 q_2\sqrt{1 - \theta_2}\right)^{\frac{1}{1-\alpha_2}}$$

$$+ e^{-rt}(C_1\theta_1 + C_2\theta_2),$$

With the terminal condition $W(T, \theta_1, \theta_2, R) = 0$ by constructing the backward difference scheme;
- Generate $\theta_1, \theta_2, b_1, b_2$, and V from $t = 0$ to $t = T$ according to Eq. (6.1) and the following equations

$$b_1 = \left(\frac{W_{\theta_1}\rho_1 q_1\alpha_1\sqrt{1 - \theta_1}}{(W_R + 1)e^{-rt}}\right)^{\frac{1}{1-\alpha_1}}, b_2 = \left(\frac{W_{\theta_2}\rho_2 q_2\alpha_2\sqrt{1 - \theta_2}}{(W_R + 1)e^{-rt}}\right)^{\frac{1}{1-\alpha_2}}, \quad (6.11)$$

we get the optimal control b_1, b_2, and the optimal payoff V.

Algorithm 2 (to find the minimum budget to achieve the producer equilibrium).

- Solve the partial differential equation

$$V_t + (1 - \alpha_1)(e^{rt}\alpha_1)^{\frac{\alpha_1}{1-\alpha_1}}\left(\rho_1 q_1\sqrt{1 - \theta_1}V_{\theta_1}\right)^{\frac{1}{1-\alpha_1}}$$

$$+ (1 - \alpha_2)(e^{rt}\alpha_2)^{\frac{\alpha_2}{1-\alpha_2}}\left(\rho_2 q_2\sqrt{1 - \theta_2}V_{\theta_2}\right)^{\frac{1}{1-\alpha_2}}$$

$$+ e^{-rt}(C_1\theta_1 + C_2\theta_2) = 0, \quad (6.12)$$

with the terminal condition $V(T, \theta_1, \theta_2) = 0$;
- Generate $\theta_1, \theta_2, b_1, b_2$, and V from $t = 0$ to $t = T$ according to Eq. (6.1) and the following equations

$$b_1 = \left(e^{rt}\rho_1 q_1\alpha_1\sqrt{1 - \theta_1}V_{\theta_1}\right)^{\frac{1}{1-\alpha_1}}, b_2 = \left(e^{rt}\rho_2 q_2\alpha_2\sqrt{1 - \theta_2}V_{\theta_2}\right)^{\frac{1}{1-\alpha_1}}. \quad (6.13)$$

We then obtain the minimum budget B needed to achieve the producer equilibrium.

6.4 Experimental Validation

6.4.1 Data Descriptions

In this section, we design numerical experiments to evaluate our optimal budget allocation model and some identified properties. We generate experimental datasets from historical advertising logs including operations and effects collected from real-world advertising campaigns of sponsored search auctions. In the following we will provide experimental steps and some relevant results to evaluate our model with respect to budget constraints and the advertising elasticity.

6.4.2 Experimental Design

The experimental evaluation focuses on the following two aspects. First, we intend to prove some desirable properties of our budget model as discussed in Section 6.3.2. Secondly, we try to evaluate our budget model with respect to budget constraints and the advertising elasticity. We also try to discuss whether the adverting effort u is increasing with time because the experience curve effect will lead to more profitable equilibrium strategies for an advertiser. According to Hax and Majluf (1982), with the experience accumulated in the process of search advertising campaigns, the advertiser's capacity to make advertising decisions improves, and then his/her advertising elasticity increases. Thus the same amount of advertising budget will result in more advertising efforts. Thirdly, we intend to figure out the influence of budget constraints on the advertiser's budget allocation strategies. As follows, we provide details of our experimental setup and results.

Let us discuss the budget decision scenario where the advertising budget allocated to two search markets is constrained to $100, such that the limited budget cannot entitle the advertiser to reach the producer equilibrium point. In this situation, suppose the advertising elasticity of an advertiser is fixed in market 2, we consider three cases in terms of her advertising elasticity in market 1: constant (Case1-constant), increases over time (Case2-increase), and decreases over time (Case3-decrease), while the advertiser has the same average advertising elasticity in these three cases.

6.4.3 Experimental Results

From Figures 6.1–6.3, we can see that the advertiser's budget allocation strategy is more stable in the Case2-increase, followed by that in the Case1-constant, and then that in the Case3-decrease. In other words, the level of an advertiser's advertising elasticity to a large degree determines his/her budget allocation strategy: the higher advertising elasticity means the same size of budget has a better effect, thus encouraging the advertiser to invest more in the budget to gain more net profits. Thus, the advertiser with increasing advertising elasticity is encouraged to invest more in the budget in the late stages, but the advertiser with decreasing

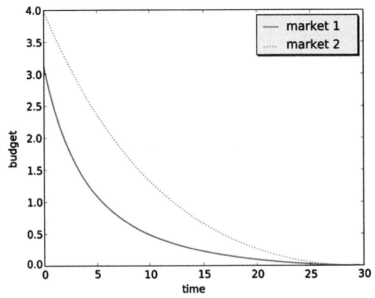

Figure 6.1   Constrained budget allocation to two markets in Case3-decrease.

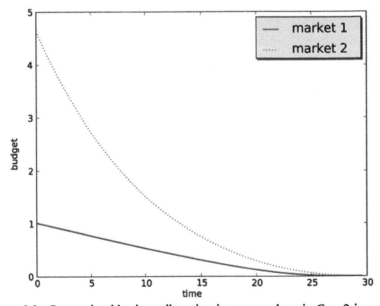

Figure 6.2   Constrained budget allocation in two markets in Case2-increase.

advertising elasticity should invest more in the budget in the initial stage, in order to maximize net profits.

Then we discuss optimal budget allocation strategies in these three cases, without budget constraints. Experimental results are described in Figures 6.4–6.6. From Figures 6.1–6.3, we

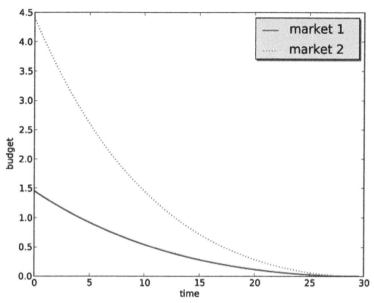

Figure 6.3   Constrained budget allocation in two markets in Case1-constant.

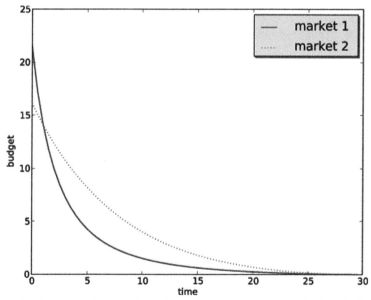

Figure 6.4   Unconstrained budget allocation in two markets in Case3-decrease.

can make similar conclusions in terms of the advertising elasticity to those in a setting without budget constraints. However, percentages of the budget allocated to these two markets are different in settings with and without budget constraints.

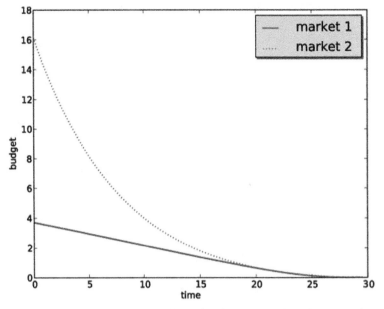

Figure 6.5   Unconstrained budget allocation in two markets in Case2-increase.

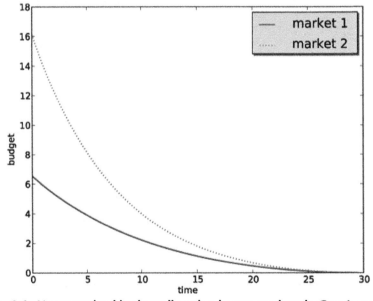

Figure 6.6   Unconstrained budget allocation in two markets in Case1-constant.

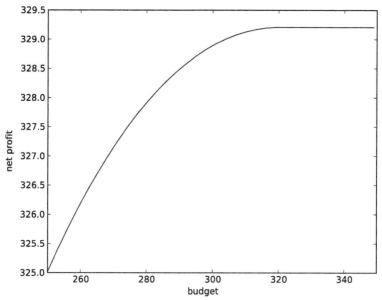

Figure 6.7 The map of the total budget relative to net profit.

After 100 computations we obtain the map showing the advertising budget relative to the net profit, as shown in Figure 6.7. The convexity feature of this map is consistent with Algorithm 2 in Section 6.3.3, which also validates Proposition 1.

6.5 Conclusions

In this chapter, we present a novel optimal budget model to dynamically allocate the advertising budget to several markets simultaneously, under a finite time horizon. Our model captures some distinctive features of search advertisements by introducing the dynamical advertising effort u and quality score q to extend the advertising response function to fit search advertising scenarios. We also discuss some desirable properties and present a feasible solution for our model. We conduct a computational experimental study to evaluate our model and identified properties, and experimental results show that the advertiser with increasing advertising elasticity is encouraged to invest more budget in the late stages, but the advertiser with decreasing advertising elasticity should invest more budget in the initial stage, in order to maximize net profits.

We are in the process of extending our model in the following directions: (a) relaxing the homogeneous assumption of the search advertising structure and contents to explore a more flexible model for budget allocations across markets, (b) studying budget allocation strategies in uncertain marketing environments of sponsored search auctions, and (c) studying optimization of the algorithm implementation to improve space and time efficiencies, and thus to facilitate budget decisions in practice.

References

Bass, F. M. 1969. A simultaneous equation regression study of advertising and sales of cigarettes, Journal of Marketing Research 6(3):291–300.

Erickson, G. M. 1992. Empirical analysis of closed-loop duopoly advertising strategies, Management Science 38(12):1732–1749.

Feinberg, F. M. 2001. On continuous-time optimal advertising under S-shaped response, Management Science 47(1):1476–1487.

Fruchter, G. E., W. Dou. 2005. Optimal budget allocation over time for keyword ads in web portals, Journal of Optimization Theory and Applications 124(1):157–174.

Hax, A. C., N. S. Majluf. 1982. Competitive cost dynamics: the experience curve, Interfaces 12(5):50–61.

Little, J. D. C. 1979. Aggregate advertising models: the state of the art, Operations Research 27(4):629–667.

Prasad, A., S. P. Sethi. 2004. Competitive advertising under uncertainty: A stochastic differential game approach, Journal of Optimization Theory and Applications 123(1):163–185.

Sasieni, M. W. 1971. Optimal advertising expenditure, Management Science 18(4):64–72.

Sethi, S. P. 1977. Dynamic optimal control models in advertising: a survey, SIAM Review 19(4):685–725.

Sethi, S. P. 1977. Optimal advertising for the Nerlove-arrow model under a budget constraint, Operation Research Quarterly, 28(3):683–693.

Sethi, S. P. 1983. Deterministic and stochastic optimization of a dynamic advertising model, Optimal Control Applications and Methods 4, 179–184.

Shakun, M. F. 1965. Advertising expenditures in coupled markets–a game-theory approach, Management Science 11(4):42–47.

Simon, J. L., J. Arndt. 1980. The shape of the advertising response function, Journal of Advertising Research 20(4):11–30.

Vidale M. L., H. B. Wolfe. 1957. An operations research study of sales response to advertising, Operations Research 5(3):370–381.

Yang, Y., J. Zhang, R. Qin, J. Li, F. Wang, Q. Wei. 2012. A budget optimization framework for search advertisements across markets, IEEE Transactions on Systems, Man, and Cybernetics, Part A, 42(5):1141–1151.

Budget Allocation In Competitive Search Advertisements, Part I: In Static Environments

7.1 Introduction

As a modern Internet advertising format, sponsored search auctions have been favored by a lot of advertisers. However, major sponsored search auction platforms (e.g. Google Adwords) provide only 8–10 advertising slots on the Search Engine Result Page (SERP). Thus advertisers have to compete for opportunities to display their advertisements. Moreover, most advertisers, especially those from small and medium enterprises (SMEs), have serious budget constraints. In other words, serious budget constraints aggravate advertising competitions in sponsored search auctions. Thus, they have to carefully determine their budget strategies in order to maximize the expected revenue from search promotional activities.

Recently many research efforts directed at advertising budget decision problems have emerged. Fruchter and Dou (2005) employed dynamic programming methods to study optimal budget allocation problems among web portals. According to Maille et al. (2010), most current research on budget decisions in competitive environments is directed at search engines, with the purpose of optimizing mechanism designs (Ashlagi et al., 2010; Borgs et al., 2005; Feldman et al., 2008; Edelman et al., 2007; Abrams et al., 2008), rather than at the advertisers' standpoint of maximizing their advertising revenues. By considering the entire lifecycle of advertising campaigns in sponsored search auctions, Yang et al. (2012) proposed a budget optimization framework (BOF) to facilitate budget decisions at three different decision levels: budget allocation across search advertising markets at the system level, temporal distribution over a series of slots (e.g. day) at the campaign level, and budget adjustment of the remaining budget (e.g. the daily budget) at the keyword level. This chapter focuses on the budget decision problem at the system level of the BOF framework, with special attention to competitive search advertising environments, specifically the budget competition problem among a group of advertisers.

Yang and Wang: Budget Constraints and Optimization in Sponsored Search Auctions. http://dx.doi.org/10.1016/B978-0-12-411457-9.00007-0
© 2014 Elsevier Inc. All rights reserved.

In competitive environments, an advertiser cannot achieve optimal budget allocation strategies without consideration of other advertisers' actions. Competition not only cancels out part of the advertisers' advertising effects (Friedman, 1958), but also makes the advertiser pay more for the same number of potential clicks. There are several serious challenges in studying the budget allocation problem in competitive environments. First, budget constraints restrict an advertiser's feasible strategy space, such that he/she might have less access to optimal budget allocation strategies. Secondly, in budget competitions, an advertiser's optimal strategy also depends on whether it is an equilibrium strategy and is stable. Thirdly, usually an advertiser cannot know exactly the type of his/her competitors. Fourthly, the underlying architecture of sponsored search auctions is essentially complicated. It is beyond an advertiser's capability to catch all parameters to make a reasonable budget decision, especially in competitive search advertising environments.

The objective of this research is to explore optimal budget allocation strategies in competitive settings by using a game-theoretical approach. Normative findings from our current research can be summarized as follows: (1) If the advertiser's type is public, then the budget competition is a complete-information game, then Nash equilibriums and corresponding budget strategies are available. (2) If the advertiser's type is private, the budget competition is an incomplete-information game, and then Bayesian Nash equilibriums and corresponding budget strategies exist. Whether or not the total budget is public is another important factor in the budget competition. Then we study whether the advertising campaigns are profitable using our proposed budget allocation strategies, given the total budget is determined. We present an evaluation approach based on the present value model to evaluate these equilibrium budget strategies in search advertising environments. Furthermore, some computational experiments are conducted to validate our budget strategies as identified in this work. Experimental results prove the superiority of our game-theoretical budget strategies over those neglecting budget competitions in sponsored search auctions.

The remainder of the chapter is organized as follows. Section 7.2 analyzes the budget allocation game in competitive search advertising environments, either with the complete-information settings or with incomplete-information settings. Section 7.3 presents an evaluation approach to evaluate whether these budget strategies are profitable. Section 7.4 reports some experimental results to validate our budget allocation strategies. Section 7.5 concludes the chapter.

7.2 The Budget Allocation Game

7.2.1 The Complete-Information Budget Game

Competition makes budget decisions at the system level more complicated. When there are two or more advertisers in a market, they must fight each other to get better opportunities and resources, e.g. potential clicks in search advertising markets. In the following we will analyze the budget competition problem using a game-theoretic approach. The notations used in this chapter are shown in Table 7.1.

Suppose the players of the budget game include m advertisers. For the advertiser i, she has a total budget b_i to allocate for her advertising campaigns during a given promotional period. In a static game, actions of the advertiser can be viewed as budget strategies. In the following analysis we will define the strategy space for the advertiser. Generally, we use $S_i = \{s_i\}$ to denote the strategy set for advertiser i, and the strategy is the budget allocation decision across several search advertising markets. So $s_i = (b_{i,1}, \ldots, b_{i,j}, \ldots, b_{i,n})$, where the condition $\sum_{j=1}^{n} b_{i,j} \leq b_i$ must be satisfied. Every advertiser chooses a certain budget strategy, and their strategies can form a strategy profile $s = (s_1, \ldots, s_i, \ldots, s_m)$.

Another important factor in the budget game is the advertiser's payoff. The payoff represents the exact utility or the expected utility that an advertiser can obtain for a certain strategy profile. Every advertiser in the budget game aims to maximize his/her own payoff. For advertiser i, the payoff can be described as $u_i = u_i(s_1, \ldots, s_i, \ldots, s_m)$. In the context of sponsored search auctions, it is measured as the total profit generated by the obtained clicks.

In the jth search advertising market, there are $q_j C_j$ potential clicks for all m advertisers. Besides the average cost-per-click (CPC) in the jth market, the cost-per-click of advertiser i in jth market (e.g. $p_{i,j}$) is also affected by her own quality score. In this research we use the advertiser i's individual click-through rate $c_{i,j}$ to describe the quality score because major search engines take it as the main component of the quality score and keep the quality score as a business secret. The higher $c_{i,j}$ implies that advertiser i can pay less for the same number of clicks in market j. Please note that C_j is estimated based on the rank of the advertisement and $c_{i,j}$ is influenced by the advertiser's advertising quality. In this research, we take C_j as the comprehensive click-through rate in market j with consideration of click-through rates of all advertisements displayed on the Search Engine Result Page (SERP).

As we described above, for advertiser i, $b_{i,j}$ is proportional to the number of clicks that she can obtain in market j. Thus we can use $b_{i,j} c_{i,j}$ to represent the ability to gain clicks in market j.

Table 7.1 List of notations.

Notation	Definition
b_i	The total budget of advertiser i, $i = 1, 2, \ldots, m$
$c_{i,j}$	The click-through rate (CTR) for advertiser i in the jth market, $j = 1, 2, \ldots, n$
$b_{i,j}$	The budget allocated to the jth market by advertiser i
$v_{i,j}$	The value-per-click (VPC) for advertiser i in the jth market
$p_{i,j}$	The cost-per-click (CPC) for advertiser i in the jth market
q_j	The total query demand in the jth market
C_j	The average click-through rate (CTR) in the jth market
r^k	The interest rate of the kth year

We assume that the number of clicks gained by an advertiser is proportional to (1) the total potential clicks and (2) the ability to gain clicks. Thus, we can define the payoff as follows:

$$u_i = \sum_{j=1}^{n} (v_{i,j} - p_{i,j}) \frac{b_{i,j} c_{i,j}}{\sum_{i=1}^{m} b_{i,j} c_{i,j}} q_j C_j.$$

Assumption (1) can be justified by the fact that $q_j C_j$ relies mainly on the search demands, rather than by the advertising budget. Assumption (2) is also rational because more budget means the advertiser can get more clicks or get better ranks, and the higher individual click-through rate indicates the advertiser's ad can attract more clicks at the same cost level. In the budget game, advertiser i must choose from a set of $b_{i,j}$, subject to the restriction $\sum_{j=1}^{n} b_{i,j} \leq b_i$.

If the advertiser knows the competitors' decision information exactly such as the total budget, strategy sets, and corresponding payoffs, and the competitors know that he/she knows, in other words, every player's total budget, strategy set, and payoffs are **common knowledge**, then the game is a **complete-information static game** in competitive search advertising environments. It was proved by Nash (1950) that there exists at least one Nash equilibrium for a finite game, and the equilibrium might be either pure strategic or mixed strategic. In the following we will try to explore the equilibrium of the budget allocation game with the complete-information setting.

Because every unit of the budget can be used to generate clicks and usually the net profit of each click is positive, it is reasonable for the advertiser to use up all the budget to gain maximum profit. Then the restriction is transformed to be $\sum_{j=1}^{n} b_{i,j} = b_i$. In the complete-information competitive environment, the budget allocation problem can be solved by Lagrangian function,

$$L_i = \sum_{j=1}^{n} (v_{i,j} - p_{i,j}) \frac{b_{i,j} c_{i,j}}{\sum_{i=1}^{m} b_{i,j} c_{i,j}} q_j C_j + \lambda \left(\sum_{j=1}^{n} b_{i,j} - b_i \right).$$

Differentiating L_i with respect to the unknown $b_{i,j}$ and the Lagrangian multiplier λ, we can obtain the following equations

$$(v_{i,j} - p_{i,j}) \frac{c_{i,j} \left(\sum_{i=1}^{m} b_{i,j} c_{i,j} - b_{i,j} c_{i,j} \right)}{\left(\sum_{i=1}^{m} b_{i,j} c_{i,j} \right)^2} q_j C_j + \lambda = 0,$$

$$\sum_{j=1}^{n} b_{i,j} - b_i = 0.$$

Then, we have the response function

$$b_{i,j} = b_{i,j}(b_{-i,j}) = b_{i,j}(b_{1,j}, \ldots, b_{i-1,j}, b_{i+1,j}, \ldots, b_{m,j}),$$

and

$$b_{i,j} = \frac{\left(b_i + \sum\limits_{j=1}^{n} A_{i,j}\right) \sqrt{(v_{i,j} - p_{i,j})q_j C_j A_{i,j}}}{\sum\limits_{j=1}^{n} \sqrt{(v_{i,j} - p_{i,j})q_j C_j A_{i,j}}} - A_{i,j},$$

where

$$A_{i,j} = \frac{\sum\limits_{-i \neq i} b_{-i,j} c_{-i,j}}{c_{i,j}}$$

and $-i$ represents the competitors of i (e.g. other players besides i). The response function indicates that each advertiser's optimal strategy for budget allocation is a function of their competitors' strategies. Through computing the mn response functions, we can finally find the equilibrium which is the profile of every advertiser's optimal strategy. It generally can be given as follows,

$$s^* = (s_1^*, \ldots, s_i^*, \ldots, s_m^*),$$

where $s_i^* = (b_{i,1}^*, \ldots, b_{i,j}^*, \ldots, b_{i,n}^*)$ and $b_{i,j}^*$ is the optimal budget allocated to market j by advertiser i. The solution for this budget allocation problem shows that the budget game described above has a **pure strategic Nash equilibrium**.

Let $p_{i,j}$ denote the cost-per-click (CPC) for advertiser i in the jth market, then $\frac{b_{i,j} c_{i,j}}{\sum_{i=1}^{m} b_{i,j} c_{i,j}} q_j C_j$ is the total clicks that she can obtain in market j. We can easily notice

$$p_{i,j} \frac{b_{i,j} c_{i,j}}{\sum\limits_{i=1}^{m} b_{i,j} c_{i,j}} q_j C_j = b_i.$$

Thus the payoff function can be simplified as follows:

$$u_i = \sum\limits_{j=1}^{n} v_{i,j} \frac{b_{i,j} c_{i,j}}{\sum\limits_{i=1}^{m} b_{i,j} c_{i,j}} q_j C_j.$$

In the simplified model, it is suggested the advertiser allocates the budget across markets with the following strategy:

$$b_{i,j} = \frac{\left(b_i + \sum\limits_{j=1}^{n} A_{i,j}\right) \sqrt{v_{i,j} q_j C_j A_{i,j}}}{\sum\limits_{j=1}^{n} \sqrt{v_{i,j} q_j C_j A_{i,j}}} - A_{i,j},$$

where

$$A_{i,j} = \frac{\sum\limits_{-i \neq i} b_{-i,j} c_{-i,j}}{c_{i,j}}$$

and $-i$ represent all the competitors of i.

7.2.2 The Incomplete-Information Budget Game

In practical promotional activities of sponsored search auctions, it is hard for an advertiser to access the complete information relevant to the competitors' payoff function. In such a situation, budget decisions in competitive environments are much more complicated, and it can be viewed as an **incomplete-information static game**. It is also termed a **static Bayesian game**. Similar to the complete-information static game, for advertiser i, the strategy set S_i is equivalent to the strategy space A_i in the incomplete-information static game. The difference lies in that her action set is type-contingent in the incomplete-information static game. In other words, an advertiser's budget allocation strategy depends on their type. In this work, we use the total budget b_i to represent an advertiser i's type. Then we have $S_i = S_i(b_i)$, and for a certain b_i, there is an exclusive S_i. The advertiser knows their own type exactly, other players only know the distribution of this type. We assume that several factors such as the individual click-through rate $c_i = (c_{i,1}, \ldots, c_{i,j}, \ldots, c_{i,n})$ and the value-per-click $v_i = (v_{i,1}, \ldots, v_{i,j}, \ldots, v_{i,n})$ are common knowledge.

Through Harsanyi transformation (Harsanyi and Selten, 1972), the incomplete-information game can be converted into the game with complete but imperfect information. We introduce a dummy player called "nature." It acts at first to choose the advertiser's type. For an advertiser i, the competitors know the distribution of their type, but don't know the exact type and strategy to take. The advertiser i knows what the competitors know. That is, the distribution of advertiser i's type is public information.

In the budget game with incomplete-information settings, the advertiser i tries to maximize her expected payoff, given as follows:

$$E(u_i) = \sum_{j=1}^{n} v_{i,j} E\left(\frac{b_{i,j} c_{i,j}}{\sum\limits_{i=1}^{m} b_{i,j} c_{i,j}}\right) q_j C_j,$$

under the restriction $\sum_{j=1}^{n} b_{i,j} = b_i$.

Then we have

$$E\left(\frac{b_{i,j} c_{i,j}}{\sum\limits_{i=1}^{m} b_{i,j} c_{i,j}}\right) = \frac{b_{i,j} c_{i,j}}{\sum\limits_{-i \neq i} E(b_{-i,j}) c_{-i,j} + b_{i,j} c_{i,j}}.$$

It can be proved that (1) the budget game with incomplete-information settings has at least one **Bayesian Nash equilibrium** (Gibbons, 1992), and (2) when in equilibrium state, advertisers maximize their expected payoffs, given that their type and competitors' type distributions are known.

Given an exact type b_i of the advertiser i, the advertiser $-i$ can figure out the reaction function $b_{-i,j} = g_{-i}(b_{-i}, b_{i,j})$, and the advertiser i also has access to the function in the complete-information budget game. Thus, if b_{-i} is a continuous random variable and it has probability density function $f_{-i}(b_{-i})$, then

$$E(b_{-i,j}) = \int_{-\infty}^{+\infty} g_{-i} f_{-i} d(b_{-i}).$$

Suppose b_{-i} is subject to the normal distribution function $N(\mu, \sigma^2)$. Because

$$b_{-i,j} = \frac{(b_{-i} + \sum\limits_{j=1}^{n} A_{-i,j})\sqrt{v_{-i,j} q_j C_j A_{-i,j}}}{\sum\limits_{j=1}^{n} \sqrt{v_{-i,j} q_j C_j A_{-i,j}}} - A_{-i,j}$$

is a linear function of b_{-i}, where

$$A_{-i,j} = \frac{\sum\limits_{i \neq -i} b_{i,j} c_{i,j}}{c_{-i,j}},$$

then we can prove that $b_{-i,j}$ also follows the normal distribution, and

$$E(b_{-i,j}) = \frac{\sqrt{v_{-i,j} q_j C_j A_{-i,j}}}{\sum\limits_{j=1}^{n} \sqrt{v_{-i,j} q_j C_j A_{-i,j}}} \mu + \frac{\left(\sum\limits_{j=1}^{n} A_{-i,j}\right)\sqrt{v_{-i,j} q_j C_j A_{-i,j}}}{\sum\limits_{j=1}^{n} \sqrt{v_{-i,j} q_j C_j A_{-i,j}}} - A_{-i,j},$$

$$D(b_{-i,j}) = \left(\frac{\sqrt{v_{-i,j} q_j C_j A_{-i,j}}}{\sum\limits_{j=1}^{n} \sqrt{v_{-i,j} q_j C_j A_{-i,j}}} \sigma\right)^2.$$

Substitute $E(b_{-i,j})$ into the advertiser i's expected payoff function $E(u_i)$ to get the final form. Differentiating the Lagrangian function with respect to $b_{i,j}$ and Lagrangian multiplier, the advertiser i's response function

$$b_{i,j} = b_{i,j}[E(b_{-i,j})] = b_{i,j}[E(b_{1,j}), \ldots, E(b_{i-1,j}), E(b_{i+1,j}), \ldots, E(b_{m,j})]$$

can be obtained, given the competitors' budget allocation strategy set $S'_{-i} = \{s'_{-i}\}$, where

$$s'_{-i} = [E(b_{-i,1}), \ldots, E(b_{-i,j}), \ldots, E(b_{-i,n})].$$

Through mutual substitution of the mn reaction functions, we can find the optimal strategy for each advertiser, and the profile of all advertisers' optimal strategies, stays at the equilibrium of the budget game with incomplete-information settings.

7.3 An Evaluation Approach

In Section 7.2, we provide the solution to the budget allocation game with incomplete-information settings in the competitive environment of sponsored search auctions. Given the total budget, the allocation decisions computed from these budget models can yield the maximum revenue for each advertiser in the equilibrium state. This section aims to figure out whether the revenue generated from our budget model in sponsored search auction campaigns can outperform that generated by other forms of investment, such as savings in a bank or buying public debt.

For the advertiser i, let b_i denote the total budget for a three-year sponsored search auction campaign and the advertiser will settle her budget decisions every year.

Suppose that clicks in the jth market during three years have the distribution $f^t_{i,j}$

$$\int_0^1 t f^t_{i,j}\, dt = c^1_{i,j} \quad \int_1^2 t f^t_{i,j}\, dt = c^2_{i,j} \quad \int_2^3 t f^t_{i,j}\, dt = c^3_{i,j}.$$

At the end of each year, the advertiser transfers revenues into cash. It is known that in financial economics when comparing values of money at different periods of time, people will consider the time value of money. The time value of money refers to the fact that the money in hand today is worth more than the expectation of the same amount to be received in the future. Thus, here we use the concept of present value (pv for short) (Friedman, 1957) of the revenues gained at different periods to compute the total value of revenues during three years, then compare it against the original budget in order to figure out whether our decision in the budget game with incomplete-information settings in sponsored search auction campaigns is profitable for the advertiser i (See Table 7.2).

If the Net pv of revenues from advertising activities at the end of the third year satisfies the following condition

$$pv^1 + pv^2 + pv^3 - b_i \geq 0,$$

then we can reckon that our decision in the budget game with incomplete-information settings in sponsored search auction campaigns is profitable for the advertiser i. Thus a wise advertiser will follow our budget game model in sponsored search auction campaigns. Otherwise, if it

Table 7.2 The present value of revenues.

Year	*Pv* of revenues	Net *pv* of revenues
1	$pv^1 = \frac{\sum c_{i,j}^1 v_{i,j}}{(1+r^1)}$	$pv^1 - b_i$
2	$pv^2 = \frac{\sum c_{i,j}^2 v_{i,j}}{(1+r^1)(1+r^2)}$	$pv^1 + pv^2 - b_i$
3	$pv^3 = \frac{\sum c_{i,j}^3 v_{i,j}}{(1+r^1)(1+r^2)(1+r^3)}$	$pv^1 + pv^2 + pv^3 - b_i$

does not satisfy the condition, our decisions in the budget game with incomplete-information settings in sponsored search auction campaigns are not profitable for the advertiser i. Then it is suggested the advertiser does not participate in search advertising campaigns. The upper boundary for the advertiser to participate in search advertising campaigns and follow our budget game model is when b_i satisfies the condition, e.g.

$$pv^1 + pv^2 + pv^3 - b_i = 0.$$

7.4 Experiments

In this section, we conduct a numerical experiment to validate the budget game model and corresponding strategies.

Note that the complete-information game-theoretical analysis of the budget allocation can be viewed as a special case of incomplete information game-theoretical analysis where the variance in the advertisers' total budget is 0. Thus in this research we focus on experiments to reveal the effectiveness of our budget allocation analysis in the competitive environment with incomplete-information settings, which is termed a Bayesian Nash equilibrium strategy (BNES for short). In the following experiment, we take a baseline strategy for the purpose of comparison, e.g. a budget allocation strategy without consideration of competition (e.g. termed the uncompetitive strategy, UCS for short).

We consider the budget competition scenario in sponsored search auctions, where two advertisers allocate their budgets across two search advertising markets. The main experimental data is described in Table 7.3.

As for our budget decision strategy BNES, the total budget for these two advertisers has the distribution $b_1 \sim N(200, 8)$ and $b_2 \sim N(150, 5)$, respectively. Experimental results show that:

Table 7.3 Experimental data.

$v_{1,1} = 1.5$	$v_{1,2} = 1$	$v_{2,1} = 1.2$	$v_{2,2} = 1.2$
$c_{1,1} = 0.4$	$c_{1,2} = 0.3$	$c_{2,1} = 0.3$	$c_{2,2} = 0.6$
$q_1 = 300$	$q_2 = 400$	$C_1 = 0.5$	$C_2 = 0.4$

1. The advertiser-1 should allocate 114.409 to market-1 and 85.591 to market-2, then he/she gets revenue of 209.830.
2. The advertiser-2 should allocate 70.682 to market-1 and 79.318 to market-2, then he/she gets revenue of 180.595.

We can also compute the average cost-per-click for both advertisers in two markets.

1. For advertiser-1, it is 1.246 in market-1 and 1.265 in market-2.
2. For advertiser-2, it is 1.246 in market-1 and 0.843 in market-2.

Let us consider that the advertiser's sponsored search auction campaigns last for three years. Suppose that the clicks gained for both advertisers follow the normal distribution in the two markets and the interest rate is kept at 2% during the three-year period. Then we can get the following results:

1. The present value of the revenue for advertiser-1 is 201.708 (obviously larger than 200). However, if the interest rate increases slightly, the revenue for advertiser-1 is minus. Thus he/she is advised to take sponsored search auction campaigns with reserved opinions.
2. The present value of revenue for advertiser-2 is 173.605 (obviously larger than 150). Only if the interest rate is higher than 9.9%, should the advertiser transfer the advertising budget to other forms of investment.

As for the baseline strategy UCS, the total budget for advertiser-1 and advertiser-2 is given as 200 and 150, respectively. Using the same method in competitive situations, then advertiser-1 should put all the budget into market-1 to gain revenue of 240.750, and advertiser-2 should allocate all the budget to market-2 to gain revenue of 213.494. With the same assumptions about clicks distribution over time and the interest rate in competitive situations, the present value of revenues for advertiser-1 and advertiser-2 are 231.432 and 205.231, respectively.

From experimental results, someone might say that the budget decision strategy UCS outperforms our BNES because it can generate more revenue for both advertisers. However, in fact the budget allocation strategy UCS is not applicable for advertisers in competitive environments, because the optimal budget allocation strategy without consideration of competitors' strategies is unstable. If an advertiser chooses to use the UCS strategy, their competitor has the motivation to violate the UCS to get more revenue. Then the budget game between these two advertisers will cease until the equilibrium is reached where both advertisers use the BNES strategy to allocate their advertising budget.

7.5 Conclusions

In sponsored search auctions, the advertiser should allocate the limited budget across search advertising markets at the very beginning of the promotion project. There are many advertisers in a search market and they compete against each other for the limited opportunities to display their advertisements and resources such as clicks. An advertiser cannot optimize budget decision strategies without consideration of the competition.

In this chapter, we employ the game-theoretical approach to analyze the budget allocation problem in competitive search advertising environments with and without complete information settings. For these two scenarios, Nash equilibrium strategies and Bayesian Nash equilibrium strategies are explored, respectively. We also evaluate whether the allocation strategies of our budget competition model are profitable using the present value model. Furthermore, computational experiments are conducted to validate the budget competition model and allocation strategies proposed. Experimental results illustrate the superiority of our allocation strategies over a baseline strategy.

In an ongoing work, we are studying the dynamic budget allocation problem in a competitive scenario where the information is incomplete.

References

Abrams, Z., S. S. Keerthi, O. Mendelevitch, J. A. Tomlin. 2008. Ad delivery with budgeted advertisers: A comprehensive LP approach, Journal of Electronic Commerce Research, 9:16–32.

Ashlagi, I., M. Braverman, A. Hassidim, R. Lavi, M. Tennenholtz. 2010. Position auctions with budgets: existence and uniqueness, In Proceedings of the Sixth Workshop on Ad Auctions,Cambridge, MA, USA, June 2010.

Borgs, C., J. Chayes, N. Immorlica, M. Mahdian, A. Saberi. 2005. Multi-unit auctions with budget-constrained bidders, In ACM Conference on Electronic Commerce (EC), 44–51.

Edelman, B., M. Ostrovsky, M. Schwarz. 2007. Internet advertising and the generalized second price auction: Selling billions of dollars worth of keywords, American Economic Review, 97(1):242–259.

Feldman, J., S. Muthukrishnan, E. Nikolova, M. Pál. 2008. A truthful mechanism for offline ad slot scheduling, In First International Symposium on Algorithmic Game Theory, Lecture Notes in Computer Science, 4997:182–193.

Friedman, M. 1957. A Theory of the Consumption. Princeton University Press.

Friedman, L. 1958. Game-theory models in the allocation of advertising expenditures, Operations Research, 6:699–709.

Fruchter G. E., W. Dou. 2005. Optimal budget allocation over time for keyword ads in Web portals, Journal of Optimization Theory and Applications, 124 (1):157–174.

Gibbons, R. 1992. A primer on Game Theory. New York:Wheatsheaf.

Harsanyi, J. C., R. Selten. 1972. A generalized Nash solution for two-person bargaining games with incomplete information, Management Science, 18(5):80–106.

Maille, P., E. Markakis, M. Naldi, G.D Stamoulis, B. Tuffin. 2010. Sponsored search auctions: An overview of research with emphasis on game theoretic aspects. Working Paper.

Nash, J. 1950. Equilibrium points in n-person games, Proceedings of the National Academy of Sciences, 36:48–49, USA.

Yang, Y., J. Zhang, R. Qin, J. Li, F. Wang, Q. Wei. 2012. A budget optimization framework for search advertisements across markets, IEEE Transactions on Systems, Man, and Cybernetics, Part A, 42(5):1141–1151.

Budget Allocation in Competitive Search Advertisements, Part II: In Dynamic Environments

8.1 Introduction

The growing prosperity of markets of sponsored search auctions is vastly driven by the influx of millions of advertisers. However, most search engine companies currently provide a limited number of advertising slots (e.g. 8–10) on the Search Engine Result Pages (SERPs). The unbalanced relationship between a large number of advertisers and limited advertising space leads to high levels of advertising competition. On the other hand, advertisers or brand managers, especially those from small and medium enterprises (SMEs), usually have serious budget constraints. Therefore, advertisers have to make advertising decisions wisely in order to survive the fierce competition and to get maximized profits.

Advertising competition cancels out part of the effect of promotional expenditure (Friedman, 1958). Thus, an advertiser cannot fully optimize his own budgeting strategy without consideration of his competitors' strategies. Thus, turning to pursue a best response becomes a feasible issue, that is, to find the best strategies while fixing other competitors' strategies. In early literature related to advertisements, the decision about advertising levels was incorporated with advertising/sale response functions to parsimoniously capture the relationship between advertising spending and unit sales (Sasieni, 1971; Little, 1979, Rao and Rao, 1983; Sethi, 1983). Because the marketing environment is time-varying, differential game (Fruchter and Kalish, 1998; Prasad and Sethi, 2004; Erickson, 1992, 1995; Leitmann and Schmitendorf, 1978) and optimal control methods (Sethi, l977; Archak et al., 2010) are used to capture advertising dynamics and competitive advertising strategies.

There are several challenges in determining optimal budget strategies with distinctive features relevant to sponsored search auctions. First, millions of advertisers with serious budget constraints aggravate the competitive status in sponsored search auctions, and budget constraints define the strategy space and thus possible equilibrium solutions. Secondly,

Yang and Wang: Budget Constraints and Optimization in Sponsored Search Auctions. http://dx.doi.org/10.1016/B978-0-12-411457-9.00008-2
© 2014 Elsevier Inc. All rights reserved.

the underlying architecture (e.g. auction mechanism, ranking, and pricing processes) are complex and thus beyond the reach of advertisers. It's not a straightforward task to build effective budget strategies amidst so many parameters. Thirdly, the large volume of search demands makes search advertising a continuous, dynamic process. Fourthly, similar to general markets, a search market has a saturation level of search demands. However, it splits into millions of interweaving pieces corresponding to keywords, and thus is difficult to estimate.

In this chapter, we employ a differential game approach to formulate budget allocation problems in a competitive search market, within a finite time horizon. We amend the response function as given in Prasad and Sethi (2004) to fit advertising scenarios in sponsored search auctions through introducing advertising effort u and quality score q, as major search engines have adopted a quality-based ranking and pricing mechanism recently. Because an advertiser usually has no way to get knowledge about the competitors' market share and time-varying advertising performance, we derive open-loop Nash equilibria (OLNEs) for our budget model with and without budget constraints, and study some desirable properties. In the case of budget constraints, there exist two kinds of OLNEs: "budget-stable" and "budget-unstable" OLNEs. The budget-stable OLNE refers to when an advertiser slightly changes the budget, but the old equilibrium points still apply to the new situation. The budget-unstable OLNE refers to when an advertiser slightly changes the budget, but the old equilibrium points either don't apply to the new situation or stay outside of the feasible region. We also perform experiments to validate our budget allocation model and some desirable properties. The results show that budget strategies with dynamic advertising elasticity are superior to those with the advertising elasticity fixed and our finds in OLNEs are helpful for advertisers to make budget decisions. The advertiser is encouraged to allocate the advertising budget to a certain market to get BS-OLNE, that is to make the equilibrium stay within the budget boundary.

The remainder of this chapter is organized as follows. Section 8.2 analyzes budget decision problems under consideration. Section 8.3.1 illustrates the response function in competitive search advertisements, respectively. Section 8.3.2 proposes our budget model for budget allocation in competitive search advertisements, then studies some desirable properties and gives solutions. Section 8.4 reports some experimental evaluation results of our model and identified properties. Section 8.5 concludes this research and discusses several future directions.

8.2 Problem Statement

Millions of advertisers with serious budget constraints aggravate the competitive status in sponsored search auctions. Competition can cancel out part of the advertising effect. In other words, competition forces an advertiser to pay more either to maintain current market share, or to gain new parts of market share. Thus, advertisers have to optimize budget allocation

Table 8.1 List of notations.

Notation	Definition
$u_j(t)$	The advertising effort advertiser j at time t
$b_j(t)$	The allocated budget of advertiser j at time t
$m(t)$	The search demand at time t
$\theta_j(t)$	The market share of advertiser j at time t
$\alpha_j(t)$	The advertising elasticity of advertiser j at time t
$c(t)$	The click-through rate at time t
B_j	The total budget of advertiser j
q_j	The quality score of advertiser j
v_j	The value-per-click for advertiser j
ρ_j	The response constant of advertiser j

strategies given that their competitors' strategies are accessed. In an equilibrium state, no advertiser would like to change the budget allocation strategies because no more revenue is available for such actions. However, when advertisers have serious budget constraints, especially in sponsored search auctions, equilibria free of budget constraints might not be feasible or become "unstable," because budget constraints define the strategy space and thus possible equilibrium solutions. In such a situation, it's not easy for an advertiser to figure out competitors' budget strategies, and thus he cannot set down his own optimal budget decisions. This chapter aims to study budget optimization problems in a competitive search market within a finite time horizon, and find "stable" equilibria for budget decisions in a differential game setting.

The notations used in this chapter are shown in Table 8.1.

8.3 Budget Competition

8.3.1 The Response Function

The advertising response function is introduced as a formula to show the cumulative advertising effect for an individual advertiser. We extend the advertising response function given by Prasad and Sethi (2004) to fit sponsored search auction scenarios from three aspects. First, besides the advertising budget, an advertiser's quality score q can also have significant influence on their capacity to gain market share. A higher quality score entitles an advertiser to pay less for each click, so the same amount of the advertising budget can result in more market share than other advertisers with a lower quality score. Because an advertiser's click-through rate (CTR) is the core component for the quality score, in this work we use the CTR to denote quality score. Let us consider two advertisers allocating the advertising budget to compete for market share θ in sponsored search auctions. Therefore, we give the advertising response function for competitive search advertisements as:

$$d\theta_1/dt = \rho_1 q_1 u_1 \sqrt{1-\theta_1} - \rho_2 q_2 u_2 \sqrt{1-\theta_2}$$

and

$$d\theta_2/dt = \rho_2 q_2 u_2 \sqrt{1-\theta_2} - \rho_1 q_1 u_1 \sqrt{1-\theta_1},$$

where q_1, q_2 are the quality scores of advertiser-1 and advertiser-2, respectively, and ρ_1, ρ_2 are the response constants for advertiser-1 and advertiser-2, respectively, and they determine the effectiveness of the advertising effort.

Secondly, the search advertising elasticity α is time-varying as described previously. In this work we take an advertiser's market share as private information. Thus we prefer to employ an open-loop method to study the budget allocation problem. Thus with $u = b^{\alpha(t)}$ (Section 6.2.1), we have

$$d\theta_1/dt = \rho_1 q_1 b_1^{\alpha_1(t)} \sqrt{1-\theta_1} - \rho_2 q_2 b_2^{\alpha_2(t)} \sqrt{1-\theta_2}$$

for advertiser-1 and

$$d\theta_2/dt = \rho_2 q_2 b_2^{\alpha_2(t)} \sqrt{1-\theta_2} - \rho_1 q_1 b_1^{\alpha_1(t)} \sqrt{1-\theta_1}$$

for advertiser-2.

8.3.2 The Model

In this section, we build a differential game model to study two advertisers' budget optimization to get more market share in a competitive setting of sponsored search auctions. Let B_j denote the total budget for the advertiser j, m the search demand, and c the click-through rate (CTR). Suppose there is no advertisement differentiation. By advertisement differentiation, we mean that for an advertiser the advertising structure and content is the same (or similar) in several markets.

In a competitive setting of sponsored search auctions, an advertiser seeks optimal budget strategy to maximize expected revenues given that a competitor's budget allocation strategies are available. Let v_1, v_2 be values of a click for advertiser-1 and advertiser-2, respectively. Then the payoff of these two advertisers can be given as:

$$\int_0^T e^{-rt}(v_1 m(t) c(t) \theta_1(t) - b_1(t)) dt$$

and

$$\int_0^T e^{-rt}(v_2 m(t) c(t) \theta_2(t) - b_2(t)) dt,$$

where e^{-rt} is the discount factor.

Based on the analysis above, we provide a differential game model for budget allocation in a competitive search market, with consideration of two advertisers,

$$\max \int_0^T e^{-rt}(v_1 m(t) c(t) \theta_1(t) - b_1(t)) \mathrm{d}t$$

$$\max \int_0^T e^{-rt}(v_2 m(t) c(t) \theta_2(t) - b_2(t)) \mathrm{d}t$$

$$\text{s.t. } \mathrm{d}\theta_1/\mathrm{d}t = \rho_1 q_1 (b_1(t))^{\alpha_1(t)} \sqrt{1 - \theta_1} - \rho_2 q_2 (b_2(t))^{\alpha_2(t)} \sqrt{1 - \theta_2} \qquad (8.1)$$

$$\mathrm{d}\theta_2/\mathrm{d}t = \rho_2 q_2 (b_2(t))^{\alpha_2(t)} \sqrt{1 - \theta_2} - \rho_1 q_1 (b_1(t))^{\alpha_1(t)} \sqrt{1 - \theta_1}$$

$$\int_0^T e^{-rt} b_j(t) \mathrm{d}t \leqslant B_j, \ j = 1, 2$$

$$b_j(t) \geqslant 0.$$

8.3.3 Properties

In this section, we will discuss open-loop Nash equilibria (OLNEs) in two cases: one case without consideration of budget constraints, and the other with consideration of budget constraints. First, let us discuss the case without budget constraints. We use the Pontryagin Maximum Principle (Kopp, 1962) to find Nash equilibria. Let $u_j(t)$ be the advertising effort function, i.e.

$$u_j(t) = b_j(t)^{\alpha_j(t)}, b_j(t) = u_j(t)^{\beta_j(t)}, \beta_j(t) = 1/\alpha_j(t) > 1.$$

For simplicity, set

$$C_j(t) = v_j(t) m_j(t) c_j(t), \beta_j = \beta_j(t), b_j = b_j(t), u_j = u_j(t).$$

Notice that $\theta_1(t) + \theta_2(t) \equiv 1$. Then we can reduce the dynamic system to a dynamic equation and write $\theta_1 = \theta$. In the case without budget constraints:

$$\max \int_0^T e^{-rt}(C_1(t)\theta(t) - u_1(t)^{\beta_1(t)}) \mathrm{d}t$$

$$\max \int_0^T e^{-rt}(C_2(t)(1 - \theta(t)) - u_2(t)^{\beta_2(t)}) \mathrm{d}t \qquad (8.2)$$

$$\text{s.t. } \mathrm{d}\theta/\mathrm{d}t = \rho_1 q_1 u_1(t) \sqrt{1 - \theta} - \rho_2 q_2 u_2(t) \sqrt{\theta}$$

$$u_j(t) \geqslant 0.$$

We give a Nash equilibrium solution in terms of open-loop controls for the differential game model without budget constraints, as follows.

Step 1: The optimal controls can be determined in terms of adjoint variables:

For any $Q_1, Q_2 \in \mathbb{R}$,

$$u_1^{\#}(t, \theta, Q_1, Q_2) = \text{argmax}_{w \geq 0}\{Q_1 \rho_1 q_1 w \sqrt{1 - \theta} - w^{\beta_1} e^{-rt}\}$$

$$= \left(Q_{1,+} \frac{\rho_1 q_1 \sqrt{1 - \theta}}{\beta_1 e^{-rt}}\right)^{1/(\beta_1 - 1)},$$

$$u_2^{\#}(t, \theta, Q_1, Q_2) = \text{argmax}_{w \geq 0}\{-Q_2 \rho_2 q_2 w \sqrt{\theta} - w^{\beta_2} e^{-rt}\}$$

$$= \left((-Q_2)_+ \frac{\rho_2 q_2 \sqrt{\theta}}{\beta_2 e^{-rt}}\right)^{1/(\beta_2 - 1)}.$$

Here, $Q_+ = Q$, if $Q \geq 0$, otherwise, $Q_+ = 0$.

Step 2: The state $\theta(\cdot)$ and adjoint variables $Q_1(\cdot)$, $Q_2(\cdot)$ can be determined by solving the boundary value problem

$$
\begin{cases}
\frac{d\theta}{dt} = \left(\frac{1}{\beta_1 e^{-rt}}\right)^{\frac{1}{\beta_1 - 1}} \left(\rho_1 q_1 \sqrt{1 - \theta}\right)^{\frac{\beta_1}{\beta_1 - 1}} (Q_{1,+})^{\frac{1}{\beta_1 - 1}} \\
\quad - \left(\frac{1}{\beta_2 e^{-rt}}\right)^{\frac{1}{\beta_2 - 1}} \left(\rho_2 q_2 \sqrt{\theta}\right)^{\frac{\beta_2}{\beta_2 - 1}} ((-Q_2)_+)^{\frac{1}{\beta_2 - 1}}, \\
\frac{dQ_1}{dt} = \frac{1}{2}(\rho_1 q_1)^{\frac{\beta_1}{\beta_1 - 1}} \left(\frac{1}{\beta_1 e^{-rt}}\right)^{\frac{1}{\beta_1 - 1}} (Q_{1,+})^{\frac{1}{\beta_1 - 1}} \left(\sqrt{1 - \theta}\right)^{\frac{2 - \beta_1}{\beta_1 - 1}} \\
\quad + \frac{1}{2}(\rho_2 q_2)^{\frac{\beta_2}{\beta_2 - 1}} \left(\frac{1}{\beta_2 e^{-rt}}\right)^{\frac{1}{\beta_2 - 1}} Q_1((-Q_2)_+)^{\frac{1}{\beta_2 - 1}} \left(\sqrt{\theta}\right)^{\frac{2 - \beta_2}{\beta_2 - 1}} - e^{-rt}C_1(t), \quad (8.3) \\
\frac{dQ_2}{dt} = \frac{1}{2}(\rho_1 q_1)^{\frac{\beta_1}{\beta_1 - 1}} \left(\frac{1}{\beta_1 e^{-rt}}\right)^{\frac{1}{\beta_1 - 1}} Q_2(Q_{1,+})^{\frac{1}{\beta_1 - 1}} \left(\sqrt{1 - \theta}\right)^{\frac{2 - \beta_1}{\beta_1 - 1}} \\
\quad - \frac{1}{2}(\rho_2 q_2)^{\frac{\beta_2}{\beta_2 - 1}} \left(\frac{1}{\beta_2 e^{-rt}}\right)^{\frac{1}{\beta_2 - 1}} ((-Q_2)_+)^{\frac{\beta_2}{\beta_2 - 1}} \left(\sqrt{\theta}\right)^{\frac{2 - \beta_2}{\beta_2 - 1}} + e^{-rt}C_2(t), \\
\theta(0) = \theta_1(0), \\
Q_1(T) = Q_2(T) = 0.
\end{cases}
$$

Once a solution $t \rightarrow (\theta(t), Q_1(t), Q_2(t))$ to the two-point boundary value problem (8.3) is available, the trajectory θ^* and the controls (u_1^*, u_2^*) can determined by

$$\theta^*(t) = x(t), u_1^*(t) = u_1^{\#}(t, \theta(t), Q_1(t), Q_2(t)), u_2^*(t) = u_2^{\#}(t, \theta(t), Q_1(t), Q_2(t)).$$

Secondly, let us discuss the case with budget constraints. We try to get open-loop Nash equilibria (OLNEs) for the case with budget constraints (model (8.1)) through introducing a boundary value of the advertising budget to the case without budget constraints (model (8.2)). Thereafter, we can find two kinds of OLNEs of model (8.1): "budget-stable" and "budget-unstable" OLNEs.

Definition 8.1 (Budget-Stable Open-Loop Nash Equilibrium). If an open-loop Nash equilibrium point $(b_1^*(t), b_2^*(t))$ of model (8.2) stays inside the budget boundary of model (8.1), it is called a budget-stable open-loop Nash equilibrium (BS-OLNE) point.

The following theory provides necessary conditions for the BS-OLNEs in model (8.1).

Theorem 8.1 (Necessary conditions for BS-OLNE). *Assuming $(b_1^*(t), b_2^*(t))$ is a "budget-stable" open-loop Nash equilibrium (BS-OLNE) point of model (8.1), we have*

1. *for advertiser j, $\int_0^T e^{-rt} b_j^*(t)\mathrm{d}t < B_j$;*
2. *for $u_j^*(t) = b_j^*(t)^{\alpha_j(t)}, \theta^*(t)$ (derived from the equation*
   $\mathrm{d}\theta/\mathrm{d}t = \rho_1 q_1 u_1^* \sqrt{1-\theta} - \rho_2 q_2 u_2^* \sqrt{\theta}, \theta(0) = \theta_1(0))$, *and*

$$Q_1(t) = \frac{(u_1^*)^{\beta_1-1} e^{-rt}}{\rho_1 q_1 \sqrt{1-\theta^*}}, \quad Q_2(t) = -\frac{(u_2^*)^{\beta_2-1}\beta_2 e^{-rt}}{\rho_2 q_2 \sqrt{\theta^*}},$$

satisfy the ordinary differential system (8.3).

Definition 8.2 (Budget-Unstable Open-Loop Nash Equilibrium (BUS-OLNE)). If an open-loop Nash equilibrium point $(b_1^*(t), b_2^*(t))$ of model (8.1) stays at the budget boundary, it is called a budget-unstable open-loop Nash equilibrium (BS-OLNE) point.

In the case of a Budget-Stable Open-loop Nash Equilibrium (BS-OLNE), when an advertiser slightly changes the budget, the old equilibrium points still apply to the new situation. In this sense, the advertiser is encouraged to decrease the budget as much as possible until the equilibrium is outside the feasible region.

In the case of a Budget-Unstable Open-loop Nash Equilibrium (BUS-OLNE), when an advertiser slightly changes the budget, the old equilibrium points either don't apply to the new situation, or stay outside the feasible region.

Theorem 8.2. *There is no other open-loop Nash equilibrium (OLNE) of model (8.1), besides Budget-Stable Open-Loop Nash Equilibrium (BS-OLNE) and Budget-Unstable Open-Loop Nash Equilibrium (BUS-OLNE).*

Proof. If there exists a third kind of open-loop Nash equilibrium of model (8.1), it must be an equilibrium reached inside the budget boundary, but not the equilibrium of model (8.2). However, if this equilibrium is inside the budget boundary, then at the equilibrium point an advertiser cannot improve revenues through investing in a greater budget. Thus, it is the equilibrium of model (8.2) which is a contradiction of the assumption.

As a result, we suggest that an advertiser sets a rational budget constraint in a specific market to make the budget competition game reach a budget-stable equilibrium. Because, if the budget constraint of an advertiser makes the game reach a budget-unstable equilibrium, the competitors may not use the equilibrium budget strategies, because these competitors can improve expected revenues through changing their budget constraints.

8.4 Experimental Evaluation

In this section, we design numerical experiments to evaluate our budget allocation model and some identified properties. We generate experimental datasets from historical advertising logs including operations and effects collected from real-world advertising campaigns of sponsored search auctions. In the following we will provide experimental steps and some relevant results with respect to modeling parameters, to illustrate the superiority of our model.

The experimental evaluation focuses on the following two aspects. First, we intend to prove some desirable properties of model (8.1), and computational algorithms of the proposed solution. Secondly, we try to evaluate whether the advertising effort u increasing with time because of the experience curve effect will lead to more profitable equilibrium strategies for an advertiser. As for different advertisers, the change in the rate of advertising elasticity should be different. In the following we provide details about our experimental setup and results.

8.4.1 Experimental Results

The first experimental scene can be simply described as follows: two advertisers participate in search advertisements within a finite time horizon to compete for market share from each other. We try to find open-loop Nash equilibria in the case without budget constraints, then to figure out necessary conditions in terms of two advertisers' total budgets (B_1, B_2) for the existence of budget-stable open-loop Nash equilibria (BS-OLNEs) in the case with budget constraints.

The equilibrium budget strategies for these two advertisers are as follows: The total budgets for advertiser-1 and advertiser-2 are 5671.542 and 4387.396, respectively. As described in Section 8.3.3, the advertiser is encouraged to set a budget constraint leading to budget-stable equilibria. In this sense, the optimal budget of these two advertisers should be $B_1^* > 5671.542$ and $B_2^* > 4387.396$, respectively. Figure 8.2 illustrates the evolution path of OLNEs in the case without budget constraints, which is depicted with the advertising budget.

For comparison purposes, we set a baseline budget strategy where the advertising elasticity is fixed as a constant during advertising campaigns, which is denoted as "StaticElast". In the static case, the advertiser has a constant of advertising elasticity, e.g. 1/2. In the dynamic case, the advertiser is assigned an initial advertising elasticity, e.g. 2/3, which then changes over time.

From Figure 8.1, we can see that (a) in the static case, the advertiser stably invests the advertising budget; (b) in the dynamic case, the advertiser gradually increases the advertising

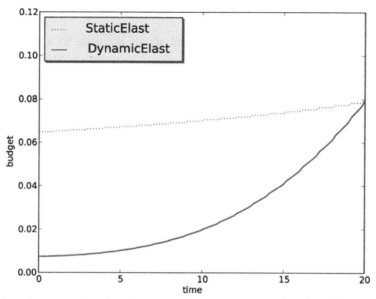

Figure 8.1   Budget allocation in cases of static and dynamic advertising elasticity.

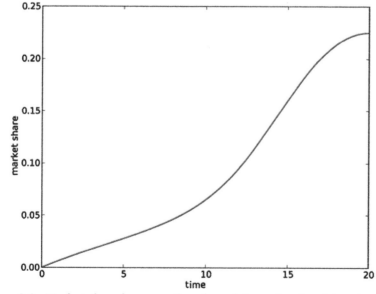

Figure 8.2   Market share in cases of static and dynamic advertising elasticity.

budget; (c) the advertiser tends to invest more budget to gain the same portion of market share when he/she has lower advertising elasticity. Figure 8.2 shows that when OLNEs are reached, the evolution paths of market share are the same in both cases.

8.4.2 Experimental Analysis

Through analysis of the experimental results given above, we come to some interesting facts as follows: (a) The market share is positively proportional to the advertising budget; (b) the increasing rate of the former decreases gradually; (c) the increasing rate of the latter increases gradually; (d) the higher advertising elasticity entitles advertisers to pay less for the same portion of market share; (e) when the advertising elasticity increases, the advertiser prefers to increase the budget gradually to get more market share, because the same amount of budget can exert more effect, but the budget will never surpass the budget of another advertiser with lower advertising elasticity.

8.5 Conclusions

In this study we propose a novel budget allocation model based on differential games, aiming to help advertisers allocate the advertising budget in competitive search advertisements, within a finite time horizon. We also derive open-loop Nash equilibria (OLNEs) for our model with and without budget constraints, and study some desirable properties of two kinds of OLNEs. The preliminary evaluation of numerical experiments indicates that budget strategies with dynamic advertising elasticity are superior to those with the advertising elasticity fixed and our finds in OLNEs are helpful for advertisers to make budget decisions.

Our ongoing research focuses on (a) evolutionary paths of OLNEs with different information settings and budget constraints, (b) budget allocation across multiple search advertising markets with competitive features, and (c) efficient computation of OLNEs for these situations.

References

Archak, N., V. S. Mirrokni, S. Muthukrishnan. 2010. Budget optimization for online advertising campaigns with carryover effects. In Proceedings of the Sixth Workshop on Ad Auctions, June 8, 2010, Cambridge, Massachusetts.

Erickson, G. M. 1992. Empirical analysis of closed-loop duopoly advertising strategies, Management Science 38(12):1732–1749.

Erickson, G. M. 1995. Differential game models of advertising competition, European Journal of Operational Research 83(2):431–438.

Friedman, L. 1958. Game-theory models in the allocation of advertising expenditures, Operations Research, 6(5):699–709.

Fruchter, G. E., S. Kalish. 1998. Dynamic promotional budgeting and media allocation, European Journal of Operational Research, 111(1):15–27.

Kopp, R. E. 1962. Mathematics in science and engineering, Mathematics in Science and Engineering, 5:255–279.

Leitmann, G., W. Schmitendorf. 1978. Profit maximization through advertising: a nonzero sum differential game approach, IEEE Transactions on Automatic Control, 23(4):645–650.

Little, J. D. C. 1979. Aggregate advertising models: The state of the art, Operations Research, 27(4):629–667.

Prasad, A., S. P. Sethi. 2004. Competitive advertising under uncertainty: A stochastic differential game approach, Journal of Optimization Theory and Applications, 123(1):163–185.

Rao, J. L. N., V. R. Rao. 1983. Nitrogenase activity in the rice rhizosphere soil as affected by *Azospirillum* inoculation and fertilizer nitrogen under upland conditions, Current Science, 52(14):686–688.

Sasieni, M. W. 1971. Optimal advertising expenditure, Management Science, 18(4):64–72.

Sethi, S. P. 1977. Optimal advertising for the Nerlove-Arrow model under a budget constraint, Operation Research Quarterly, 28(3):683–693.

Sethi, S. P. 1983. Deterministic and stochastic optimization of a dynamic advertising model, Optimal Control Applications and Methods, 4(2):179–184.

CHAPTER 9

Stochastic Budget Strategies at the Campaign Level: A Preliminary Investigation*

9.1 Introduction

Sponsored search auctions can be viewed as complex systems that could evolve with feeds from the outside environment and intra-interactions (Wang, 2010). This is also reflected in various factors including the diversity of sponsored search auction mechanisms (Aggarwal et al., 2009, 2006; Varian, 2007; Colini-Baldeschi et al., 2012), the unprecedented complexity and dynamics of bidding processes (Mahdian and Wang, 2009; Feldman et al., 2007; Ravi et al., 2009; Gummadi et al., 2011), and the strong-coupling and unpredictability of search markets with imperfect information (Borgs et al., 2005).

In sponsored search auctions, bidding is triggered once an information request is submitted. A high volume of search demands makes the bidding a continuous, infinite process. Ranking results and prices might be changed when any advertiser alters the keywords and/or bids over these keywords at any time. Thus, advertisers have to monitor and adjust their advertising strategies in real time, in order to capture and react to marketing dynamics in sponsored search auctions.

On the one hand, advertisers, especially those from small corporations, usually face serious budget constraints due to their financial conditions. This demands that advertisers should appropriately allocate their limited budget in order to obtain the best advertising performance. On the other hand, advertisers usually do not have sufficient knowledge and time for advertising budget operations in sponsored search auctions. Moreover, there are plenty of uncertainties in the mapping from the budget into the advertising performance

---

* This chapter is a modified version of an article accepted in IEEE Transactions on Services Computing.

Yang and Wang: Budget Constraints and Optimization in Sponsored Search Auctions. http://dx.doi.org/10.1016/B978-0-12-411457-9.00009-4
© 2014 Elsevier Inc. All rights reserved.

(Du et al., 2007). It is difficult to predict some important factors such as queries, clicks, cost-per-click (CPC), and click-through rate (CTR), due to uncertainties and dynamics of search advertising markets. An efficient advertising strategy for budget decisions should be capable of dynamically allocating and adjusting the advertising budget on the fly, according to actual conditions of marketing environments.

In Chapter 4 we take the initiative to develop a hierarchical budget optimization framework (BOF) with consideration of the entire lifecycle of advertising campaigns in sponsored search auctions. The BOF framework could support a set of closed-loop strategies across different levels of abstraction (e.g. system, campaign, and keyword), thus providing an environment/testbed for various budget strategies. The objective of this work is to investigate optimal budget strategies to deal with uncertainties at the campaign level in the BOF. Uncertainties of random factors at the campaign level lead to risk at the market/system level.

Following the BOF framework and identified principles, this work proposes a stochastic, risk-constrained optimization strategy for budget operations at the campaign level. In detail, our budget strategy takes a random factor of clicks per unit cost (e.g. a multiplicative inverse for the cost-per-click) which could reflect a kind of uncertainty at the campaign level, and the variance of revenues obtained from one or more search markets to measure advertiser's risk tolerances, in order to balance the expected revenue (e.g. effective clicks) and risk exposure. We analyze some desirable properties of our budget strategy (in the BOF framework), thus proving its theoretical soundness. Furthermore, some computational experiments are made to evaluate our strategy with real-world data collected from field reports and logs of search advertising campaigns, through comparing them with two baseline strategies. Experimental results verify some assumptions of our approach, which outperforms these two baseline strategies. We also notice that (1) the risk tolerance to a large degree determines optimal budget solutions; (2) the higher risk tolerance usually leads to more expected revenues. These conclusions coincide with the rule of positive correlation between risk exposure and expected return in financial economics.

The contributions to this work can be summarized as follows.

- We propose a stochastic budget optimization strategy to deal with uncertainties at the campaign level in the BOF framework.
- We prove the theoretical soundness of our strategy through the analysis of some desirable properties.
- We design some experiments to validate the effectiveness of our strategy.

The remainder of this chapter is organized as follows. The next section briefly reviews relevant literature. In Section 9.2 we state the problems under consideration. In Section 9.3 we present a stochastic strategy for budget optimization and analyze its properties. Section 9.4 reports some experimental results to evaluate our strategy through comparing with two baseline strategies. Section 9.5 concludes this work.

9.2 Problem Statement

The complexity of budget decisions lies in the following facts inherent in sponsored search auctions. First, the complex structure of sponsored search auction mechanisms together with a high volume of search demands lead to continual dynamics in auction processes, which raises serious challenges to various decision-making activities (e.g. budget decisions) in sponsored search auctions. Secondly, large uncertainties exist in the mapping from the search advertising budget to expected profits. Thirdly, the budget is structured over the entire lifecycle of search advertising activities, rather than a simple constraint as in traditional economic phenomena. This makes budget decisions in sponsored search auctions a set of structured optimization problems. Thus, a great concern of advertisers in sponsored search auctions is to obtain not only local optimizations but global optimal outcomes with structured budget constraints. Our previous work on the BOF framework in Chapter 4 took an initial step in this direction.

Uncertainty is one of the crucial factors to be considered in budget decisions. On the one hand, search demands are of high volumes and thus uncertain in terms of both user intentions and search volumes. On the other hand, participants of sponsored search auctions (e.g. advertisers) and their advertisements change over time. Moreover, the outside environment of sponsored search auctions is dynamical and unpredictable. Dynamics and uncertainties from those factors have great influence on bidding behavior and results. It is well known that in economics uncertainties lead to risk in various degrees for investors. It is also true for advertisers in sponsored search auctions. Then, advertisers with different individual risk tolerances will choose different budget strategies, in order to balance risk exposures and expected revenues. That is, if the risk is beyond an advertiser's risk tolerance, the strategy is not acceptable even if the expected revenue is very high. This work considered the randomness of clicks per unit cost to deal with uncertainties in budget decisions at the campaign level, following principles of the BOF. The uncertainties at the campaign level lead to different risk exposures at the market/system level. Thus we try to provide a stochastic budget strategy at the campaign level to maximize the expected revenue (e.g. effective clicks) under certain risk tolerances at the market/system level. We take clicks per unit cost as the random factor because it is a multiplicative inverse for the cost-per-click (CPC) which is a crucial factor to measure the performance of online advertisements.

Table 9.1 List of notations.

Notation	Definition
B	The overall budget for search advertisements
n_1	The number of search markets
n_2	The number of temporal slots during a promotion period
x	The allocated budget vector at the search market level
y_i	The allocated budget vector at the campaign level in the ith search market
z_{ij}	The allocated budget vector at the keyword level for the jth temporal slot in the ith search market
$r(t, y_{ij})$	The remaining budget at time t of the jth temporal slot in the ith search market
α_{ij}	Clicks per unit cost of the jth temporal slot in the ith search market
ψ_{ij}	The consuming speed of budget of the jth temporal slot in the ith search market
σ	The risk tolerance of an advertiser

The notations used in this chapter are listed in Table 9.1.

9.3 Budget Distribution Over Time

9.3.1 A Stochastic Strategy

In this section we propose a stochastic, risk-constrained strategy for budget optimization at the campaign level in the BOF framework. We assume that the advertising budget available to advertisers is limited, or at least less than the sufficient amount. This assumption can be easily justified by the fact that most advertisers, especially those from small enterprises, have to face serious constraints on the advertising budget. Moreover, advertisers with serious budget constraints usually have low risk tolerances.

In sponsored search auctions, a click is an action initiating a visit to a website via a sponsored link. If a click is an intentional click that has a realistic probability of generating values once the visitor arrives at the website, then it is a *valid click*; otherwise it is *invalid* (Jansen, 2008). In this work, we consider the generated value obtained through some kinds of user behavior including purchase, registration, staying on the landing page for more than 5s, surfing more than two links, bookmarking, and downloading. We give a concept of effective click-through rate (CTR) as follows.

Definition 9.1 (Effective CTR).   Effective CTR is the ratio of valid clicks and total clicks, i.e.

$$\text{Effective CTR} = \frac{\text{valid clicks}}{\text{total clicks}}.$$

Note that the effective CTR is equivalent to the conversion rate if this kind of user behavior is defined as conversion actions by advertisers.

Let B denote the total amount of the advertising budget, x_i the allocated budget in search market i, $i = 1, 2, \ldots, n_1$, then we have the following constraint:

$$\sum_{i=1}^{n_1} x_i \leq B.$$

Let $\xi(x_i)$ denote effective clicks obtained through the allocated budget x_i in market i. Then the objective is to maximize the total of effective clicks in n_1 search markets, i.e. $\sum_{i=1}^{n_1} \xi(x_i)$.

In the following let us analyze the value of $\xi(x_i)$. Let ψ_{ij} denote the consuming speed of the budget in temporal slot j in market i, $j = 1, 2, \cdots, n_2$, $r(t, y_{ij})$ the remaining budget in temporal slot j in market i at time t, where y_{ij} denotes the initial budget, i.e. $r(0, y_{ij}) = y_{ij}$. Since ψ is time-varying, we take $\psi(r, t)$ to denote the consuming speed of the budget at time t.

We assume that ψ satisfies the following three properties:

- The consuming speed is always non-negative, i.e. $\psi(r, t) \geq 0$.
- When the budget is used up, the consuming speed becomes 0, i.e. $\psi(0, t) = 0$.
- At time t, the consuming speed is monotone increasing with the remaining budget, i.e. $\psi(r_1, t) \geq \psi(r_2, t)$, if $r_1 > r_2$.

Then the actual daily expenditure is $\int_0^T \psi(r(y_{ij}), t)dt$ when an advertiser allocates the initial budget y_{ij} in temporal slot j in market i, where T represents the period of a temporal slot. Let α_{ij} be the clicks per unit cost in slot j in market i, $f(\cdot)$ the advertising utility function of expenditures. Then $f(\int_0^T \psi(r(y_{ij}), t)dt)$ and $\alpha_{ij} f(\int_0^T \psi(r(y_{ij}), t)dt)$ represent the section of the actual expenditure that generates effective clicks and effective clicks obtained in slot j in market i, respectively. Thus, $\xi(x)$ can be given as the optimal value of the following programming problem:

$$\max \sum_{j=1}^{n_2} \alpha_{ij} f\left(\int_0^T \psi(r(y_{ij}), t)dt\right)$$

$$\text{s.t.} \sum_{j=1}^{n_2} \int_0^T \psi(r(y_{ij}), t)dt \leq x_i$$

$$y_{ij} \leq (1 - k_{ij}) \left(x_i - \sum_{l=1}^{j-1} \int_0^T \psi(r(y_{il}), t)dt\right)$$

$$y_{ij} \geq 0, j = 1, 2, \ldots, n_2,$$

(9.1)

where $r(0, y_{ij}) = y_{ij}$ and $r(t, y_{ij}) = r(0, y_{ij}) - \int_0^t \psi(r(s, y_{ij}), s)ds$ for any $t \in [0, T]$, k_{ij} is the reserve rate of advertising budget in slot j in market i, and $0 \leq k_{ij} < 1$. The intuition of the reserve rate is the fact that an advertiser needs to reserve some proportion of the available budget for possible opportunities in the future, similar to the concept of the deposit reserve rate in the financial economy.

Suppose $\alpha_i = (\alpha_{i,1}, \alpha_{i,2}, \ldots, \alpha_{i,n_2})$ is a random vector with distribution $g_i(t)$. Each realization of α_i can be represented as $\bar{\alpha}_i = (\bar{\alpha}_{i,1}, \bar{\alpha}_{i,2}, \ldots, \bar{\alpha}_{i,n_2})$, then $\xi(x_i)$ becomes

$$\xi(x_i, \bar{\alpha}_i) = \max \sum_{j=1}^{n_2} \bar{\alpha}_{ij} f\left(\int_0^T \psi(r(y_{ij}), t)\mathrm{d}t\right)$$

$$\text{s.t.} \sum_{j=1}^{n_2} \int_0^T \psi(r(y_{ij}), t)\mathrm{d}t \le x_i \tag{9.2}$$

$$y_{ij} \le (1 - k_{ij})\left(x_i - \sum_{l=1}^{j-1} \int_0^T \psi(r(y_{il}), t)\mathrm{d}t\right)$$

$$y_{ij} \ge 0, j = 1, 2, \ldots, n_2.$$

Then we can notice that $\xi(x_i)$ is a random variable with probability density function $g_i(t)$.

In the following we consider the risk in budget operations of sponsored search auctions. In this chapter we take the variance per unit budget of random variable $\sum_{i=1}^{n_1} \xi(x_i)$ (at the market/system level) as the risk, given as

$$\text{Var}\left(\sum_{i=1}^{n_1} \xi(x_i)\right) / B \le \sigma,$$

where σ is the risk tolerance of an advertiser.

Based on the above analysis and relevant principles of the BOF, we formulate the budget optimization problem at the campaign level as follows.

The overall objective concerns maximizing the advertising revenue (e.g. effective clicks) expected in n_1 search markets (at the system level), given as

$$\max E\left[\sum_{i=1}^{n_1} \xi(x_i)\right]$$

$$\text{s.t.} \sum_{i=1}^{n_1} x_i \le B \tag{9.3}$$

$$\text{Var}\left(\sum_{i=1}^{n_1} \xi(x_i)\right) / B \le \sigma$$

$$x_i \ge 0, i = 1, 2, \ldots, n_1,$$

where $\xi(x_i)$ is the maximum of effective clicks obtained in search market i (at the campaign level), given as

$$\xi(x_i) = \max \sum_{j=1}^{n_2} \alpha_{ij} f \left(\int_0^T \psi(r(y_{ij}), t) dt \right)$$

$$\text{s.t.} \sum_{j=1}^{n_2} \int_0^T \psi(r(y_{ij}), t) dt \leq x_i$$

$$(9.4)$$

$$y_{ij} \leq (1 - k_{ij}) \left(x_i - \sum_{l=1}^{j-1} \int_0^T \psi(r(y_{il}), t) dt \right)$$

$$y_{ij} \geq 0, \ j = 1, 2, \dots, n_2,$$

where $f(\cdot)$ denotes the advertising utility obtained at the keyword level.

9.3.2 The Advertising Utility

In Erickson (1992), the advertising effort is given as $g(A) = (A)^E$, where $A \in [0, 1]$ denotes the advertising rate, $E \in (0, 1)$ is a constant that is assumed empirically to be 1/2 in traditional advertising. In the following let us determine the advertising utility function of advertising expenditures $f(c)$.

Let C denote the total advertising cost (expenditure), A_{ij} be the advertising rate in slot j in market i, then $c_{ij} = A_{ij}C$ represents the cost in slot j in market i. Thus the advertising effort of A_{ij} can be given as

$$g(A_{ij}) = (A_{ij})^E = C^{-E}(A_{ij}C)^E = C^{-E}(c_{ij})^E.$$

We assume that the advertising budget is limited, and thus the optimal budget allocated will be used up in each slot, i.e. $C = B$. This can be easily justified in the case where an advertiser has a serious advertising budget. Thus, we have $g(A_{ij}) = B^{-E}(c_{ij})^E$. Therefore, in this work f is represented as $f(c) = (c)^E = g(A_{ij})B^E$. This is consistent with the Lanchester model of advertising competition described in (Erickson, 1992), in terms of the advertising effort.

We take the consuming speed function as the following,

$$\psi(r(b_{ij}), t) = \begin{cases} \bar{\psi}_{ij}, & \text{if } 0 \leq t \leq \bar{t}_{ij} \\ 0, & \text{otherwise,} \end{cases}$$

where $\bar{\psi}_{ij} \geq 0$ is a constant and $\bar{t}_{ij} = \min\{b_{ij}/\bar{\psi}_{ij}, T\}$, then model (9.4) can be written as the following convex programming (the proof is given in the following section):

$$\xi(x_i) := \max \sum_{j=1}^{n_2} \alpha_{ij} \left(\int_0^T \psi(r(y_{ij}), t)dt \right)^E$$

$$\text{s.t.} \sum_{j=1}^{n_2} \int_0^T \psi(r(y_{ij}), t)dt \leq x_i$$

$$y_{ij} \leq (1 - k_{ij}) \left(x_i - \sum_{l=1}^{j-1} \int_0^T \psi(r(y_{il}), t)dt \right)$$

$$y_{ij} \geq 0, \ j = 1, 2, \ldots, n_2.$$

(9.5)

9.3.3 Properties

In the following we discuss the computable conditions for the proposed budget optimization model.

Lemma 9.1. *If f is a positive concave function, ψ is a positive and second-order continuous differential function with $\int_0^T \psi_{rr}(r(t, y_{ij}), t)\frac{\partial r}{\partial y}(t, y_{ij})dt \leq 0$, then model (9.3) is a convex programming problem.*

Proof.   We can verify that $r(t, y_{ij})$ satisfies the following ordinary differential equations:

$$\frac{\partial r}{\partial t} = -\psi(r, t),$$

(9.6)

$$r(0) = y_{ij}.$$

(9.7)

Then the first-order and second-order partial derivatives of r with respect to the initial value y_{ij} can be computed as follows:

$$\frac{\partial r}{\partial y} = \exp\left\{ -\int_0^t \psi_r(r(s, y_{ij}), s)ds \right\}$$

(9.8)

and

$$\frac{\partial^2 r}{\partial y^2} = -\exp\left\{ -\int_0^t \psi_r(r(s, y_{ij}), s)ds \right\} \int_0^t \psi_{rr}(r(s, y_{ij}), s)\frac{\partial r}{\partial y}(s, y_{ij})ds,$$

which illustrate that $\frac{\partial r}{\partial y} > 0$ and $\frac{\partial^2 r}{\partial y^2} \geq 0$.

Since

$$\int_0^T \psi(r(t, y_{ij}), t)dt = y_{ij} - r(T, y_{ij}),$$

we have

$$f\left(\int_0^T \psi(r(y_{ij}), t)\mathrm{d}t\right) = f(y_{ij} - r(T, y_{ij}))$$

which is concave. Then we can get the conclusion.

The conditions of Lemma 1 are not easy to verify in practice. In the following theorem we present a stronger condition with practical values.

Theorem 9.1. *If f is a concave function, ψ is a positive and second-order continuous differential function with $\psi_{rr} \leq 0$ for any i, j, then model (9.3) is a convex programming problem.*

Proof. From calculations described above, we can notice

$$\frac{\partial r}{\partial y}(t, y_{ij}) > 0$$

for any $t \in [0, T]$.

Given $\psi_{rr} \leq 0$, we have

$$\psi_{rr}(r(t, y_{ij}), t)\frac{\partial r}{\partial y}(t, y_{ij}) \leq 0$$

for any $t \in [0, T]$.

Then,

$$\int_0^T \psi_{rr}(r(t, y_{ij}), t)\frac{\partial r}{\partial y}(t, y_{ij})\mathrm{d}t \leq 0.$$

Thus, all conditions in Lemma 9.1 can be satisfied. The proof is complete.

Following the above discussions, we can employ the sequential least squares method to find the optimal solution for models (9.3) and (9.4). In the next section, we will present some experiments to illustrate our approach in detail.

9.4 Experimental Evaluation

9.4.1 Data Descriptions

In this section, we use some real-world data collected from search advertising campaigns to verify our budget strategy, where the random factor (e.g. clicks per unit cost) is represented as a random vector. In our case, we take a five-day promotion period during which the total budget is $B = 400.0$ for advertising activities in two markets, and $k_{ij} = 0$ to give more flexibility for budget strategies. The value of function ψ (namely the consuming speed of the

Table 9.2 Values of budget consuming speed $\bar{\psi}_{ij}$.

$\bar{\psi}_{ij}$	$j = 1$	$j = 2$	$j = 3$	$j = 4$	$j = 5$
$i = 1$	3.875	6.5	8.75	10.0	11.25
$i = 2$	3.75	7.5	8.125	6.875	12.5

budget) in the jth temporal slot in search market i is assumed to be a constant (denoted as $\bar{\psi}_{ij}$), as given in Table 9.2.

From advertising logs and reports, α_1 and α_2 (during a five-day period) can be given as random normal vectors with the following distribution

$$p(x) = \frac{1}{(2\pi)^{\frac{5}{2}}|\Sigma|^{\frac{1}{2}}} \exp\left\{-\frac{1}{2}(x - \mu)^T \Sigma^{-1}(x - \mu)\right\},$$

where expected values of α_1 and α_2 are

$$\mu_1 = (0.9, 0.95, 0.6, 0.35, 0.15),$$

$$\mu_2 = (0.85, 0.85, 0.25, 0.1, 0.3),$$

and variances of α_1 and α_2 are

$$\Sigma_1 = 0.1 \cdot I, \quad \Sigma_2 = 0.09 \cdot I,$$

where I is the identity matrix.

9.4.2 Experimental Design

We will perform some computational experiments to validate our budget strategy as proposed in Section 9.3. The experimental scene is described as an advertiser with risk tolerance σ with a total budget B for search advertisements to promote his products in two markets during a five-day period.

Our budget strategy considers the randomness of an advertising factor (clicks per unit cost) to support optimal distribution of the budget for a campaign over a series of temporal slots, for advertisers with different risk preferences. A risk-averse advertiser prefers certainty to risk, and low risk to high risk, and thus prefers a strategy within his/her risk tolerance; while a risk-loving advertiser would prefer the chance of getting more revenue at the cost of high risk. A risk neutral advertiser would not have any preference. In our work, we consider two versions of our strategy in terms of risk: StoRiskAverse and StoRiskLoving. The StoRiskAverse strategy concerns the optimal solution of model (9.5), while the StoRiskLoving strategy can be viewed as a special case of the former with $\sigma = \infty$.

For comparison purposes, we implement two baseline strategies. The first benchmark, called BASE1-Average-SC, represents a strategy to even out the distribution of the search advertising budget across these two markets and then among a series of temporal slots during a given promotion period. The second benchmark is called BASE2-Average-C, which can be viewed as a special case of BASE1-Average-SC with budgets allocated in these two markets available (from the StoRiskLoving strategy in our case).

In the following, we give the concept of strategy acceptability for a risk-averse advertiser.

Definition 9.2 (Strategy Acceptability).   A strategy is acceptable if the actual risk of this strategy is within an advertiser's risk tolerance, otherwise it is unacceptable.

Based on the concept of strategy acceptability, we provide some criteria to evaluate the performance of two strategies for comparison.

Criteria:

1. If both strategies are acceptable, then the strategy generating more revenue (e.g. effective clicks) is better.
2. If a strategy is acceptable and another is unacceptable, then the acceptable strategy is better.
3. If both strategies are unacceptable, then the strategy with lower risk is better.

9.4.3 Experimental Results

During the five-day period, effective clicks obtained through these four strategies (two baselines and two versions of our proposed strategy) are illustrated in Table 9.3 and Figure 9.1. The experimental results are described as follows:

1. As for the baseline strategy BASE1-Average-SC: the optimal result in terms of effective clicks is 32.119, with the actual risk 0.70.
2. As for the baseline strategy BASE2-Average-C: the optimal result in terms of effective clicks is 32.265, with the actual risk 0.71.
3. As for the StoRiskLoving strategy: the budget allocated in market 1 is 220.0, and in market 2 is 180.0; the optimal result in terms of effective clicks is 34.792, with the actual risk 0.8.

Table 9.3 Optimal budget solutions.

Cases	Optimal budget	Effective clicks	Risk
BASE1-Average-SC	(40.0,40.0,40.0,40.0,40.0,40.0,40.0,40.0,40.0,40.0)	32.119	0.70
BASE2-Average-C	(44.0,44.0,44.0,44.0,44.0,36.0,36.0,36.0,36.0,36.0)	32.265	0.71
StoRiskLoving	(31.0,52.0,61.0,75.0,1.0,30.0,60.0,40.0,7.0,43.0)	34.792	0.80
StoRiskAverse, $\sigma = 0.7$	(31.0,52.0,70.0,27.0,4.6,30.0,60.0,42.8,7.1,75.5)	34.771	0.68

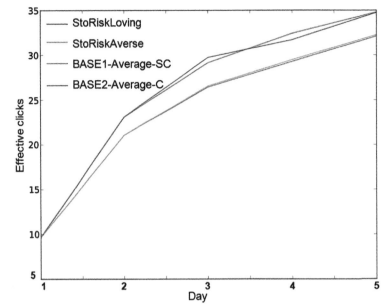

Figure 9.1   Comparison of accumulated effective clicks.

4. As for the StoRiskAverse strategy with risk tolerance $\sigma = 0.7$: the budget allocated in market 1 is 184.6, and in market 2 is 215.4; the optimal result in terms of effective clicks is 34.771, with the actual risk 0.68.

From Table 9.3 and Figure 9.1, we can draw conclusions as follows:

1. The two versions of our proposed strategy outperform these two baseline strategies.
2. As for the two baseline strategies, BASE2-Average-C performs better than BASE1-Average-SC in terms of accumulated effective clicks. Moreover, these two strategies have similar performance in the first two days; and in the remaining three days, BASE2-Average-C performs better than BASE1-Average-SC. The reason might be that the former takes budgets allocated in these two markets (from the StoRiskLoving strategy) as inputs for budget distributions over temporal slots. This also proves the effectiveness of the StoRiskLoving strategy.
3. As for the two versions of our proposed strategy, the StoRiskLoving strategy performs better than the StoRiskAverse strategy in terms of accumulated effective clicks. Moreover, the StoRiskLoving strategy performs better than the StoRiskAverse strategy, except on the 4th day. The reason behind this is that the actual risk on these days (except the 4th day) is beyond the advertiser's risk tolerance. This proves that the risk attitude plays an important role in budget decisions.
4. In the case of a risk-loving advertiser, the StoRiskLoving strategy is slightly better than the StoRiskAverse strategy (with risk tolerance $\sigma = 0.7$).

5. In the case where an advertiser is risk-averse, with risk tolerance $\sigma = 0.7$, both BASE1-Average-SC and the StoRiskAverse strategy (with risk tolerance $\sigma = 0.7$) are acceptable, and the latter is better.

Our experimental results also coincide with the rule of positive correlation between risk exposures and expected revenues in financial economics. Specifically, risk tolerances influence the determination of the optimal solution in budget decisions, and the higher risk tolerance usually leads to more expected revenues.

9.5 Conclusions

This chapter proposes a stochastic, risk-constrained budget optimization strategy to distribute the budget for an advertising campaign over a series of temporal slots. Following principles of the BOF framework, our strategy considers the random factor of clicks per unit of cost to capture uncertainties at the campaign level and the variance per unit budget of revenues at the market/system level to measure the advertiser's risk tolerances. We also perform a mathematical analysis of some desirable properties of our proposed strategy. Furthermore, we report some experimental results to illustrate the effectiveness of our strategy, with real-world data collected from search advertising campaigns. Experimental results show that our strategy outperforms the two baseline strategies, and risk tolerances have a great influence on the determination of optimal strategies.

This work presents a preliminary investigation on stochastic strategies for budget optimization in sponsored search auctions. There is still the need to invest more effort in this direction. In an ongoing work, we are attempting to develop more sophisticated budget strategies considering a set of interwoven random factors, and to find possible approximation solutions. Another interesting and challenging issue is to probe uncertainties in budget operations of the real-time adjustment of the remaining budget at the keyword level.

References

Aggarwal, G., A. Goel, R. Motwani. 2006. Truthful auctions for pricing search keywords, ACM Conference on Electronic Commerce, 1–7.

Aggarwal, G., S. Muthukrishnan, D. Pál, M. Pál. 2009. General auction mechanism for search advertising. In: Proceedings of the 18th International Conference on World Wide Web, April 20–24, 2009, Madrid, Spain.

Borgs C., J. Chayes, N. Immorlica, M. Mahdian, A. Saberi. 2005. Multi-unit auctions with budget-constrained bidders. In Proceedings of the 6th ACM Conference on Electronic Commerce, June 5–8, 2005, Vancouver, BC, Canada.

Colini-Baldeschi, R., M. Henzinger, S. Leonardi, M. Starnberger. 2012. On multiple keyword sponsored search auctions with budgets, ICALP'12 Proceedings of the 39th international colloquium conference on Automata, Languages, and Programming – Volume Part II, 1–12.

Du, R., Q. Hu, S. Ai. 2007. Stochastic optimal budget decision for advertising considering uncertain sales responses, European Journal of Operational Research, 183(3):1042–1054.

Erickson, G.M. 1992. Empirical analysis of closed-loop duopoly advertising strategies, Management Science, 38(12):1732–1749.

Feldman J., S. Muthukrishnan, M. Pál, C. Stein. 2007. Budget optimization in search-based advertising auctions. Proceedings of the 8th ACM Conference on Electronic Commerce, June 11–15, 2007, San Diego, California, USA.

Gummadi, R., P. B. Key, A. Proutiere. 2011. Optimal bidding strategies in dynamic auctions with budget constraints, 49th Annual Allerton Conference on Communication, Control, and Computing, 588.

Jansen, B. J. 2008. Click fraud, IEEE Computer, 40(7):85–86.

Mahdian, M., G. Wang. 2009. Clustering-based bidding languages for sponsored search. In: Proceedings of the 17th Annual European Symposium on Algorithms, September 7–9, 2009, Copenhagen, Denmark.

Ravi, R., I. Hafalir, A. Sayedi. 2009. Sort-cut: A pareto-optimal and semi-truthful mechanism for multi-unit auctions with budget-constrained bidders. In Fifth Workshop on AdAuctions, July 6, 2009.

Varian, H. 2007. Position auctions, International Journal of Industrial Organization, 25(6):1163–1178.

Wang, F. Y. 2010. The emergence of intelligent enterprises: From CPS to CPSS. IEEE Intelligent Systems, 25(4):85–88.

CHAPTER 10

A Stochastic Budget Distribution Model in Search Advertisements

10.1 Introduction

Recently, sponsored search auctions have become more and more popular due to some advantages such as low costs and quick promotion effects. Google has successfully found and monetized the long tails of both advertisers and publishers that contribute at least half of the revenue for Google long tail (Anderson, 2005). The long tail advertisers include millions of small companies and individuals that have limited resources (e.g. advertising budgets). Thus, this demands an effective way to manipulate limited budgets in order to maximize revenues expected from search promotions (Abrams, 2006; Ashlagi et al., 2010; Abrams et al., 2007; Colini-Baldeschi et al., 2012).

Most of the current works on search advertising strategies simply take the budget as constraints (Archak et al., 2010; Borgs et al., 2007; Drosos et al., 2010; Muthukrishnan et al., 2010; Ozluk and Cholette, 2007) to determine bids over keywords of interest. We argue that these works fall into the category of bidding strategies. With consideration of the entire lifecycle of search advertising, budget decisions in sponsored search auctions occur at three levels (Yang et al., 2012): allocation across search markets, temporal distribution over a series of slots (e.g. day), and adjustment of the remaining budget (e.g. the daily budget). This work aims to deal with the budget allocation problem over a series of sequential slots. First, there are plenty of uncertainties in the mapping from the budget into the advertising performance (Du et al., 2007). Secondly, advertisers have to adapt the daily budget to an optimal level according to some key factors such as cost-per-click (CPC) and click-through rate (CTR). However, due to the complexity and uncertainty of sponsored search auctions, such as the dynamics of the market and some important parameters (e.g. CTR, CPC), the demand of budget for each temporal slot cannot be known in advance. Thirdly, the search marketing environment is essentially dynamic and thus it is difficult to precisely predict the optimal daily budget. If the allocated budget is less than the demand of budget, the advertiser will lose some

Yang and Wang: Budget Constraints and Optimization in Sponsored Search Auctions. http://dx.doi.org/10.1016/B978-0-12-411457-9.00010-0
© 2014 Elsevier Inc. All rights reserved.

potential clicks (customers), and if the allocated budget is set too high, the advertiser will waste money on clicks without valuable actions.

In this work, we formulate the budget distribution over a series of sequential temporal slots (e.g. a day) as a stochastic programming problem. First, we take the demand of budget as a random variable, because we cannot know its precise value, but its probability distributions can be obtained according to some experiences or promotion logs. Secondly, we present a stochastic model for budget distribution for a series of temporal slots, with the consideration of the total budget. Thirdly, we discuss some properties and possible solutions to our model, by taking the demand of the budget for a temporal slot as uniform random variable and normal random variable. On the one hand, when the demand of budget is uniformly distributed, the proposed model is convex, and we can compute the solutions of the model. On the other hand, when the demand of the budget is normally distributed, the proposed model is also convex, but the solutions cannot be given directly since they contain the standard normal distribution function Φ. For computational purpose, we provide an algorithm to compute Φ. Furthermore, we perform some experiments to evaluate our model, and experimental results show that budget allocation according to the normal distribution can achieve better revenues than that according to the uniform distribution, which illustrates that the demand of the budget is more likely to be normally distributed than uniformly distributed, and both of our two strategies outperform one baseline strategy that is commonly used in practice, in terms of total effective clicks.

The remainder of this chapter is organized as follows. In Section 10.2 we state the problem under consideration, then propose a stochastic budget distribution model over a series of temporal slots. In Section 10.3 we discuss some properties and solutions of our model when the demand of the budget can be represented by a uniform random variable and normal random variable. In Section 10.4 we present some experimental results to evaluate our budget distribution model. Section 10.5 concludes this chapter.

10.2 A Stochastic Budget Distribution Model

We consider the following decision scenario in sponsored search auctions: given the total budget $B_{campaign}$ in a search market, an advertiser has to distribute the budget to a series of temporal slots in order to maximize the revenue.

The notations used in this chapter are given in Table 10.1.

10.2.1 The Basic Model

Let d_j represent the demand of budget in the jth temporal slot. By saying demand of budget, we mean that if the advertiser allocates budget b_j in temporal slot j according to the demand of budget, i.e. $b_j = d_j$, she can get the maximum revenue. Thus, the demand of budget is of great importance for the advertiser, and if the entire budget $B_{campaign}$ is sufficient and

Table 10.1 List of notations.

Notation	Definition
n	The number of temporal slots during a promotion period
$B_{campaign}$	The total budget for a campaign
p_j	Clicks per unit cost of the jth temporal slot $j = 1, 2, \ldots, n$
b_j	The budget allocated in the jth temporal slot $j = 1, 2, \ldots, n$
d_j	The random demand of the budget for the jth temporal slot, $j = 1, 2, \ldots, n$
$f(d_j)$	The probability distribution function of d_j $j = 1, 2, \ldots, n$
c_j	The effective CTR of the jth temporal slot (below the demand of the budget), $j = 1, 2, \ldots, n$
c'_j	The effective CTR of the jth temporal slot (above the demand of the budget), $j = 1, 2, \ldots, n$

the demand of budget for each temporal slot can be precisely known in advance, then the budget allocation becomes very easy for the advertiser, and she just needs to allocate the budget b_j as d_j to obtain the maximum revenue. However, the entire budget $B_{campaign}$ is limited, and the advertiser cannot know the demand of budget d_j precisely in advance, since there exist a lot of uncertainties in sponsored search auctions, which makes her budget decision-making difficult. Though the advertiser cannot know the precise demand of the budget, she can obtain some information (e.g. the lower bound $\underline{b}$ and the upper bound $\overline{b}$) of the demand of budget, according to experience and promotion logs. Thus, we can represent the demand of budget d_j as a random variable on $[\underline{b}, \overline{b}]$ with probability distribution $f(d_j)$.

Thus, in this chapter, we discuss the case where d_j, $j = 1, 2, \ldots, n$ are mutually independent random variables on $[\underline{b}, \overline{b}]$, where $\underline{b} \leq \overline{b}$. On the one hand, if the advertiser allocates $\underline{b}$ in the jth temporal slot, i.e. $b_j = \underline{b}$, then the total budget $B_{campaign}$ cannot be used up, that is $n\underline{b} < B_{campaign}$. On the other hand, if the advertiser allocates $\overline{b}$ in the jth temporal slot, i.e. $b_j = \overline{b}$, then the total budget $B_{campaign}$ is insufficient, that is $n\overline{b} > B_{campaign}$. Thus, we have $n\underline{b} < B_{campaign} < n\overline{b}$, and the allocated budget satisfies $\underline{b} \leq b_j \leq \overline{b}$. Since the total budget $B_{campaign}$ is limited, it will be used up in n temporal slots, that is $\sum_{i=1}^{n} b_j = B_{campaign}$.

Let $C(b_j, d_j)$ be the revenue of the jth temporal slot with budget b_j in the case that the demand of budget is d_j, then $\sum_{i=1}^{n} C(b_j, d_j)$ is the total revenue of the n temporal slots. Since d_j is a random variable, $C(b_j, d_j)$ and $\sum_{i=1}^{n} C(b_j, d_j)$ are also random variables. Thus, the purpose of the advertiser is to maximize the total expected revenue, i.e. $E\left[\sum_{i=1}^{n} C(b_j, d_j)\right]$. Since d_j, $j = 1, 2, \ldots, n$ are independent random variables, we have

$$E\left[\sum_{i=1}^{n} C(b_j, d_j)\right] = \sum_{i=1}^{n} E[C(b_j, d_j)].$$

10.2.2 The Objective Function

In the following, we discuss how to compute the total expected revenue, which is characterized by total expected effective clicks.

Let p_j be clicks per unit cost of the jth temporal slot, then $p_j b_j$ represents the clicks obtained in the jth temporal slot. Let c_j be the effective CTR of the budget below the demand of budget in the jth temporal slot, and c'_j the effective CTR of the budget above the demand of budget in the jth temporal slot, $j = 1, 2, \ldots, n$. Since the number of potential users is limited and the demand of budget corresponds to the potential users, if the advertiser allocates more budget than the demand of budget, the effective CTR will become smaller, i.e. $c_j > c'_j$.

If $b_j < d_j$, then the effective clicks obtained by b_j are $p_j b_j c_j$, otherwise if $b_j \geq d_j$, then the effective clicks obtained by b_j can be divided into two parts, the first part d_j with effective CTR c_j, and another part $b_j - d_j$ with effective CTR c'_j. Thus the effective clicks will be $p_j c_j d_j + p_j c'_j (b_j - d_j)$. Since d_j is a random variable on $[\underline{b}, \overline{b}]$ with probability distribution $f(d_j)$, then based on the concept of expected value of random variable, for each j we have

$$E[C(b_j, d_j)] = \int_{\underline{b}}^{b_j} (p_j c_j d_j + p_j c'_j (b_j - d_j)) f(d_j) \mathrm{d} d_j + \int_{b_j}^{\overline{b}} p_j c_j b_j f(d_j) \mathrm{d} d_j. \quad (10.1)$$

10.2.3 The Stochastic Model

Thus, with the probability distribution $f(d_j)$ on $[\underline{b}, \overline{b}]$, we can formulate the following stochastic budget distribution model for a given campaign

$$\max \int_{\underline{b}}^{b_j} (p_j c_j d_j + p_j c'_j (b_j - d_j)) f(d_j) \mathrm{d} d_j + \int_{b_j}^{\overline{b}} p_j c_j b_j f(d_j) \mathrm{d} d_j$$

$$\text{s.t.} \sum_{i=1}^{n} b_j = B_{campaign} \quad (10.2)$$

$$\underline{b} \leq b_j \leq \overline{b}.$$

10.3 Properties and Solutions

In this section we study the properties and solutions of model (10.2) when the demand of budget is some commonly used random variable. In the following, we first study the properties when the demand of budget can be characterized by a uniform distributed random variable, and present its solutions. Then we study the case for the normally distributed demand of budget, and discuss its solution algorithms.

10.3.1 Uniform Distributed Budget

When the random demand of budget for each temporal slot is uniformly distributed, we have the following theorem.

Theorem 10.1. *If the random demand of budget for the jth day satisfies* $d_j \sim U(\underline{b}, \overline{b})$, $j = 1, 2, \ldots, n$, *then model (10.2) can be represented as*

$$\max \sum_{i=1}^{n} \left[-\frac{p_j c_j - p_j c_j'}{2(\overline{b} - \underline{b})} \left(b_j^2 + \underline{b}^2 \right) + \frac{p_j c_j \overline{b} - p_j c_j' \underline{b}}{\overline{b} - \underline{b}} b_j \right]$$

$$\text{s.t.} \sum_{i=1}^{n} b_j = B_{campaign}$$

$$\underline{b} \le b_j \le \overline{b},$$

(10.3)

and it is a convex programming.

Proof. Since $d_j \sim U(\overline{b}, \overline{b})$, $j = 1, 2, \ldots, n$, the probability distribution of d_j is

$$f(d_j) = \begin{cases} \frac{1}{\overline{b} - \underline{b}}, & \text{if } \underline{b} < x < \overline{b} \\ 0, & \text{otherwise.} \end{cases}$$

Thus, we have

$$E[C(b_j, d_j)] = \int_{\underline{b}}^{b_j} (p_j c_j d_j + p_j c_j'(b_j - d_j)) \frac{1}{\overline{b} - \underline{b}} \mathrm{d}d_j + \int_{b_j}^{\overline{b}} p_j c_j b_j \frac{1}{\overline{b} - \underline{b}} \mathrm{d}d_j$$

$$= \frac{p_j c_j - p_j c_j'}{2(\overline{b} - \underline{b})} \left(b_j^2 - \underline{b}^2 \right) + \frac{cc_j' b_j (b_j - \underline{b})}{\overline{b} - \underline{b}} + \frac{c_j b_j (\overline{b} - b_j)}{\overline{b} - \underline{b}}$$

$$= -\frac{p_j c_j - p_j c_j'}{2(\overline{b} - \underline{b})} \left(b_j^2 + \underline{b}_j^2 \right) + \frac{p_j c_j \overline{b} - p_j c_j' \underline{b}}{\overline{b} - \underline{b}} b_j,$$

(10.4)

and model (10.2) can be represented as

$$\max \sum_{i=1}^{n} \left[-\frac{p_j c_j - p_j c_j'}{2(\overline{b} - \underline{b})} \left(b_j^2 + \underline{b}^2 \right) + \frac{p_j c_j \overline{b} - p_j c_j' \underline{b}}{\overline{b} - \underline{b}} b_j \right]$$

$$\text{s.t.} \sum_{i=1}^{n} b_j = B_{campaign}$$

$$\underline{b} \le b_j \le \overline{b}.$$

(10.5)

Since the constraints of model (10.5) are linear, we need only to prove that the objective function of programming (10.5) is convex.

Let

$$g(x) = \sum_{i=1}^{n} \left(-\frac{p_j c_j - p_j c_j'}{2(\overline{b} - \underline{b})} \left(b_j^2 + \underline{b}^2 \right) + \frac{p_j c_j \overline{b} - p_j c_j' \underline{b}}{\overline{b} - \underline{b}} b_j \right).$$

Differentiating $g(x)$ with b_j, we can obtain

$$\frac{\partial g}{\partial b_j} = -\frac{p_j c_j - p_j c'_j}{\overline{b} - \underline{b}} b_j + \frac{p_j c_j \overline{b} - p_j c'_j \underline{b}}{\overline{b} - \underline{b}} = \frac{p_j}{\overline{b} - \underline{b}} (c_j(\overline{b} - b_j) + c'_j(b_j - \underline{b})).$$

Since $\underline{b} < b_j < \overline{b}$, we have $\overline{b} - b_j > 0$, $b_j - \underline{b} > 0$, and $\overline{b} - \underline{b} > 0$. Thus $\frac{\partial g}{\partial b_j} > 0$, which concludes that $g(x)$ is a convex function.

Thus, model (10.5) is a convex programming. The proof is completed.

Based on Theorem 10.1 and the properties of the convex programming, if b_j^* is the local optimal solution of model (10.5), then it is also its global optimal solution. Thus, we have the following theorem.

Theorem 10.2. *If the random demand of budget for the jth day satisfies $d_j \sim U(\underline{b}, \overline{b})$, $j = 1, 2, \ldots, n$, then the optimal solutions of model (10.2) are*

$$b_j^* = \frac{p_j c_j \overline{b} - p_j c'_j \underline{b}}{p_j c_j - p_j c'_j} - \frac{\overline{b} - \underline{b}}{p_j c_j - p_j c'_j} \lambda, \quad i = 1, 2, \ldots, n, \tag{10.6}$$

where

$$\lambda = \left(\sum_{i=1}^{n} \frac{p_j c_j \overline{b} - p_j c'_j \underline{b}}{p_j c_j - p_j c'_j} - B_{campaign} \right) \bigg/ \left(\sum_{i=1}^{n} \frac{\overline{b} - \underline{b}}{p_j c_j - p_j c'_j} \right) \tag{10.7}$$

and the corresponding optimal value is

$$\sum_{i=1}^{n} \left[-\frac{p_j c_j - p_j c'_j}{2(\overline{b} - \underline{b})} \left(b_j^{*2} + \underline{b}^2 \right) + \frac{p_j c_j^{(1)} \overline{b} - p_j c'_j \underline{b}}{\overline{b} - \underline{b}} b_j^* \right].$$

Proof. By removing the constant items, the optimal solution of model (10.2) also solves the following model

$$\max \sum_{i=1}^{n} \left[-\frac{p_j c_j - p_j c'_j}{2(\overline{b} - \underline{b})} b_j^2 + \frac{p_j c_j \overline{b} - p_j c'_j \underline{b}}{\overline{b} - \underline{b}} b_j \right]$$

$$\text{s.t.} \sum_{i=1}^{n} b_j = B_{campaign}. \tag{10.8}$$

Using the Lagrange method, model (10.8) can be transformed into the following unconstrained programming

$$\max \sum_{i=1}^{n} \left[-\frac{p_j c_j - p_j c'_j}{2(\overline{b} - \underline{b})} b_j^2 + \frac{p_j c_j \overline{b} - p_j c'_j \underline{b}}{\overline{b} - \underline{b}} b_j \right] - \lambda \left(\sum_{i=1}^{n} b_j - B_{campaign} \right), \tag{10.9}$$

where λ is the Lagrange multiplier. Differentiating the objective of model (10.9) with b_j, $j = 1, 2, \ldots, n$. If b_j^* $(j = 1, 2, \ldots, n)$ is the optimal solution, then it satisfies

$$-\frac{p_j c_j - p_j c_j'}{\overline{b} - \underline{b}} b_j^* + \frac{p_j c_j \overline{b} - p_j c_j' \underline{b}}{\overline{b} - \underline{b}} - \lambda = 0,$$

thus we have

$$\lambda = -\frac{p_j c_j - p_j c_j'}{\overline{b} - \underline{b}} b_j^* + \frac{p_j c_j \overline{b} - p_j c_j' \overline{b}}{\overline{b} - \underline{b}}, \tag{10.10}$$

and

$$b_j^* = \frac{p_j c_j \overline{b} - p_j c_j' \underline{b}}{p_j c_j - p_j c_j'} - \frac{\overline{b} - \underline{b}}{p_j c_j - p_j c_j'} \lambda, \quad i = 1, 2, \ldots, n. \tag{10.11}$$

Since b_j^*, $i = 1, 2, \ldots$, satisfy the following condition

$$\sum_{i=1}^{n} b_j^* = B_{campaign},$$

we have

$$\sum_{i=1}^{n} \frac{p_j c_j \overline{b} - p_j c_j' \underline{b}}{p_j c_j - p_j c_j'} - \sum_{i=1}^{n} \frac{\overline{b} - \underline{b}}{p_j c_j - p_j c_j'} \lambda = B_{campaign}.$$

From the above equation, we can obtain

$$\lambda = \left(\sum_{i=1}^{n} \frac{p_j c_j \overline{b} - p_j c_j' \underline{b}}{p_j c_j - p_j c_j'} - B_{campaign} \right) \Big/ \left(\sum_{i=1}^{n} \frac{\overline{b} - \underline{b}}{p_j c_j - p_j c_j'} \right). \tag{10.12}$$

Substitute the optimal solutions b_j^* into the objective function of problem (10.2), and we can obtain the corresponding optimal value

$$\sum_{i=1}^{n} \left[-\frac{p_j c_j - p_j c_j'}{2(\overline{b} - \underline{b})} \left(b_j^{*2} + \underline{b}^2 \right) + \frac{p_j c_j \overline{b} - p_j c_j' \underline{b}}{\overline{b} - \underline{b}} b_j^* \right],$$

where b_j^* is defined by formula (10.11). The proof is completed.

Theorem 10.2 presents a method to find the optimal solutions and optimal value of model (10.2), which is convenient in practice.

10.3.2 Normal Distributed Budget

In this section we discuss the properties and solutions of model (10.2) when the random demand of budget for each temporal slot is normally distributed.

Theorem 10.3. *If the random demand of budget for the jth day satisfies $d_j \sim \mathcal{N}(\mu, \sigma)$ on $[\mu - 2\sigma, \mu + 2\sigma]$, $j = 1, 2, \ldots, n$, then model (10.2) becomes*

$$
\max \sum_{i=1}^{n} \left[-p_j(c_j - c_j') \left(\frac{\sigma}{\sqrt{2\pi}} \left(\exp\left(-\frac{(b_j - \mu)^2}{2\sigma^2} \right) - \exp(-2) \right) \right. \right.
$$
$$
\left. -(\mu - b_j)\Phi\left(\frac{b_j - \mu}{\sigma} \right) \right) + (p_j(c_j - c_j')\mu + p_j(c_j + c_j')b_j)\Phi(2)
$$
$$
\left. - p_j(c_j - c_j')\mu - p_j c_j' b_j \right]
$$

$$(10.13)$$

$$
\text{s.t. } \sum_{i=1}^{n} b_j = B_{campaign}
$$
$$
\mu - 2\sigma \leq b_j \leq \mu + 2\sigma,
$$

and it is a convex programming.

Proof. Since $d_j \sim U(\mu, \sigma)$ on $[\mu - 2\sigma, \mu + 2\sigma]$, $j = 1, 2, \ldots, n$, the probability distribution of d_j is

$$
f(d_j) = \begin{cases} \frac{1}{\sqrt{2\pi}\sigma} \exp\left(-\frac{(d_j - \mu)^2}{2\sigma^2} \right), & \text{if } \mu - 2\sigma \leq x \leq \mu + 2\sigma \\ 0, & \text{otherwise.} \end{cases}
$$

Thus, we have

$$
E[C(b_j, d_j)]
$$
$$
= \frac{1}{\sqrt{2\pi}\sigma} \int_{\mu - 2\sigma}^{b_j} (p_j c_j d_j + p_j c_j'(b_j - d_j)) \exp\left(-\frac{(d_j - \mu)^2}{2\sigma^2} \right) dd_j
$$
$$
+ \frac{1}{\sqrt{2\pi}\sigma} \int_{b_j}^{\mu + 2\sigma} p_j c_j b_j \exp\left(-\frac{(d_j - \mu)^2}{2\sigma^2} \right) dd_j
$$
$$
= \frac{\sigma}{\sqrt{2\pi}} p_j(c_j - c_j') \int_{\mu - 2\sigma}^{b_j} \frac{d_j - \mu}{\sigma^2} \exp\left(-\frac{(d_j - \mu)^2}{2\sigma^2} \right) dd_j
$$
$$
+ (p_j(c_j - c_j')\mu + p_j c_j' b_j) \int_{\mu - 2\sigma}^{b_j} \frac{1}{\sqrt{2\pi}\sigma} \exp\left(-\frac{(d_j - \mu)^2}{2\sigma^2} \right) dd_j
$$
$$
+ p_j c_j b_j \int_{b_j}^{\mu + 2\sigma} \frac{1}{\sqrt{2\pi}\sigma} \exp\left(-\frac{(d_j - \mu)^2}{2\sigma^2} \right) dd_j
$$
$$
= -\frac{\sigma}{\sqrt{2\pi}} p_j(c_j - c_j') \left(\exp\left(-\frac{(b_j - \mu)^2}{2\sigma^2} \right) - \exp\left(-\frac{(\mu - 2\sigma - \mu)^2}{2\sigma^2} \right) \right)
$$

$$+(p_j(c_j - c_j')\mu + p_jc_j'b_j)\left(\Phi\left(\frac{b_j - \mu}{\sigma}\right) - \Phi\left(\frac{\mu - 2\sigma - \mu}{\sigma}\right)\right)$$

$$+p_jc_jb_j\left(\Phi\left(\frac{\mu + 2\sigma - \mu}{\sigma}\right) - \Phi\left(\frac{b_j - \mu}{\sigma}\right)\right)$$

$$= -\frac{\sigma}{\sqrt{2\pi}}p_j(c_j - c_j')\left(\exp\left(-\frac{(b_j - \mu)^2}{2\sigma^2}\right) - \exp(-2)\right)$$

$$+(p_j(c_j - c_j')\mu + p_jc_j'b_j)\left(\Phi\left(\frac{b_j - \mu}{\sigma}\right) - \Phi(-2)\right)$$

$$+p_jc_jb_j\left(\Phi(2) - \Phi\left(\frac{b_j - \mu}{\sigma}\right)\right)$$

$$= -p_j(c_j - c_j')\left(\frac{\sigma}{\sqrt{2\pi}}\left(\exp\left(-\frac{(b_j - \mu)^2}{2\sigma^2}\right) - \exp(-2)\right) - (\mu - b_j)\Phi\left(\frac{b_j - \mu}{\sigma}\right)\right)$$

$$+(p_j(c_j - c_j')\mu + p_j(c_j + c_j')b_j)\Phi(2) - p_j(c_j - c_j')\mu - p_jc_j'b_j, \qquad (10.14)$$

where $\Phi(\cdot)$ is the standard normal probability distribution function.

Thus, model (10.2) can be given as follows

$$\max \sum_{i=1}^{n}\left[-p_j(c_j - c_j')\left(\frac{\sigma}{\sqrt{2\pi}}\left(\exp\left(-\frac{(b_j - \mu)^2}{2\sigma^2}\right) - \exp(-2)\right)\right.\right.$$

$$\left.-(\mu - b_j)\Phi\left(\frac{b_j - \mu}{\sigma}\right)\right) + (p_j(c_j - c_j')\mu + p_j(c_j + c_j')b_j)\Phi(2)$$

$$\left. - p_j(c_j - c_j')\mu - p_jc_j'b_j\right] \qquad (10.15)$$

$$\text{s.t. } \sum_{i=1}^{n}b_j = B_{campaign}$$

$$\mu - 2\sigma \leq b_j \leq \mu + 2\sigma.$$

Since the constraints of model (10.15) are linear, we need only to prove that the objective function of programming (10.15) is convex.

Let

$$g(x) = \sum_{i=1}^{n}\left[-p_j(c_j - c_j')\left(\frac{\sigma}{\sqrt{2\pi}}\left(\exp\left(-\frac{(b_j - \mu)^2}{2\sigma^2}\right) - \exp(-2)\right)\right.\right.$$

$$\left.-(\mu - b_j)\Phi\left(\frac{b_j - \mu}{\sigma}\right)\right) + (p_j(c_j - c_j')\mu + p_j(c_j + c_j')b_j)\Phi(2)$$

$$\left. - p_j(c_j - c_j')\mu - p_jc_j'b_j\right].$$

Differentiating $g(x)$ with b_j, we can obtain

$$\frac{\partial g}{\partial b_j} = -p_j(c_j - c'_j)\left(-\frac{1}{\sqrt{2\pi}\sigma}(b_j - \mu)\exp\left(-\frac{(b_j - \mu)^2}{2\sigma^2}\right)\right.$$

$$+ \Phi\left(\frac{b_j - \mu}{\sigma}\right) - \frac{1}{\sqrt{2\pi}\sigma}(\mu - b_j)\exp\left(-\frac{(b_j - \mu)^2}{2\sigma^2}\right)\right)$$

$$+ p_j(c_j + c'_j)\Phi(2) - p_j c'_j$$

$$= -p_j(c_j - c'_j)\Phi\left(\frac{b_j - \mu}{\sigma}\right) + p_j(c_j + c'_j)\Phi(2) - p_j c'_j$$

and

$$\frac{\partial g^2}{\partial b_j^2} = -p_j(c_j - c'_j)\frac{1}{\sqrt{2\pi}\sigma}\exp\left(-\frac{(b_j - \mu)^2}{2\sigma^2}\right).$$

Since $c_j > c'_j$, we have $\frac{\partial g^2}{\partial b_j^2} < 0$, which concludes that $g(x)$ is a convex function.

Thus, model (10.15) is a convex programming. The proof is completed.

According to Theorem 10.1, if b_j^* is the local optimal solution of model (10.15), then it is also its global optimal solution.

Since the objective function of model (10.15) contains probability distribution function Φ, it is difficult to get the precise optimal solutions. In the following, we use MC simulation to evaluate it.

From the definition of the standard normal distribution function, we have

$$\Phi(h(x)) = \int_{-\infty}^{h(x)} \frac{1}{\sqrt{2\pi}}\exp\left(-\frac{u^2}{2}\right)du,$$

where $h(x)$ is a function of x. The algorithm for evaluating $\Phi(h(x))$ is given in the following.

$N \leftarrow$ iteration times
$num \leftarrow 0$
$y \leftarrow 0$
while $num \leq N$
  $q \leftarrow r \sim \mathcal{N}(0, 1)$
  if $q \leq h(x)$ **then**
    $y \leftarrow y + 1$
  $num \leftarrow num + 1$
return y/N

In the following section, we provide some computational experiments to validate our model and its properties.

10.4 Experiments

In this section we perform some experiments with field logs of real campaigns in search markets to illustrate the effectiveness of the proposed strategy, named StoStrategy_uniform and StoStrategy_normal.

For comparison purposes, we implement one baseline strategy, called BASE-Average, which represents a strategy to allocate the budget to a series of temporal slots averagely. That is, it neglects the differences between these temporal slots. The reason for us choosing the BASE-Average is that it is easy to implement, and thus is usually adopted by advertisers.

10.4.1 Experimental Data

In this experiment, we use the data during a month (e.g. 30 days), and the data such as clicks per unit cost, effective CTR, and effective clicks per unit cost are shown in Figures 10.1–10.3. The total budget is $B_{campaign} = 3000$. From the logs, we can know that the demand of budget for every day is on interval [80, 150]. Thus, StoStrategy_uniform and StoStrategy_normal regard the random optimal daily budget for the promotion period as satisfying $U(80, 150)$ and $\mathcal{N}(115, 17.5^2)$, respectively.

10.4.2 Result Analysis

The optimal daily budgets for the three strategies are shown in Figure 10.4, and the corresponding total cumulative effective clicks are shown in Figure 10.5, where "cumulative

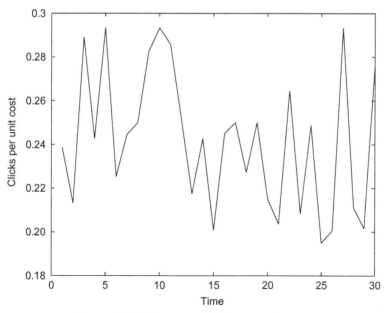

Figure 10.1   Pattern of clicks per unit cost.

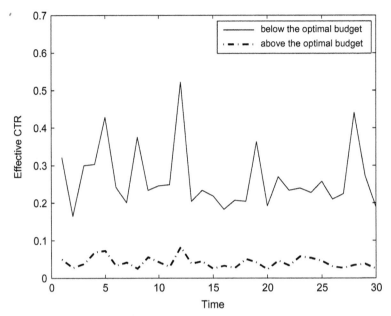

Figure 10.2 Pattern of the effective CTR.

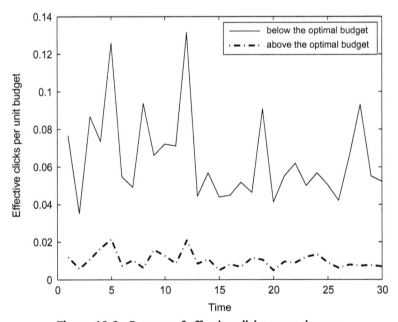

Figure 10.3 Pattern of effective clicks per unit cost.

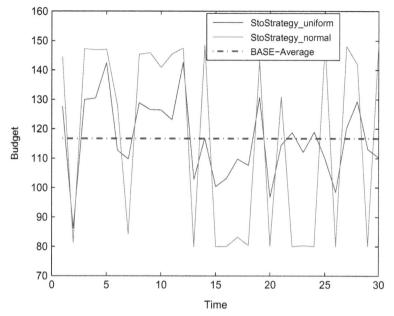

Figure 10.4 Comparisons of the daily budget by the three strategies.

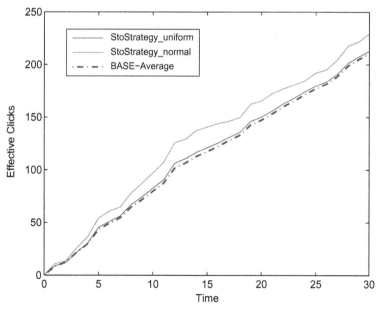

Figure 10.5 Comparisons of the total cumulative effective clicks by the three strategies.

effective clicks" on the jth day represent the total effective clicks from the 1st day to the jth day, $j = 1, 2, \ldots, 30$.

From Figures 10.4 and 10.5, we can obtain the following results:

1. StoStrategy_normal and StoStrategy_uniform can obtain 229.17 and 212.80 effective clicks, respectively, and BASE-Average can obtain 210.49 effective clicks.
2. StoStrategy_normal strategy outperforms StoStrategy_uniform strategy (by about 7.69%), in terms of the total effective clicks. The reason is that the StoStrategy_normal strategy can allocate more budget in the more profitable days that have high effective clicks per unit cost (both below and above the demand of budget), and allocate less budget in the days with low effective clicks per unit cost (both below and above the demand of budget), which makes the budget more profitable.
3. Both our StoStrategy_normal strategy and StoStrategy_uniform strategy outperform BASE-Average by about 8.86–1.10%, respectively, in terms of the total effective clicks. The reason is that both of our strategies consider the differences in parameters for these days and BASE-Average neglects the differences between these days in budget decisions.

10.4.3 Managerial Insights

This chapter provides critical managerial insights for advertisers facing such budget distribution problems in sponsored search auctions. On the one hand, if the advertiser can get both the upper and lower bound of the demand of budget for each temporal slot, assuming the demand of budget as a random variable can help the advertiser obtain more revenues than allocating the budget averagely. On the other hand, the demand of budget is more likely to be normally distributed than uniformly distributed. Thus, if the advertiser takes the demand of budget as a normally distributed random variable, she can get more revenues than with uniform distribution.

10.5 Conclusions

In this chapter we mainly discuss how to distribute the budget for a campaign to a series of sequential temporal slots during a certain promotion period, with the consideration of serious budget constraints. Considering the demand of budget for each temporal slot as a random variable to characterize the uncertainties in sponsored search auctions, we formulate a stochastic budget distribution model over a series of temporal slots for a given campaign. When the demand of budget can be represented by uniform random variables and normal random variables, we study some properties and solutions of the proposed model. With field logs of real campaigns in search markets, we perform some experiments to validate our model, and the results show that our strategies outperform a baseline strategy commonly used in piratical search advertisement campaigns in terms of optimal effective clicks. Comparing the revenues for the budget strategies according to uniform distribution and normal distribution, we can conclude that the demand of budget is more likely to be normally distributed than uniformly distributed.

In our future work we will attempt to study more complex cases, with consideration of the randomness for two or more parameters, and study the properties and solutions of our model when the randomness can be represented by other kinds of random variables. Another interesting and challenging perspective is to consider the dynamics and randomness of the demand of budget simultaneously.

References

Abrams, Z. 2006. Revenue maximization when bidders have budgets, In Proceedings of the Seventeenth Annual ACM-SIAM Symposium on Discrete Algorithms.

Abrams, Z., O. Mendelevitch, J. A. Tomlin. 2007. Optimal delivery of sponsored search advertisements subject to budget constraints, EC'07, June 11–15, 2007, San Diego, California, USA.

Anderson, C. 2005, February 12. Google's Long Tail. Available from: <http://longtail.typepad.com/the_long_tail/2005/02/googles_long_ta.html>.

Archak, N., V. S. Mirrokni, S. Muthukrishnan. 2010. Budget optimization for online advertising campaigns with carryover effects, In Sixth Workshop on Ad auctions.

Ashlagi, I., M. Braverman, A. Hassidim, R. Lavi, M. Tennenholtz. 2010. Position auctions with budgets: Existence and uniqueness. The BE Journal of Theoretical Economics, 10(1).

Borgs, C., J. Chayes, O. Etesami, N. Immorlica, K. Jain, M. Mahdian. 2007. Dynamics of bid optimization in online advertisement auctions, In Proc. WWW, 531–540.

Colini-Baldeschi, R., M. Henzinger, S. Leonardi, M. Starnberger. 2012. On multiple keyword sponsored search auctions with budgets, In ICALP'12 Proceedings of the 39th International Colloquium Conference on Automata, Languages, and Programming - Volume Part II, 1–12.

Drosos, D., E. Markakis, G. D. Stamoulis. 2010. Budget constrained bidding in sponsored search auctions. Working Paper.

Du, R., Q. Hu, S. Ai. 2007. Stochastic demand of budget decision for advertising considering uncertain sales responses, European Journal of Operational Research, 183:1042–1054.

Muthukrishnan, S., M. Pál, Z. Svitkina. 2010. Stochastic models for budget optimization in search-based advertising, Algorithmica, 58:1022–1044.

Özlük, Ö., S. Cholette. 2007. Allocating expenditures across keywords in search advertising, Journal of Revenue and Pricing Management, 6(4):347–356.

Yang, Y., J. Zhang, R. Qin, J. Li, F. Wang, Q. Wei. 2012. A budget optimization framework for search advertisements across markets, IEEE Transactions on Systems, Man, and Cybernetics, Part A, 42(5):1141–1151.

CHAPTER 11

A Two-Stage Fuzzy Programming Approach for Budget Allocation in Sponsored Search Auctions

11.1 Introduction

Sponsored search auctions (SSA) have become an important marketing field for many advertisers. In sponsored search auctions, major search engines such as Google and Yahoo! provide several advertising slots for advertisers to display their advertisements along with organic search results on search engine results pages (SERPs). Advertisers participating in keyword auctions should first select a set of keywords that are relevant to their products or services, and then submit a bid for each keyword. When a search user submits a query, an auction process happens among the advertisers who bid for keywords matching the query. The advertisers will not pay unless a search user clicks their advertisements.

In sponsored search auctions, how to effectively allocate the limited budget is an important decision issue. Moreover, budget decisions are also viewed as important inputs to various kinds of advertising strategies. Fruchter and Dou (2005) used techniques of dynamic programming to find analytical solutions for the optimal budgeting decisions between a generic market and a specialized market. They found that, in the long run, an advertiser should always spend more in the specialized market. The budget optimization problem can also be cast as an online (multiple-choice) knapsack problem (Babaioff et al., 2007; Chakrabarty et al., 2007) to achieve a provably optimal competitive ratio for advertisers. Several stochastic models have also been established (Du et al., 2007; DasGupta and Muthukrishnan, 2012; Feldman et al., 2007; Hosanagar and Cherepanov, 2008; Muthukrishnan et al., 2010) to spread a given budget over a set of keywords of interest, to maximize the expected number of clicks.

However, most of these works focused on the budget allocation at the keyword level (Archak et al., 2010; Borgs et al., 2005; Mahdian and Wang, 2009; Zhou et al., 2008; Zluk and Cholette, 2007). It is not suitable in real practice. With consideration of the entire lifecycle of

Yang and Wang: Budget Constraints and Optimization in Sponsored Search Auctions. http://dx.doi.org/10.1016/B978-0-12-411457-9.00011-2
© 2014 Elsevier Inc. All rights reserved.

sponsored search auctions, there exist three budget allocation scenarios at different phases, including long-term budget allocation across markets, budget distribution over a series of intervals (e.g. daily budget constraints) for a specific SSA campaign, and real-time budget adjustment within a given interval (Yang et al., 2012). Strategies for budget allocation and adjustment in these three scenarios construct a closed-loop, composite allocation strategy for sponsored search auctions through forms of constraints and feedbacks. This chapter aims to explore the budget decision problem at the campaign level, e.g. budget distribution over a series of intervals. Specifically, this chapter focuses on how to allocate the budget to a series of sequential "temporal slots" for a specific SSA campaign in a search market.

The optimal budget in each temporal slot is influenced by many factors, e.g. search demands from search users and the click-through rate of advertisements. Thus it not easy to be known in advance. In this research we assume that (1) the effective click-through rate is kept constant when the budget does not exceed the optimal budget in a temporal slot; (2) clicks generated from the exceeded budget are ineffective. We give more detailed justifications for these two assumptions in Section 11.2.

By taking optimal budgets in these temporal slots as fuzzy variables (Liu and Liu, 2002), we establish a two-stage fuzzy budget allocation model with the two-stage fuzzy programming approach as proposed by Liu (2005). Specifically, advertisers give an initial budget at the first stage, and then adjust the budget according to the distribution of these optimal budgets at the second stage. The particle swarm optimization (PSO) algorithm is utilized to find the best solution for our budget allocation model in the case where optimal budgets are represented as discrete fuzzy variables. We also conduct some computational experiments to validate our budget allocation model and algorithm. Experimental results show that our model performs better in terms of optimal values, compared with five other budget allocation operations.

The main contributions of this research can be summarized as follows:

(*i*)   We establish a two-stage fuzzy budget allocation model, with optimal budgets characterized by fuzzy variables.

(*ii*)   We develop a feasible solution procedure for the proposed budget model with PSO algorithm in the case where optimal budgets are represented as discrete fuzzy variables.

(*iii*)   We conduct some experiments to validate the proposed budget allocation method and its solution algorithm, and experimental results proved our allocation model is more effective in terms of optimal value.

The remainder of this chapter is organized as follows. In Section 11.2, we define the budget allocation problem over a series of sequential temporal slots, and then establish a two-stage fuzzy programming model to solve this problem. In Section 11.3, we propose a solution method to solve the established budget model. In Section 11.4, we make experiments to illustrate the effectiveness of our budget allocation model and corresponding solution method. Section 11.5 concludes this chapter.

11.2 Problem Formulation

11.2.1 Problem Statement

Suppose the budget allocated to a search market during a certain period is given, then consider the budget allocation problem over a series of sequential temporal slots (e.g. days/weeks/months) during the promotional period.

The potential search demands in each temporal slot is finite, thus the marginal clicks generated from certain expenditures cannot always be positive, as illustrated in Figure 11.1. Specifically, when the budget is less than a critical value, the clicks will increase as the allocated budget increases; when the budget is larger than the critical value, the growth rate of clicks decreases and gradually approaches zero as the allocated budget increases. The critical value is regarded as the *optimal budget*, represented by the symbol "*" in Figure 11.1. For simplicity, we assume that the part of the allocated budget that is greater than the optimal budget will be used up and the clicks generated from it are ineffective. This assumption can be justified by the fact that the allocated budget $\gg$ optimal budget will never happen in each temporal slot due to budget constraints, especially for advertisers from small and medium enterprises. The effective clicks are by no means infinite in each temporal slot.

Besides the concept of *optimal budget*, there are two relevant concepts called *exceeded budget* and *lacking budget*, represented by I^+ and I^-, respectively, as shown in Figure 11.2. We define the three terms as follows:

- *Optimal budget*: That is the best budget to satisfy the search demands. In Figure 11.2, we use the symbol "*" to represent the optimal budget in temporal slots t_1, t_2, t_3, and t_4. In a search market, when the budget during the whole period is given, the case where the allocated budget $\gg$ optimal budget will never happen. Thus we can suppose that the budget allocated in each temporal slot will be used up.

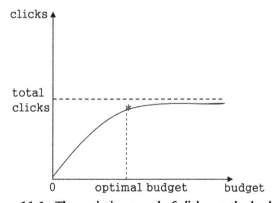

Figure 11.1 The variation trend of clicks on the budget.

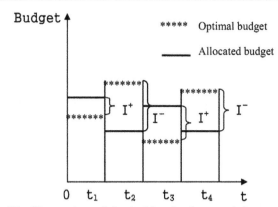

Figure 11.2 **The illustration of the lacking budget and the exceeded budget.**

- *Exceeded budget*: In the temporal slots t_1 and t_3 in Figure 11.2, the allocated budget, which is represented by the real line, is larger than the optimal budget. The difference between the allocated budget and the optimal budget is referred to as *exceeded budget*, represented by I^+. We suppose this part of budget will be used up and clicks generated from it are ineffective. Thus it is a loss for the advertiser.
- *Lacking budget*: In the temporal slots t_2 and t_4 in Figure 11.2, the shortage of budget between the allocated budget and the optimal budget is referred to as *lacking budget*, represented by I^-. The loss of effective clicks for the advertiser will increase as this part of the budget increases. Thus it is also a loss for the advertiser.

From the above descriptions, it is obvious that the optimal budget is of great significance for the advertiser in dealing with the budget allocation problem, e.g. budget distribution over a series of intervals. However, the optimal budget in each temporal slot is influenced by many factors, e.g. search demands from search users and click-through rate of advertisements. Thus it is not easy to be known in advance. In the following section, we will characterize optimal budgets by fuzzy variables, and establish a two-stage fuzzy budget allocation model to solve this problem.

11.2.2 The Two-Stage Fuzzy Budget Allocation Model

As we described previously, optimal budgets over these temporal slots cannot be known with certainty in advance. Thus we characterize them by fuzzy variables to establish a budget allocation model. The notations used in this chapter are shown in Table 11.1.

In practical search advertising campaigns, clicks per unit cost in the ith temporal slot (c_i) can be obtained from the average cost-per-click (CPC) in the ith temporal slot through the

Table 11.1 List of notations.

Notations	Definition
n	The number of total temporal slots in the whole period
B	The total budget in the search market during a certain period
c_i	Clicks per unit cost in the ith temporal slot, $i = 1, 2, \ldots, n$
x_i	The allocated budget in the ith temporal slot, $i = 1, 2, \ldots, n$
$\tilde{d}_i$	The fuzzy optimal budget for the ith temporal slot, $i = 1, 2, \ldots, n$
p_i	The effective click-through rate in the ith temporal slot, $i = 1, 2, \ldots, n$
I_i^+	The exceeded budget in the ith temporal slot, $i = 1, 2, \ldots, n$
I_i^-	The lacking budget in the ith temporal slot, $i = 1, 2, \ldots, n$

following formula

$$c_i = \frac{1}{c_i'},$$

where c_i' is the average CPC of the ith temporal slot.

For an advertiser, the aim of the search advertising campaign is to maximize the revenue, which can be represented by the obtained clicks. If the loss in terms of clicks decreases, then the obtained clicks will increase. Thus, the objective of maximizing the obtained clicks can be transformed into that of minimizing the loss in terms of clicks.

From the analysis above, in the objective function of our budget model, we consider minimizing the loss in terms of clicks for the advertiser. In the ith temporal slot, $i = 1, 2, \ldots, n$, the loss in terms of clicks contains the following three parts:

- If $I_i^+ = I_i^- = 0$, then the loss is represented by the ineffective clicks generated from x_i, i.e. $c_i x_i (1 - p_i)$.
- If $I_i^+ > 0$, then the loss is represented by the ineffective clicks generated from $x_i - I_i^+$ and I_i^+, i.e. $c_i (x_i - I_i^+)(1 - p_i) + c_i I_i^+ = c_i x_i (1 - p_i) + c_i I_i^+ p_i$.
- If $I_i^- < 0$, then the loss is represented by the ineffective clicks generated from x_i and the loss of effective clicks by I_i^-, i.e. $c_i x_i (1 - p_i) + c_i I_i^- p_i$.

As the optimal budget for each temporal slot cannot be known in advance, an advertiser can give the initial budget at the first stage, and then adjust the budget based on the realization of the fuzzy optimal budget at the second stage. Using the notations in Table 11.1, the two-stage fuzzy budget allocation model can be established as follows

$$\min \sum_{i=1}^{n} c_i x_i (1 - p_i) + \mathcal{Q}(\mathbf{x})$$

$$\text{s.t.} \ \sum_{i=1}^{n} x_i \leq B \tag{11.1}$$

$$x_i \geq 0, i = 1, 2, \ldots, n,$$

where

$$Q(\mathbf{x}) = E_{\tilde{\mathbf{d}}}[Q(\mathbf{x}, \tilde{\mathbf{d}}(\gamma)] \tag{11.2}$$

and

$$Q(\mathbf{x}, \mathbf{d}(\tilde{\gamma})) = \min \left[\sum_{i=1}^{n} c_i I_i^+ p_i + \sum_{i=1}^{n} c_i I_i^- p_i \right]$$
$$\text{s.t.} \quad I_i^+ = [x_i - \tilde{d}_i(\gamma)] \vee 0 \tag{11.3}$$
$$I_i^- = [\tilde{d}_i(\gamma) - x_i] \vee 0, \, i = 1, 2, \dots, n,$$

where $Q(\mathbf{x})$ is called the recourse function (Liu 2005), and E denotes the expected value of a fuzzy variable (Liu and Liu 2002).

11.3 The Solution Algorithm

11.3.1 The Recourse Function

Let the optimal budget $\tilde{\mathbf{d}} = (\tilde{d}_1, \tilde{d}_2, \dots, \tilde{d}_n)$ be a discrete fuzzy vector, given as follows:

$$\hat{\mathbf{d}}^1 = (\hat{d}_1^1, \hat{d}_2^1, \dots, \hat{d}_n^1) \text{ with possibility } \mu_1 > 0,$$
$$\hat{\mathbf{d}}^2 = (\hat{d}_1^2, \hat{d}_2^2, \dots, \hat{d}_n^2) \text{ with possibility } \mu_2 > 0,$$
$$\dots$$
$$\hat{\mathbf{d}}^N = (\hat{d}_1^N, \hat{d}_2^N, \dots, \hat{d}_n^N) \text{ with possibility } \mu_N > 0,$$

and $\max\limits_{j=1}^{N} \mu_j = 1$.

Then, according to Liu (2005), the recourse function (11.2) can be computed in the following way. Without the loss of generality, we assume that for a fixed $\mathbf{x}$, the second-stage objective function satisfies the condition $Q(\mathbf{x}, \hat{\mathbf{d}}^1) \leq Q(\mathbf{x}, \hat{\mathbf{d}}^2) \leq \dots \leq Q(\mathbf{x}, \hat{\mathbf{d}}^N)$, and then the recourse function (11.2) at $\mathbf{x}$ can be described by the following formula

$$Q(\mathbf{x}) = \sum_{j=1}^{N} \omega_j Q(\mathbf{x}, \hat{\mathbf{d}}^j), \tag{11.4}$$

where the corresponding weights ω_j, $j = 1, 2, \dots, N$ are given by the following formulas

$$\omega_j = \frac{1}{2} \left(\max_{k=1}^{j} \mu_k - \max_{k=0}^{j-1} \mu_k \right) + \frac{1}{2} \left(\max_{k=j}^{N} \mu_k - \max_{k=j+1}^{N+1} \mu_k \right), \quad j = 1, 2, \dots, N \tag{11.5}$$

$(\mu_0 = 0, \mu_{N+1} = 0)$ and satisfy the following constraints

$$\omega_j \geq 0, \sum_{j=1}^{N} \omega_j = \max_{j=1}^{N} \mu_j = 1.$$

11.3.2 The PSO Algorithm

In this section we utilize the particle swarm optimization (PSO) algorithm to solve the proposed budget allocation model as proposed in Section 11.2.

The PSO algorithm, as inspired by the social behavior of bird flocking or fish schooling, is a population-based stochastic optimization technique developed by Kennedy and Eberhart (1995). Compared with other evolutionary algorithms, the PSO algorithm has much faster convergence speed and fewer parameters to adjust. This makes it particularly easy to implement. Recently, the PSO algorithm has attracted much attention and been successfully applied in evolutionary computing, unconstrained continuous optimization problems, and many other fields.

The system is initialized with a population of random solutions and searches for optima by updating generations. In PSO, the potential solutions, called particles, fly through the problem space by following the current optimum particles. In the search process, the velocity and position of the ith particle are updated by the following formulas

$$V_i(t + 1) = wV_i(t) + \alpha_1 r_1(P_i(t) - X_i(t)) + \alpha_2 r_2(P_g(t) - X_i(t)), \tag{11.6}$$

$$X_i(t + 1) = X_i(t) + V_i(t + 1), \tag{11.7}$$

where $i = 1, 2, \ldots, pop\_size$; w is the inertia coefficient; α_1 and α_2 are learning rates, and r_1 and r_2 are two numbers randomly generated from [0,1].

The PSO algorithm for solving our budget model as proposed in Section 11.1 is described as follows:

Step 1. Initialize pop_size particles with random positions and velocities, and evaluate the objective values for all particles. For each particle, the objective value is evaluated in the following way:

> Step 1.1. Compute the optimal value Q_i^* of the second-stage programming (11.3), $i = 1, 2, \ldots, n$.
> Step 1.2. Rearrange Q_i^*, $i = 1, 2, \ldots, n$ such that $Q_1^* \le Q_2^* \le \cdots \le Q_n^*$.
> Step 1.3. Compute the corresponding weights according to the formula (11.5).
> Step 1.4. Compute the recourse function (11.2) according to the formula (11.4) and then the objective value.

Step 2. Set *pbest* of each particle and its objective value equal to its current position and objective value, and set *gbest* and its objective value equal to the position and objective value of the best initial particle.

Step 3. Update the velocity and position of each particle according to the formulas (11.6) and (11.7), respectively, and then compute the objective values for all the particles.

Step 4. For each particle, compare the current objective value with that of its *pbest*. If the current objective value is smaller than that of *pbest*, renew *pbest* and its objective value with the current position and objective value.

Step 5. Find the best particle from the current particle swarm with the smallest objective value. If the objective value is smaller than that of *gbest*, then renew *gbest* and its objective value with the position and objective value of the current best particle.

Step 6. Repeat Step 3 to Step 5 for a given number of cycles.

Step 7. Report *gbest* and its objective value as the optimal solution and optimal value.

11.4 Experiments

In this section we conduct some experiments to validate the established two-stage fuzzy budget allocation model and its solution as proposed in Section 11.2.

Let the total budget in a search engine during a week (e.g. 5 days) be $B = 300$, and clicks per unit cost $c_i = 0.7$, and the effective click-through rate of the ith temporal slot $p_i = 0.8$, $i = 1, 2, \ldots, 5$. The optimal budgets for the 5 days are represented by a discrete fuzzy vector with the following possibility distributions

$$\tilde{\mathbf{d}} = \begin{cases} (47, 51, 65, 62, 75), & \text{with possibility } 0.6 \\ (40, 50, 78, 59, 73), & \text{with possibility } 0.8 \\ (38, 58, 62, 64, 78), & \text{with possibility } 1 \\ (50, 54, 68, 68, 60), & \text{with possibility } 0.7. \end{cases}$$

In the following experiment, we set the learning rates $\alpha_1 = \alpha_2 = 2$, and the population size $pop\_size = 100$. By using the proposed solution, we run the PSO algorithm with 5000 generations, then get the following optimal solution

$$\mathbf{x}^* = (38, 54, 62, 64, 73),$$

and the corresponding optimal value is 51.380.

To illustrate the effectiveness of our method, we compare our solution with five other budget allocation operations. Suppose there are five advertisers who allocate their budgets according to their own preferences of budget allocation. Without the loss of generality, the first advertiser adopts the average budget allocation strategy, i.e. the budget on every day is the same; and the other four advertisers allocate their budgets according to the four possible optimal budgets, respectively. The results are compared in terms of the optimal value above, as shown in Table 11.2.

From experimental results in Table 11.2, we notice that the optimal value of our budget model is better than the objectives of the five budget allocation operations.

Table 11.2   Comparisons in terms of the objective value.

Advertiser	Preference of Budget Allocation	Budget	Objective Value
Advertiser 1	average	(60,60,60,60,60)	68.880
Advertiser 2	possibility 0.6	(47,51,65,62,75)	52.640
Advertiser 3	possibility 0.8	(40,50,78,59,73)	52.056
Advertiser 4	possibility 1	(38,58,62,64,78)	51.632
Advertiser 5	possibility 0.7	(50,54,68,68,60)	58.464
–	optimal solution	(38,54,62,64,73)	51.380

11.5 Conclusions

Budget optimization is a critical issue for different advertising strategies in sponsored search auctions. An advertiser, given a budget constraint during a specific period, has to allocate the budget to a series of sequential temporal slots in order to maximize the expected revenue. Given that the budget allocated to a search market during a certain period is determined, this research discusses how to allocate the budget to a series of sequential temporal slots within this period. We establish a two-stage fuzzy budget allocation model with the two-stage fuzzy programming approach, and propose a feasible solution based on the particle swarm optimization (PSO) algorithm. Experimental results show that our model performs better in terms of optimal values, compared with five other budget allocation operations.

In this research we discuss the solution method for our proposed budget allocation model with optimal budgets that are characterized by discrete fuzzy variables. In an ongoing work, we are studying the solution method for our budget allocation model where optimal budgets are represented as continuous fuzzy variables. Furthermore, we also consider that the effective click-through rate varies depending on the allocated budget, and a portion of clicks generated from the exceeded budget can be considered effective.

References

Archak N., V. S. Mirrokni, S. Muthukrishnan. 2010. Budget optimization for online advertising campaigns with carryover effects. The Eleventh ACM SIGECOM International Conference on Electronic Commerce, Harvard.

Babaioff, M., N. Immorlica, D. Kempe, R. Kleinberg. 2007. A knapsack secretary problem with applications, Lecture Notes in Computer Science, 4627:16–28.

Borgs, C., J. Chayes, N. Immorlica, M. Mahdian, A. Saberi. 2005. Multi-unit auctions with budget-constrained bidders, In Proceedings of the 6th ACM conference on Electronic commerce (EC '05). ACM, New York, NY, USA, 44–51.

Chakrabarty, D., Y. Zhou, R. Lukose. 2007. Budget constrained bidding in keyword auctions and online knapsack problems, Proceedings of the 16th International World Wide Web Conference.

DasGupta, B., S. Muthukrishnan. 2012. Stochastic budget optimization in Internet advertising, Algorithmica, DOI: http://dx.doi.org/10.1007/s00453-012-9614-x.

Du, R., Q. Hu, S. Ai. 2007. Stochastic optimal budget decision for advertising considering uncertain sales responses, European Journal of Operational Research, 183(3):1042–1054.

Feldman, J., S. Muthukrishnan, M. Pál, C. Stein. 2007. Budget optimization in search-based advertising auctions, Proceedings of the 9th ACM Conference on Electronic Commerce.

Fruchter, G. E., W. Dou. 2005. Optimal budget allocation over time for keyword ads in web portals. Journal of Optimization Theory and Applications 124(1):157–174.

Hosanagar, K., V. Cherepanov. 2008. Optimal bidding in stochastic budget constrained slot auctions, Proceedings of the ACM Conference on Electronic Commerce, July 8–12, 2008, Chicago, America.

Kennedy, J., R. C. Eberhart. 1995. Particle swarm optimization, Proceedings of the IEEE International Conference on Neural Networks, Piscataway, NJ, 1942–1948.

Liu, Y. K. 2005. Fuzzy programming with recourse, International Journal of Uncertainty, Fuzziness & Knowledge-Based Systems, 13:382–413.

Liu, B., Y.K. Liu. 2002. Expected value of fuzzy variable and fuzzy expected value models, IEEE Transactions on Fuzzy Systems, 10(4):445–450.

Mahdian, M., G. Wang. 2009. Clustering-based bidding languages for sponsored search, Proceedings of the 17th Annual European Symposium on Algorithms, September 7–9, 2009, Copenhagen, Denmark.

Muthukrishnan, S., M. Pál, Z. Svitkina. 2010. Stochastic models for budget optimization in search-based advertising, Algorithmica, 58:1022–1044.

Özlük Ö., S. Cholette (2007). Allocating expenditures across keywords in search advertising. Journal of Revenue and Pricing Management, 6(4):347–356.

Yang, Y., J. Zhang, R. Qin, J. Li, F. Wang, Q. Wei. 2012. A budget optimization framework for search advertisements across markets, IEEE Transactions on Systems, Man, and Cybernetics, Part A, 42(5):1141–1151.

Zhou Y., D. Chakrabarty, R. Lukose (2008). Budget constrained bidding in keyword auctions and online knapsack problems, Proceeding of the 17th International Conference on World Wide Web, Beijing, China, ACM.

CHAPTER 12

Budget Planning for Coupled Campaigns in Sponsored Search Auctions

12.1 Introduction

Sponsored search auctions have become the most successful business model accounting for 47.7% of revenues of online advertisements in 2011 (IAB, 2011). On the one hand, more and more advertisers choose sponsored search auctions to promote their products or services. On the other hand, search advertisements form the dominant revenue resource for major search engine companies. One of the most difficult tasks for advertisers is how to effectively determine and allocate the optimum level of advertising budgets in sponsored search auctions.

Budget is an endogenous factor in sponsored search auctions that heavily influences other advertising strategies. Moreover, budget-related decisions in sponsored search auctions are recognized as a structured decision problem, rather than a simple constraint (Yang et al., 2012). Specifically, throughout the entire lifecycle of search advertising campaigns, there exist three interweaving budget decisions, being affected by various factors: allocation across search markets, temporal distribution over a series of slots (e.g. day), and adjustment of the remaining budget (e.g. the daily budget). This work considers the following scenario: an advertiser usually has several campaigns simultaneously executed in a search market (e.g. Google Adwords); then given that the advertising budget in a search market is determined, how to make budgeting plans for these campaigns simultaneously over time, in order to maximize the global advertising performance? As shown by some previous research (Tull et al., 1986; Fischer et al., 2011), profit improvement from better allocation strategies is much higher than from improving the overall budget.

There have been some research efforts regarding budget-related decisions in sponsored search auctions. Most of them either take the budget as the constraint for other advertising strategies (Chakrabarty et al., 2007), or allocate the budget over keywords (Özlük and Cholette, 2007). However, these efforts are not operationally suitable to practical paradigms provided by major search engines, because they ignore the search advertising structure. Budget planning over

Yang and Wang: Budget Constraints and Optimization in Sponsored Search Auctions. http://dx.doi.org/10.1016/B978-0-12-411457-9.00012-4
© 2014 Elsevier Inc. All rights reserved.

several campaigns remains a challenging but utterly important task for advertisers in sponsored search auctions. First, the search marketing environments are essentially dynamic and uncertain, advertisers usually do not have sufficient knowledge and time to track and adjust various advertising decisions. Secondly, an advertiser's campaigns are rarely independent. Similar to the case among products (Doyle and Saunders, 1990), there are certain relationships (e.g. complementarity and substitution) between advertising campaigns, which lead to cross elasticities. For example, for a retailing advertiser, one campaign featuring smart phones might have some substitution effects on another featuring cheap cellphones, and vice versa. Thirdly, the complex structure of search advertising markets and campaigns consists of a lot of parameters, which do not make multi-campaign budgeting decisions straightforward.

The objective of this research is to explore the dynamic budget planning problem for several coupled campaigns in terms of substitution relationships in sponsored search auctions. In this chapter we formulate the multi-campaign budget planning problem as an optimal control process under a finite time horizon. First, we present a measure of coupled relationships between advertising campaigns by considering the overlapping degree (O) in terms of campaign content, promotional periods, and target regions. The overlapping degree refers to the degree to which target markets (or audiences) of these two campaigns overlap each other. Intuitively, it is defined as the probability that search users (e.g. potential customers) issued with keywords in campaign j can also be reached by campaign j' in sponsored search auctions. Secondly, we propose a random walk-based approach for the ad overlapping degree γ (e.g. campaign contents) in the context of a directed keyword graph relevant to a given advertiser. The higher the ad overlapping degree between two campaigns, the more the advertising effort is weakened. Thirdly, we provide a feasible solution to our model and study some desirable properties. Furthermore, we also conduct computational experiments to validate and evaluate our budget planning approach, with real-world data collected from logs and reports of practical campaigns. Experimental results show that (a) the overlapping degree (O) between campaigns has serious effects on optimal budgets and the advertising effort, and the advertising effort can be seriously weakened if an advertiser ignores the overlapping degree between campaigns while making advertising decisions; (b) the case with the higher ad overlapping degree (γ) leads to a lower optimal budget level and reaches the budgeting cap earlier; (c) the higher the overlapping degree is, the lower the optimal revenues that can be obtained.

The remainder of this chapter is organized as follows. In Section 12.2, we propose a measure of the three-dimensional relationship between campaigns, and present a budget planning strategy over several campaigns in sponsored search auctions. Section 12.3 studies some desirable properties and provides possible solutions for our model. Section 12.4 reports some experimental results to validate some normative findings from our model. Finally, we conclude this work and discuss future research directions in Section 12.5.

12.2 Multi-Campaign Budget Planning

12.2.1 The Three-Dimensional Relationship Between Campaigns

It is observed that the overlapping degree between two campaigns j and j' is zero if there are no overlaps from any single one of those aspects (e.g. campaign contents, promotional intervals, and target regions). Thus, the overlapping degree $O(j, j')$ is the product of overlaps from three aspects $O(j, j') = I_t(j, j') \times I_s(j, j') \times \gamma(j, j')$, where I_t and I_s represent the temporal indicator function (e.g. promotional intervals) and the spatial indicator function (e.g. target regions), respectively, and $\gamma(j, j')$ is the overlapping degree in terms of campaign contents.

The indicator function $I_A(x)$ is denoted as follows,

$$I_A(x) = \begin{cases} 1, & \text{if } x \in A \\ 0, & \text{otherwise,} \end{cases}$$

The definition of the temporal indicator and the spatial indicator is as follows.

The Temporal Indicator Function: Let T_j and $T_{j'}$ denote promotion intervals of campaign j and campaign j', respectively. The temporal indicator function is given as $I_t(j, j') = I_{T_j}(t)I_{T_{j'}}(t)$.

The Spatial Indicator Function: The overlaps with respect to target regions can be given in a similar way. Let S_j, $S_{j'}$ be target regions of campaign j and campaign j', respectively. The spatial indicator function is given as $I_s(j, j') = I_{S_j}(s)I_{S_{j'}}(s)$.

Next, we will discuss the ad overlapping degree (e.g. in terms of campaign contents) in sponsored search auctions.

12.2.2 The Ad Overlapping Degree

We construct a directed graph of keywords (K) relevant to a given advertiser (or her products/services) with the appearance probability as the edge weight. Let K_j and $K_{j'}$ be keyword sets of campaigns j and j', respectively. For each pair of k and k', we can apply a random walk approach (Doyle and Snell, 1984) to compute the appearance probability $\omega_{k,k'}$, given as $\omega_{k,k'} = P(l_k = k') = (1 - \beta_k) \sum_{(k,r) \in E} \mu_{k,r} P(l_r = k')$, where $l_k = k'$ represents starting at keyword k to hit keyword k', $\mu_{k,r} = 1/|\{r : (k, r) \in E\}|$ the transition probability from keyword k to keyword r, and $\beta_k = I_E((k, r))$. Then, $\zeta(j, j') = \sum_{k \in K_j, k' \in K_{j'}} \omega_{k,k'} / (|K_j||K_{j'}|)$ represents the probability that search users (e.g. potential customers) issued with keywords in campaign j can also be reached by campaign j', and $\zeta(j, j') \in [0, 1]$. Define $\gamma(j, j') = [d_j \zeta(j, j') + d_{j'} \zeta(j', j)]/(d_j + d_{j'})$, where d_j and $d_{j'}$ represent the potential query demands of the j th and j'th campaigns, respectively. Then γ represents the ad overlap degree between two campaigns (e.g. in terms of campaign contents).

12.2.3 The Model

In this section, we establish a budget planning model for coupled campaigns in sponsored search auctions. First, suppose the advertiser aims to maximize the total revenue from advertising activities. Let $d_{t,s}$ denote the number of query demands (relevant to an advertiser's promotions in a search market) in region s at time t, and $\theta_{j,t,s}$ campaign j's market share in region s at time t. Then the number of potential query demands that might be obtained by the advertiser in region s at time t is $d_{t,s}\theta_{j,t,s}$. Let $c_{j,t,s}$ denote the (average) click-through rate (CTR) of campaign j in region s at time t, and $v_{j,t}$ the (average) value-per-click (VPC) of campaign j at time t, and $b_{j,t,s}$ the budget segment for campaign j in region s at time t. Then the total revenue for the advertiser can be represented as $\sum_{j=1}^{m} \sum_{s\in S_j} \int_{T_j} e^{-rt}$ $(d_{t,s}\theta_{j,t,s}c_{j,t,s}v_{j,t} - b_{j,t,s})dt$, where e^{-rt} is the discount factor.

Secondly, due to marketing dynamics in sponsored search auctions, an advertiser's market share changes with time. Following Yang et al. (2011), the response function in search markets can be given as $d\theta_{j,t,s}/dt = \rho q u(t,s)\sqrt{1 - \theta_{j,t,s}}$, where ρ is the response constant, δ is the decay constant, and q is the quality score. The advertising effort u represents the effective part of advertising budget b.

Thirdly, let B_{market} denote the overall advertising budget allocated to a given search market. Then the present value of total advertising budgets (or expenditures) with a finite time horizon should not exceed it. That is, $\sum_{j=1}^{m} \sum_{s\in S_j} \int_{T_j} e^{-rt}b_{j,t,s}dt \leq B_{market}$.

Thus, we can calculate the multi-campaign budget planning problem as follows,

$$\max \sum_{j=1}^{m} \sum_{s\in S_j} \int_{T_j} e^{-rt}(d_{t,s}\theta_{j,t,s}c_{j,t,s}v_{j,t} - b_{j,t,s})dt$$

$$\text{s.t.} \sum_{j=1}^{m} \sum_{s\in S_j} \int_{T_j} e^{-rt}b_{j,t,s}dt \leq B_{market} \tag{12.1}$$

$$d\theta_{j,t,s}/dt = \rho q u(t,s)\sqrt{1 - \theta_{j,t,s}}$$

$$b_{j,t,s} \geq 0,$$

where $b_{j,t,s}$ is the control variable, and $\theta_{j,t,s}$ is the state variable.

12.3 The Solution & Properties

In this section, we study some desirable properties of our budget planning model, and provide possible solutions. Note that we focus on a case with two campaigns in this work.

Let us consider that there are two campaigns for an advertiser in a market. First, the objective function of model (12.1) can be written as $\sum_{j=1}^{2} \sum_{s \in S} \int_{0}^{T} e^{-rt} I_{T_j}(t) I_{S_j}(s)$ $(d_{t,s}\theta_{j,t,s} c_{j,t,s} v_{j,t} - b_{j,t,s}) dt$. Secondly, the budget constraint becomes $\sum_{j=1}^{2} \sum_{s \in S} \int_{0}^{T} e^{-rt}$ $I_{T_j}(t) I_{S_j}(s) b_{j,t,s} dt \leq B_{market}$. Thirdly, if the two campaigns are mutually independent, the advertising effort can be given as $u(t, s) = \sum_{j} (b_{j,t,s})^{\alpha_{j,t,s}}$, where $b_{j,t,s}$ represents the budget of campaign j at time t in region s, and $\alpha_{j,t,s}$ denotes the advertising elasticity of campaign j at time t in region s. If there are overlaps in terms of campaign contents between j and j', then the advertising effort is weakened, given as $u(t, s) = \sum_{j} (b_{j,t,s})^{\alpha_{j,t,s}} -$ $\sum_{j} (O(j, j') b_{j,t,s})^{\alpha_{j,t,s}}$, where $O(j, j')$ is the proportion of the allocated budget (for these two campaigns) where the advertising effort is weakened.

The optimal solution is $b_{j,t,s}^{*}$. It represents the optimal budget allocated to campaign j in region s at time t. With the optimal control trajectory of budget, we can also obtain the optimal budget allocated to campaign j in a finite time horizon (e.g. T): $\sum_{s} \int_{0}^{T} e^{-rt} b_{j,t,s}^{*} dt$.

Next, we study some properties and possible solutions of the model. By introducing a Lagrange multiplier λ, we employ the principle of dynamic programming and obtain the optimal feedback advertising decisions b_1^{*} and b_2^{*} that satisfy the following conditions:

$$\alpha_i (I_{T_i}(t) I_{S_i}(s) - O^{\alpha_i})(b_i^{*})^{\alpha_i - 1} = \frac{e^{-rt}(1 + \lambda)}{\rho q \sqrt{1 - \theta_i} \cdot V_{\lambda,\theta}}, \tag{12.2}$$

Then we have,

$$\lambda \left(B_{se} - \sum_{s \in S} \int_{0}^{T} e^{-rt} (I_{T_1}(t) I_{S_1}(s) b_{\lambda,1}^{*}(t, \theta) + I_{T_1}(t) I_{S_2}(s) b_{\lambda,2}^{*}(t, \theta)) dt \right) = 0. \tag{12.3}$$

With an infinite budget, we have $\lambda = 0$ and

$$\sum_{s \in S} \int_{0}^{T} e^{-rt} (I_{T_1}(t) I_{S_1}(s) b_{0,1}^{*}(t, \theta) + I_{T_2}(t) I_{S_2}(s) b_{0,2}^{*}(t, \theta)) dt < B_{market}.$$

Considering the case where the budget is limited, we choose the minimal $\lambda > 0$ so that

$$\sum_{s \in S} \int_{0}^{T} e^{-rt} (I_{T_1}(t) I_{S_1}(s) b_{\lambda,1}^{*}(t, \theta) + I_{T_2}(t) I_{S_2}(s) b_{\lambda,2}^{*}(t, \theta)) dt = B_{market}. \tag{12.4}$$

From the above analysis, we can come to the following theorems.

Theorem 12.1. *If the total budget B_{market} is less than $\sum_{s \in S} \int_{0}^{T} e^{-rt} (I_{T_1}(t) I_{S_1}(s) b_{0,1}^{*} +$ $I_{T_2}(t) I_{S_2}(s) b_{0,2}^{*}) dt$, the optimal budget allocation strategy is:*

$$b_1, b_2 = \arg\min_{b_{\lambda,1}^{*}, b_{\lambda,2}^{*}} \lambda$$

$$\text{s.t.} \quad \sum_{s \in S} \int_0^T e^{-rt}(I_{T_1}(t)I_{S_1}(s)b^*_{\lambda,1}(t,\theta) + I_{T_2}(t)I_{S_2}(s)b^*_{\lambda,2}(t,\theta))dt = B_{market}$$

$$\lambda \geq 0. \tag{12.5}$$

Theorem 12.2. *If $B > \sum_{s \in S} \int_0^T e^{-rt}(I_{T_1}(t)I_{S_1}(s)b^*_{0,1} + I_{T_2}(t)I_{S_2}(s)b^*_{0,2})dt$, the optimal way is to invest $\sum_{s \in S} \int_0^T e^{-rt}(I_{T_1}(t)I_{S_1}(s)b^*_{0,1} + I_{T_2}(t)I_{S_2}(s)b^*_{0,2})dt$ in the search advertising market.*

In reality, if we ignore the ad overlapping degrees (γ) between two campaigns, then the optimal revenue will be diminished because the corresponding advertising effort is weakened. This can be guaranteed by the following theorem.

Corollary 12.1. *Let U^* denote the optimal revenue of the model, and $\bar{U}$ the revenue corresponding to strategies $\bar{b}_1$ and $\bar{b}_2$, where $\bar{b}_1$ and $\bar{b}_2$ are optimal solutions ignoring the overlapping degree in terms of campaign contents between two campaigns, respectively. Then $U^* > \bar{U}$.*

12.4 Experimental Validation

In this section, we design computational experiments to validate the proposed model and properties. We generate experimental datasets from historical advertising logs including operations and effects collected from real-world advertising campaigns of sponsored search auctions. In the following experiments we take a search advertising scenario where two campaigns are assigned the same target regions, and different promotional intervals: one from September 1st to 20th, 2009, another from September 10th to 30th, 2009. Then we can get the ad overlapping degree (e.g. $\gamma = 0.11$) with the algorithm provided in Section 12.3.

12.4.1 The Ad Overlapping Degree

In the first experiment, we aim to prove the influence of the ad overlapping degree (γ) on the optimal budget and corresponding revenue. For this purpose we set $B = 1000$, and compute the optimal budget and corresponding revenue with different settings of ad overlapping degrees. That is, the spatial and temporal overlapping degrees are kept unchanged (as described above), and the ad overlapping degrees are assigned different values (e.g. Case 1: $\gamma = 0.0$, Case 2: $\gamma = 0.1$, Case 3: $\gamma = 0.2$). The change in the optimal budget and corresponding revenue over time are illustrated in Figures 12.1 and 12.2, respectively.

From Figures 12.1 and 12.2, we can see that

(1) As for the case with the higher ad overlapping degree (γ), the optimal budget is lower during the period when the overlapping degree $O > 0$, and is higher when the

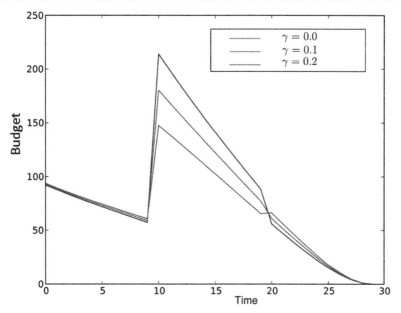

Figure 12.1   The optimal budget over time with different γ.

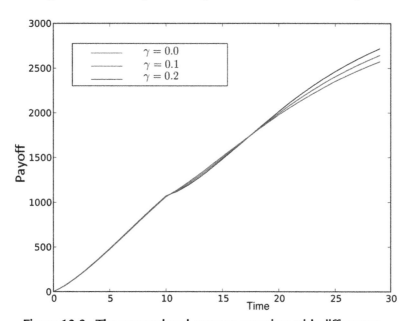

Figure 12.2   The accumulated revenue over time with different γ.

overlapping degree $O = 0$ (e.g. there is no overlapping degree), and vice versa. This phenomenon can be explained by the fact that in the case with higher γ the greater advertising effort is weakened. Thus the optimal budget and corresponding revenue are less (e.g. it is easier to reach the optimal level).

(2) Concerning the accumulated revenue, the case with larger γ is slightly bigger in the initial period, and then the increasing speed becomes lower when the overlapping degree $O > 0$, and vice versa. The reason might be that the case with larger γ allocates more budget when $O = 0$, and thus it gets a bit more revenue at the initial stage; when $O > 0$ both its optimal budget and revenue are lower, thus the increasing speed of accumulated revenue becomes slower; then, during the period from 21th to 30th, again it allocates more budget but the accumulated revenue is kept lower due to previous performance.

12.4.2 The Budgeting Level

The second experiment intends to illustrate the relationship between the optimal budget and corresponding revenue of these two campaigns with different settings of the ad overlapping degree (γ) the same as in the second experiment. We set $B \in [0, 6000]$. The experimental result is illustrated in Figure 12.3.

From Figure 12.3, we can see that

(1) The optimal revenue grows steadily until reaching the cap where the marginal revenue (e.g. the change in additional revenue) is 0, when the total budget increases. In other words, there exists a budgeting cap in the case with unlimited budgets. And the case with larger γ arrives at the budgeting cap earlier, and vice versa.

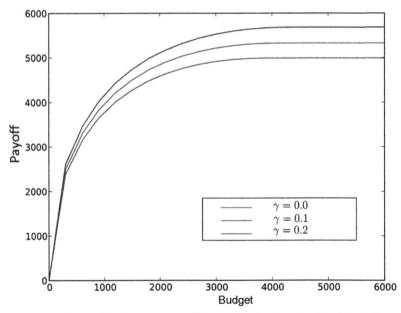

Figure 12.3 The optimal revenue at different budgeting levels with different γ.

(2) The optimal revenue in the case with larger γ is always less (than that of other cases), and vice versa.

12.4.3 The Overlapping Degree

The third experiment concerns if it is better, and how much better it is, to consider the overlapping degree (O) when doing the budget planning for multiple campaigns in a search market. We implement our multi-campaign budget planning approach (MCBP) as provided in Section 12.3 into two strategies: with (MCBP-O) and without (MCBP-I) consideration of the overlapping degree. We choose the AVERAGE strategy as a baseline strategy, which allocates the budget averagely between each campaign and over time. The optimal budget and revenue are illustrated in Figures 12.4 and 12.5, respectively.

From Figures 12.4 and 12.5, we can see that

(1) The optimal (total) budget allocated to these two campaigns is 1847.17, 2459.08, and 3000.00 by these three strategies (e.g. MCBP-O, MCBP-I, and AVERAGE), respectively. And correspondingly, the optimal payoff is 2363.70, 2340.06, and 2270.74, respectively.
(2) The MCBP-O strategy and the MCBP-I strategy can obtain 1.280 and 0.952 payoff per unit budget, respectively. In other words, the payoff per unit budget is increased 34.45% by considering the overlapping degree (O) between campaigns. This can be explained by the fact that the advertising effort is weakened when the overlapping degree between

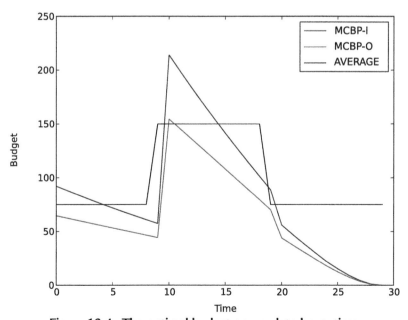

Figure 12.4 The optimal budget accumulated over time.

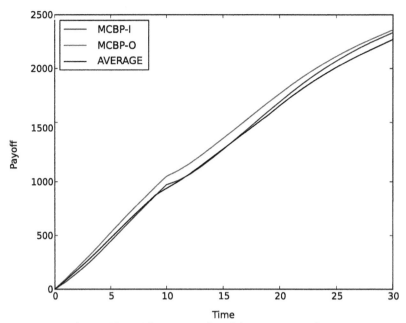

Figure 12.5 The accumulated revenue over time.

campaigns exists (e.g. $O > 0$). The situation might become even worse if the advertiser ignores the overlapping degree between campaigns while making budget planning decisions in sponsored search auctions.

(3)   The AVERAGE strategy can obtain 0.757 payoff per unit budget, and both MCBP-O and MCBP-I outperform the AVERAGE strategy from the view point of payoff per unit budget (69.09% and 25.76%), which illustrates that our multi-campaign budget planning approach can help advertisers to increase the overall payoff to a certain degree.

12.4.4 Management Insights

Our work provides critical managerial insights for advertisers to make budgeting decisions over campaigns in search auctions. First, advertisers usually pay less attention to relationships and cross-effects between their own campaigns in a search market, probably due to the fact that it is not easy to measure and manipulate the overlapping degree. This chapter indicates that the overlapping degree (O) between campaigns has serious effects on optimal budget strategies at the campaign level. Secondly, for an advertiser, the larger the overlapping degree between campaigns, the more the advertising effort is weakened, and thus the optimal revenue is less. Thus it's important for an advertiser to reduce the overlapping degree among campaigns as much as possible, and then correspondingly adjust the optimal budgets over campaigns in order to maximize the expected revenue. Thirdly, our normative findings of multi-campaign budget planning can also provide some valuable insights into other similar decision scenarios of advertising budget allocation, such as across several markets, across different media (or channels).

12.5 Conclusions

In this chapter, we present a multi-campaign budget planning approach using optimal control techniques, under a finite time horizon. Our model takes into account the overlapping degree (e.g. the substitute relationship) between campaigns in sponsored search auctions, with respect to three dimensions: target regions, promotional periods, and campaign contents. We discuss some desirable properties of our model and possible solutions. Computational experimental studies are conducted to evaluate our model and identified properties. Experimental results show that the overlapping degree between campaigns has serious effects on budgeting decisions and advertising performance, and higher overlapping degrees weaken the advertising effort and thus diminish optimal budgets and revenues.

We are in the process of extending our model in the following directions: (a) spatial heterogeneity and relationships to capture spatial effects on advertising decisions and performance; (b) stochastic budget planning strategies in uncertain marketing environments of sponsored search auctions; (c) the complementary relationship between campaigns and their effects on budgeting decisions.

References

Chakrabarty, D., Y. Zhou, R. Lukose. 2007. Budget constrained bidding in keyword auctions and online knapsack problems, Proceedings of the 16th International World Wide Web Conference.

Doyle, P., L. Snell. 1984. Random walks and electrical networks. Mathematical Association of America.

Doyle, P., J. Saunders. 1990. Multiproduct advertising budgeting, Marketing Science Spring, 9:97–113.

Fischer, M., S. Albers, N. Wagner, M. Frie. 2011. Practice prize winner—dynamic marketing budget allocation across countries, Products, and Marketing Activities, Marketing Science, 30(4):568–585.

Interactive Advertising Bureau (IAB), 2011, Internet advertising revenue report. Stable URL: <http://www.iab.net/media/file/IAB-HY-2011-Report-Final.pdf>.

Özlük, Ö., S. Cholette. 2007. Allocating expenditures across keywords in search advertising, Journal of Revenue and Pricing Management, 6(4):347–356.

Tull S., R. Wood, D. Duhan, T. Gillpatrick, R. Robertson, G. Helgeson. 1986. Leveraged decision-making in advertising: the flat maximum principle and its implications, Journal of Marketing Research, 23(1):25–32.

Yang, Y., J. Zhang, B. Liu, D. Zeng. 2011. Optimal Budget Allocation across search advertising markets, Proceedings of the 21st Workshop on Information Technologies and Systems, December 3–4, 2011, 97–102, Shanghai, China.

Yang, Y., J. Zhang, R. Qin, J. Li, F. Wang, Q. Wei. 2012. A budget optimization framework for search advertisements across markets, IEEE Transactions on Systems, Man, and Cybernetics, Part A, 42(5):1141–1151.

CHAPTER 13

Daily Budget Adjustment in Sponsored Search Auctions

13.1 Introduction

In recent years, many researchers have been attracted to explore the optimization for various advertising strategies in sponsored search auctions (Borgs et al., 2007; Rusmevichientong and Williamson, 2006; Yao and Mela, 2009), the design of the auction mechanism (Feldman et al., 2007; Feng, 2008; Gonen and Pavlov, 2007), and equilibrium analysis for the existing mechanism (Varian, 2007). The complexity of the sponsored search auction mechanism, together with the incomplete information feature and user's behavior, leads to the diversity and instability of Nash equilibriums.

In sponsored search auctions, various advertising strategies (including bid determination, keyword portfolio, and budget allocation) influence each other, which raises the complexity of decision-making for advertisers (Ashlagi et al., 2010; Abrams et al., 2007; Chaitanya and Narahari, 2010; Sissors and Baron, 2002). These strategies relevant to different decision factors must be optimized simultaneously to realize the global optimization of promotion activities. Taking the sponsored search auctions as a dynamic game being depicted as an online multi-choice knapsack problem, Zhou et al. (2008) proposed a greedy bidding strategy to guarantee best performance under budget constraints. They declared that their strategy can maximize the advertiser's revenue, while reducing the competitors' revenues (Zhou and Naroditskiy, 2008). With consideration of budget constraints, a two-bid strategy over a set of keywords was developed to gain $1-1/e$ best competition ratio (Feldman et al., 2007, 2008).

Budget adjustment is an important decision for advertisers in order to improve the expected revenue from search promotions. This chapter explores the daily budget adjustment problem and proposes a budget adjustment model. We also provide a feasible solution algorithm. Furthermore, we conduct some experiments to validate the proposed budget adjustment strategy. Experimental results show that the proposed strategy for budget adjustment can help advertisers improve the advertising performance.

Yang and Wang: Budget Constraints and Optimization in Sponsored Search Auctions. http://dx.doi.org/10.1016/B978-0-12-411457-9.00013-6
© 2014 Elsevier Inc. All rights reserved.

The remainder of this chapter is organized as follows. In Section 13.2, we propose a budget adjustment model, and discuss its properties and algorithms. In Section 13.3, we report some experimental results to evaluate our budget adjustment model. Section 13.4 concludes this chapter.

13.2 Real-Time Budget Adjustment

In a temporal slot during a certain promotional period, the advertiser has to adjust the remaining daily budget according to the advertising performance, in order to avoid wasting the budget on ineffective clicks, and reserve the budget for better opportunities in the future. In this section, we propose a real-time budget adjustment model in sponsored search auctions.

The notations used in this chapter are given in Table 13.1.

13.2.1 The Model

Let B denote the daily budget, and c the cost-per-click (CPC). In $[t, t+1]$, the potential clicks and the effective click-through rate (CTR) are $d(t)$ and $p(t)$, respectively. Let $v(t)$ denote the total clicks obtained when allocating the budget $b(t)$ in $[t, t+1]$. Then $v(t) \leq d(t)$ and $b(t) = v(t)c$. Thus, the total effective clicks that can be obtained in $[t, t+1]$ are $v(t)p(t)$.

Based on the above discussions, $\int_0^T v(t)p(t)dt$ represents the total effective clicks that can be obtained in a day, and the corresponding cost is $\int_0^T v(t)cdt$. Suppose the objective of an advertiser is to maximize the total effective clicks under a certain budget constraint. It can be formulated as follows,

$$
\begin{aligned}
\max \ & \int_0^T v(t)p(t)dt \\
\text{s.t.} \ & \int_0^T b(t)dt \leq B \\
& b(t) = v(t)c \\
& v(t) \leq d(t) \\
& B(0) = B \\
& B(T) = 0,
\end{aligned}
$$

(13.1)

Table 13.1 List of notations.

Notation	Definition
B_i	The budget allocated to a temporal slot
c_i	The average cost-per-click of a temporal slot
$p_i(t)$	The effective click-through rate of the time unit $[t, t+1]$ in a temporal slot
$v_i(t)$	Clicks gained in the time unit $[t, t+1]$ of a temporal slot

where $B(0)$ and $B(T)$ represent the remaining budget at time 0 and T, respectively. $B(T) = 0$ implies that the daily budget B is limited.

13.2.2 The Equivalent Model

The model (13.1) is a continuous time adjustment model, where the daily budget can be adjusted an infinite number of times. It is difficult to solve because the strategy space is quite large. In practice, the necessary adjustment time is somewhat finite. Thus, we can transform model (13.1) to its equivalent model with finite adjustment times.

A daily slot can be divided into m temporal intervals $T_1, T_2, \ldots, T_m$, and the corresponding effective click-through rate and the number of potential clicks for the m temporal intervals are $p_1, p_2, \ldots, p_m$ and $d_1, d_2, \ldots, d_m$, respectively. In the j th temporal interval, $j = 1, 2, \ldots, m$, if the allocated budget is b_j, then the obtained clicks are v_j, among which $v_j p_j$ are effective. Thus, the objective function and the budget constraint in model (13.1) become $\sum_{j=1}^{m} v_j p_j$ and $\sum_{j=1}^{m} b_j \leq B$, respectively.

Based the above discussions, model (13.1) is equivalent to the following model,

$$\max \sum_{j=1}^{m} v_j p_j$$
$$\text{s.t.} \sum_{j=1}^{m} b_j \leq B \tag{13.2}$$
$$b_j = v_j c$$
$$v_j \leq d_j, j = 1, 2, \ldots, m.$$

Thus, we can obtain the optimal budget adjustment strategy for model (13.1) by solving model (13.2). The latter can be implemented conveniently in practice.

13.2.3 The Solution Algorithm

In this section, we propose a solution algorithm to solve model (13.2).

From the analysis in the previous section, we can know that the parameters $p_j, j = 1, 2, \ldots$ greatly influence the budget adjustment strategy and thus the revenue in terms of effective clicks. The budget level in the temporal interval with the higher p_j can generate more effective clicks than that with the lower p_j. Thus we present the following algorithm to solve model (13.2).

Algorithm 1.

Step 1: Let $P = \{p_1, p_2, \ldots, p_m\}$, $T = \{T_1, T_2, \ldots, T_m\}$, $J = \emptyset$, and $I = \{1, 2, \ldots, m\}$.

Step 2: Choose the largest p_j in P, and compute $B = B - d_j c$.
Step 3: If $B \geq 0$, then $b_j = d_j c$. Renew P, T, and J with
$P = P \setminus \{p_j\}$, $T = T \setminus \{T_j\}$, $J = J + \{j\}$, and $I = I \setminus \{j\}$, respectively. Then repeat Step 2.
Step 4: If $B < 0$, then $b_j = B - \sum_{k \in J} b_k$ and set $b_i = 0$ for $i \in I$.
Step 5: Return the optimal budget adjustment strategy: set the daily budget at the beginning of temporal interval j as $\sum_{k \leq j} b_k$.

13.3 Experiments

In this section, we conduct some computational experiments to validate the effectiveness of our budget adjustment model and solution algorithm.

13.3.1 Experimental Data

We collected field logs of practical advertising campaigns in two search markets during Sep. 2008 and Aug. 2010. Table 13.2 illustrates the total clicks, CPC, and the daily budget in two search markets (SEAS-1 and SEAS-2). The distributions of the effective CTR in a daily slot for the two search markets are shown in Figure 13.1 and Figure 13.2, respectively.

Table 13.2 Advertising report on a certain day (from two search engines).

	SEAS-1	SEAS-2
Clicks	43	33
CPC	1.32	1.51
Schedule	09:00–18:00	09:00–18:00
Budget	56.79	50

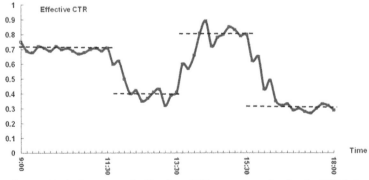

Figure 13.1 Pattern of effective CTR on a certain day in SEAS-1.

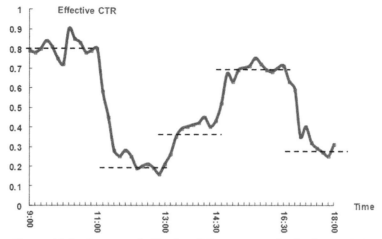

Figure 13.2   Pattern of effective CTR on a certain day in SEAS-2.

13.3.2 Experimental Results

From the distributions of the effective CTR in Figures 13.1 and 13.2, we can see that the effective CTR in either of these two search engines does not change dramatically. In SEAS-1, the effective CTR is mainly around four values; and in SEAS-2, the effective CTR is mainly distributed around five values. Thus, according to the distributions of effective CTR, we divide the promotion schedule in SEAS-1 and SEAS-2 into four and five temporal intervals, respectively. The corresponding effective CTR and clicks are shown in Table 13.3 and Table 13.4.

For comparison purposes, we implement a baseline strategy that is commonly used in practice, called BASE-Fixed. It represents a strategy that keeps the daily budget unchanged during a daily slot.

Comparisons of these two strategies in the two markets in terms of effective clicks are shown in Figures 13.3 and 13.4, and the corresponding detailed expenditures are shown in Figure 13.5 and Figure 13.6.

Table 13.3   Temporal intervals in SEAS-1 and the corresponding effective CTR and clicks.

	SEAS-1
Temporal intervals	$T_1 = [09:00 - 11:30], T_2 = [11:30 - 13:30]$ $T_3 = [13:30 - 16:00], T_4 = [16:00 - 18:00]$
Effective CTR	$p_1 = 0.7, p_2 = 0.4, p_3 = 0.8, p_4 = 0.3$
Clicks	$d_1 = 20, d_2 = 25, d_3 = 12, d_4 = 15$

Table 13.4 **Temporal intervals in SEAS-2 and the corresponding effective CTR and clicks.**

	SEAS-2
Temporal intervals	$T_1' = [09:00 - 11:00]$, $T_2' = [11:00 - 13:00]$, $T_3' = [13:00 - 14:30]$, $T_4' = [14:30 - 16:30]$, $T_5' = [16:30 - 18:00]$
Effective CTR	$p_1' = 0.8, p_2' = 0.2, p_3' = 0.4, p_4' = 0.7, p_5' = 0.3$
Clicks	$d_1' = 18, d_2' = 10, d_3' = 15, d_4' = 12, d_5' = 13$

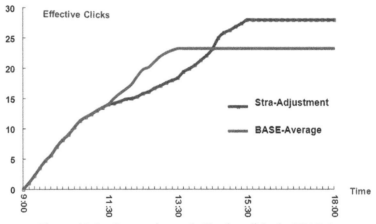

Figure 13.3 **Comparison of effective clicks in SEAS-1.**

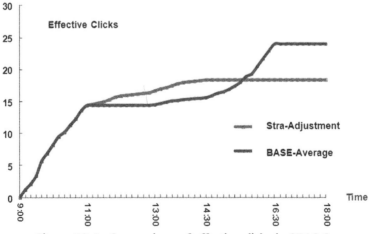

Figure 13.4 **Comparison of effective clicks in SEAS-2.**

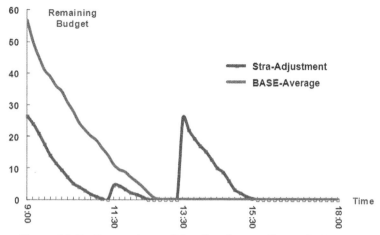

Figure 13.5 Comparison of details of expenditures in SEAS-1.

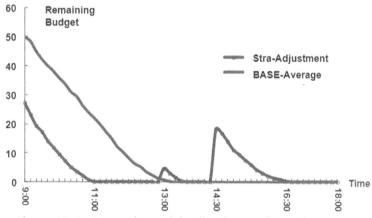

Figure 13.6 Comparison of details of expenditures in SEAS-2.

From Figures 13.3–13.6, we can obtain the following results:

(1) In SEAS-1, the optimal strategy obtained by our budget strategy (Stra-Adjustment) is as follows: set the daily budget as 26.4 at 09:00, and then at 11:30 and 13:30, and the daily budget is adjusted to 30.92 and 56.79, respectively. The corresponding total effective clicks are 28, and in the four temporal intervals the effective clicks are $v_1 = 20$, $v_2 = 11$, $v_3 = 12$, and $v_4 = 0$, respectively.

(2) In SEAS-2, the optimal strategies obtained by our budget strategy (Stra-Adjustment) are as follows: set the daily budget as 27.18 at 09:00, and then at 13:00 and 14:30, and the daily budget is adjusted to 31.71 and 50.00, respectively. The corresponding total effective clicks are 24, and in the five temporal intervals the effective clicks are $v'_1 = 18$, $v'_2 = 0$, $v'_3 = 3$, $v'_4 = 12$, and $v'_5 = 0$, respectively.

(3) With the BASE-Fixed strategy, the daily budget for SEAS-1 and SEAS-2 during 09:00–18:00 is 56.79 and 50, respectively, and the corresponding total effective clicks are 23 and 18, respectively. Moreover, the budget in SEAS-1 will be used up after gaining 20 clicks in T_1 and 23 clicks in T_2, and in SEAS-2 the budget will be used up after gaining 18 clicks in T'_1 and 5 clicks in T'_2.

(4) Our budget strategy (Stra-Adjustment) outperforms the BASE-Fixed strategy (21.7% and 33.3% in SEAS-1 and SEAS-2, respectively).

13.3.3 Experimental Analysis

From the experimental results using these two strategies in the two search markets, we can draw conclusions as follows:

(1) If the advertiser does not adjust the daily budget according to the real-time advertising performance, the budget will be used up too quickly and may result in a lot of ineffective clicks.

(2) The budget adjustment can ensure that the temporal intervals with the high effective CTR have sufficient budget, and thus can greatly increase the effective clicks and reduce the wasting of the budget on ineffective clicks.

13.4 Conclusions

In this chapter, we explore the budget adjustment problem, and present a budget model based on the variation of the effective CTR. We also provide a solution algorithm. With logs of practical search advertising campaigns, we design some computational experiments to validate our model and algorithm. Experimental results show that our strategies can greatly increase the revenue in terms of effective clicks.

References

Abrams, Z., O. Mendelevitch, J.A. Tomlin. 2007. Optimal delivery of sponsored search advertisements subject to budget constraints, EC'07, June 11–15, 2007, San Diego, California, USA.

Ashlagi, I., M. Braverman, A. Hassidim, R. Lavi, M. Tennenholtz. 2010. Position auctions with budgets: Existence and uniqueness.

Borgs, C., J. Chayes, O. Etesami, N. Immorlica, K. Jain, M. Mahdian. 2007. Dynamics of bid optimization in online advertisement auctions. 16th International Conference on World Wide Web, Banff, Alberta, Canada, May 8–12, 2007, 531–540.

Chaitanya, N., Y. Narahari. 2010. Optimal equilibrium bidding strategies for budget constrained bidders in sponsored search auctions, Oper. Res. Int. J.

Feldman, J., S. Muthukrishnan, E. Nikolova, M. Pál. 2008. A truthful mechanism for offline ad slot scheduling. 1st International Symposium on Algorithmic Game Theory, Lecture Notes in Computer Science, 4997:182–193.

Feldman J., S. Muthukrishnan, M. Pál, C. Stein. 2007. Budget optimization in search-based advertising auctions. Proceedings of the 8th ACM Conference on Electronic Commerce, June 11–15, 2007, San Diego, California, USA.

Feng, J. 2008. Research note-optimal mechanism for selling a set of commonly ranked objects. Marketing Science, 27(3):501–512.

Gonen, R., E. Pavlov. 2007. An adaptive sponsored search mechanism delta-gain truthful in valuation, time, and budget. In Proc. Workshop on Internet and Network Economics.

Rusmevichientong, P., D. P. Williamson. 2006. An adaptive algorithm for selecting profitable keywords for search-based advertising services. 7th Association for Computing Machinery (ACM) Conference on Electronic Commerce, June 11–15, 2006, Ann Arbor, Michigan, USA, 260–269.

Sissors, J.Z., R.B. Baron. 2002. Advertising media planning, McGraw-Hill, Chicago.

Varian, H. R. 2007. Position auctions. International Journal of Industrial Organization, 25(6):1163–1178.

Yao, S., C. F. Mela. 2009. Sponsored search auctions: Research opportunities in marketing. Foundations and Trends in Marketing, 3(2):75–126.

Zhou, Y., V. Naroditskiy. 2008. Algorithm for stochastic multiple-choice knapsack problem and application to keywords bidding. 17th International Conference on World Wide Web, April 21–25, 2008, Beijing, China, 1175–1176.

Zhou, Y., D. Chakrabarty, R. Lukose. 2008. Budget constrained bidding in keyword auctions and online knapsack problems, Lecture Notes in Computer Science, 5385:566–576.

CHAPTER 14

Dynamic Budget Adjustment in Sponsored Search Auctions

14.1 Introduction

Recently there has been a rapid growth of sponsored search auctions ("economics meet search"; Jansen and Spink, 2007). In sponsored search auctions, a bidding contract is triggered once an information request is submitted. The high volume of search demands makes the bidding a continuous and infinite process. Once any advertiser amends the search advertisements at any time, ranking results and cost-per-clicks will be changed accordingly. Thus, advertisers have to continuously monitor the market and adjust their advertising strategies to respond to marketing dynamics. Budget is an endogenous factor in auctions (Abrams, 2006; Abrams et al., 2007, 2008; Andelman and Mansour, 2004; Benoit and Krishna, 2001; Bhattacharya et al., 2010) that heavily influences advertising strategies in sponsored search auctions. Advertisers need to make good use of their limited budgets to maximize revenues. In sponsored search auctions, how to rationally allocate the limited budget is a critical issue. An effective advertising budget allocation strategy should be able to dynamically allocate and adjust the advertising budget according to the status of the marketing environment.

Advertisers usually do not have sufficient knowledge and/or time for real-time advertising operations in sponsored search auctions. Thus their budget is usually fixed, being taken as various constraints for other advertising strategies in search advertising practices. On the other hand, there have been some research efforts on the subject of budget allocation over keywords. However, these efforts are not operationally suitable for practical paradigms of sponsored search auctions provided by major search engines (e.g. Google). Most of these studies (Feldman et al., 2007; Muthukrishnan et al., 2010) fall into the category of bidding strategies, rather than budget strategies. By considering the entire lifecycle of search advertising, we have pointed out in Chapter 4 that budget decisions in sponsored search auctions occur at three levels: allocation across search markets, temporal distribution over a series of slots (e.g. by day), and adjustment of the remaining budget (e.g. the daily budget). The objective of this

Yang and Wang: Budget Constraints and Optimization in Sponsored Search Auctions. http://dx.doi.org/10.1016/B978-0-12-411457-9.00014-8
© 2014 Elsevier Inc. All rights reserved.

work is to explore an effective solution for the dynamic adjustment of the daily budget, in order to achieve high-return clicks and avoid less effective clicks.

In this chapter, we formulate the budget adjustment problem as a state-action decision process in the reinforcement learning (RL) framework, as the strategic decision about the advertising budget can be viewed as a special multi-stage dynamic decision problem. Since major state variables in this problem, such as the daily budget, are continuous values, we model advertising decisions of the budget adjustment based on a continuous-time, continuous-state reinforcement learning approach (Doya, 2000). We extend this continuous reinforcement learning (CRL) approach to fit budget decision scenarios in sponsored search auctions, from three perspectives. First, as some sponsored search auction providers (e.g. Google) permit only a limited number of times for daily budget adjustments, we amend CRL to deal with continuous-time, continuous-state, discrete real-time action cases with step functions, where actions can be taken at any time during a given period (e.g. a day). We take into consideration that an advertiser wants to make optimal policies of budget adjustment for *N* intervals and the advertising budget assigned to these *N* intervals is bounded. Secondly, the dynamical systems' behavior of agents is usually given in advance. However, in sponsored search auctions we don't have access to such a system of differential equations in advance. Thus we employ Back Propagation (BP) neural networks with some rules based on sponsored search auction scenarios for system fitting. Thirdly, we provide a novel numeric solution for our CRL-based budget adjustment model. The market utility is defined as discounted total clicks to be obtained during the remaining period of an advertising schedule. Furthermore, we design some experiments to validate and evaluate our strategy of budget adjustment with real-world data from search advertising campaigns. Experimental results illustrate the superiority of our strategy over the two other baseline strategies.

The remainder of this chapter is organized as follows. In Section 14.2, we state the problems and challenges of dynamical budget adjustment in sponsored search auctions. In Section 14.3, we first present our budget adjustment strategy based on continuous reinforcement learning, and then provide a numerical solution for our proposed model. Section 14.4 reports some experimental results to validate our model, through comparing them with two baseline strategies. Section 14.5 concludes this work.

14.2 Problem Statement

In sponsored search auctions an advertiser usually sets a daily budget for each campaign in which a set of keywords are selected and bids for these keywords are assigned. If the daily budget is used up before the end of the advertising schedule, the advertisements will not be shown for the rest of the day, which may result in the loss of potential clicks. On the other hand, if the daily budget is set too high, there is a risk of wasting money on ineffective clicks

Table 14.1 List of notations.

Notation	Definition
d	The daily budget
q	The bid value over keywords of interest
c	The cost-per-click (CPC)
p	The effective click-through rate (CTR)
b	The remaining daily budget during the advertising schedule

without valuable actions expected by advertisers. As the marketing environment of sponsored search auctions changes over time, an effective budget adjustment strategy should enable advertisers to dynamically adjust the daily budget.

The strategic decision concerning the advertising budget can be viewed as a special multi-stage dynamic decision problem with Markov properties (Du et al., 2007; Archak et al., 2010). Decisions at time t depend on both the current marketing state and decisions at time $t - 1$. This makes RL an appropriate technique to model budget adjustment in sponsored search auctions. Nevertheless, there are still several challenges that need to be addressed. First, sponsored search auctions are a continuous process in terms of the high volume of search demands. They demand CRL with flexible components suitable for encoding various states and actions in sponsored search auctions. Secondly, due to the dynamical complexity of sponsored search auctions, it is impossible to get an explicit dynamic system in CRL, e.g. a system of differential equations, in advance. Thirdly, budget constraints make the decision space discontinuous, which hinders the derivation of rewards in the direction of policy to obtain the necessary conditions for optimal actions. The notations used in this chapter are listed in Table 14.1.

14.3 Dynamic Budget Adjustment

14.3.1 The Budget Adjustment Model

Suppose that an advertiser has a daily budget d and bids q for keywords of interest. Let c denote the cost-per-click (CPC), p the effective CTR, and b the remaining daily budget during the advertising schedule. Then, $X = \{x_1, x_2, \ldots\}$ represents a set of environmental states $x = (c, p, b)$ in sponsored search auctions, $U = \{u_1, u_2, \ldots\}$ a set of actions $u = (d, q)$ that the advertiser can take, and a policy μ can be identified with a mapping from the set of states x to the set of actions u, that is, to select advertising actions based on the current state.

The environmental state in sponsored search auctions is time-varying, thus we represent it with differential equations

$$\dot{x}(t) = f(x(t), u(t)),$$

which denotes the changing rate of the environmental state. We don't have access to such a system of differential equations (e.g. f) in advance, thus we employ BP neural networks based on some rules of sponsored search auction scenarios for system fitting.

The number of times for budget adjustment is limited in some search markets such as Google. If an advertiser adjusts the remaining daily budget and bids simultaneously, then $\boldsymbol{u}$ can be given as a step function (e.g. N pieces)

$$\boldsymbol{u}(t) = \begin{cases} \boldsymbol{u}_1, & \text{if } 0 \leq t < t_1 \\ \boldsymbol{u}_2, & \text{if } t_1 \leq t < t_2 \\ \cdots \\ \boldsymbol{u}_N, & \text{if } t_{N-1} \leq t < T. \end{cases}$$

The control variable $\boldsymbol{u}$ consists of $\boldsymbol{u}_1, t_1, \boldsymbol{u}_2, t_2, \ldots, \boldsymbol{u}_N$. In other words, it includes $2N - 1$ parameters in total. The optimal action $\boldsymbol{u}^* = (\boldsymbol{u}_1^*, t_1^*, \boldsymbol{u}_2^*, t_2^*, \ldots, \boldsymbol{u}_N^*)$ characterizes a policy of budget adjustment with maximized profits in terms of effective clicks.

At time t_m, the values of $\boldsymbol{u}_1, t_1, \boldsymbol{u}_2, t_2, \ldots, \boldsymbol{u}_{t_m}, t_m$ are already chosen by the advertiser, leaving only $2N - 1 - 2m$ parameters to determine.

At time t, if action $\boldsymbol{u}(t)$ is taken based on state $\boldsymbol{x}(t)$, then the system state transits to $\boldsymbol{x}(t + \Delta t)$. The cost from t to $t + \Delta t$ can be represented by the advertising expenditure $b(t) - b(t + \Delta t)$, and the advertiser gets

$$\frac{p(t)(b(t) - b(t + \Delta t))}{c(t)}$$

effective clicks. Let $r(t)$ represent the instant reward at time t, when $\Delta t \to 0$,

$$r(t) = r(\boldsymbol{x}(t), \boldsymbol{u}(t)) = -\frac{b'(t)}{c(t)} p(t),$$

which is a continuous function on time t. The current estimate of the value function

$$V(t) = \int_t^T e^{-\frac{s-t}{\tau}} r(\boldsymbol{x}(s), \boldsymbol{u}(s)) \mathrm{d}s,$$

where $\tau \in (0, 1]$ is a discount factor. It represents the total discounted effective clicks from time t to T.

Then, the objective is to find a policy that can maximize the future total discounted reward $V(t)$. We formulate this problem in the reinforcement learning (RL) framework, as follows,

$$\boldsymbol{u}(t) = \underset{\boldsymbol{u} \in U(t)}{\operatorname{argmax}} V(t)$$

$$\text{s.t. } \dot{\boldsymbol{x}}(t) = f(\boldsymbol{x}(t), \boldsymbol{u}(t)) \tag{14.1}$$

$$V(t) = \int_t^T e^{-\frac{s-t}{\tau}} r(\boldsymbol{x}(s), \boldsymbol{u}(s)) \mathrm{d}s,$$

where $U(t)$ is the feasible set of actions, and varies over time.

The peculiar characteristics of model (14.1) compared to other RL models lie in three aspects specific to distinctive features in sponsored search auctions. First, rather than taking f as a determined function, it cannot be given explicitly in advance due to the dynamics of system environments, which are trained from the field data of the collected advertising performance. Secondly, u in model (14.1) is a step function with limited steps, instead of a continuous variable. However, in our case, actions of budget adjustment can be taken at any time during a given period (e.g. a day). Thirdly, the advertising schedule makes our model time-bounded.

14.3.2 The Solution

In this section, we provide a numerical solution for our CRL-based budget adjustment model. First, we deal with the function f. We can extract some prior knowledge about f from the historical field data collected from practical advertising campaigns, and get a better estimation of the function f with the optimal action u^* in the current state. Thus, we train a BP neural network to approximate the function f, and use a reward-based mechanism to make the approximation more and more perfect. In detail, we initialize f arbitrarily, then at time t it can be improved based on the reward at $t - 1$; after many iterations, the approximation function of f will approach the real f. The training and learning processes of f might be time-consuming. However, we can accelerate them with some domain knowledge in sponsored search auctions.

Secondly, we discuss the estimation of $\partial V^*(x)/\partial x$. A universal approximation $V(x; w)$ is used to approximate the total discounted reward function V. Utilizing the Hamilton-Jacobi-Bellman equation, the optimal total reward V^* should satisfy conditions (Doya, 2000)

$$\dot{V}(t) = \frac{1}{\tau}V(t) - r(t)$$

and

$$\frac{1}{\tau}V^*(x(t)) = \max_{u[t,T]}\left[r(x(t), u(t)) + \frac{\partial V^*(x)}{\partial x}f(x(t), u(t))\right].$$

If we define

$$\delta(t) \equiv r(t) - \frac{1}{\tau}V(t) + \dot{V}(t),$$

which is called the TD error. We can denote

$$E(t) \equiv \frac{1}{2}|\delta(t)|^2.$$

Minimizing E with a gradient descent algorithm, we can obtain the optimal reward $V^*(x; w)$, thus $\partial V^*(x)/\partial x$.

Thirdly, we propose a way to find the optimal action u^*. In CRL, the control variable u can be chosen in the whole action space U, so it can be obtained by many kinds of optimization algorithms such as a gradient descent algorithm. However, in the search auction, u can only be a step function with a limited number of times, which makes it extremely difficult to find the solution u^*. This problem is beyond the solving ability of traditional optimization algorithms. With consideration of some characteristics of u, we solve this problem with the following method. Suppose we are at time t, and the last time for adjustment is t_m. That is, actions $u_1^*, \ldots, u_{t_m}^*$ and the real adjustment time $t_1^*, \ldots, t_m^*$ before time t are known for certain, leaving $u_{t_{m+1}}^*, \ldots, u_{t_{N-1}}^*$ and $t_{m+1}^*, \ldots, t_{N-1}^*$ unknown. Thus, at t, we have $2N - 1 - 2m$ parameters to determine, which can be obtained by maximizing

$$r(x(t), u) + \frac{\partial V^*(x)}{\partial x} f(x(t), u).$$

We utilize Q-Learning to find the optimal action u^* that minimizes the temporal difference E during the current day. In detail, we initialize $Q(x, u)$ arbitrarily, where $Q(x, u)$ is the estimated utility function, which tells us how good the action u is in a given state x; then at time $t + 1$, we will choose $Q(x(t + 1), u(t + 1))$ based on the state and action set at time t, i.e.

$$Q(x(t), u(t)) = r(x(t), u(t)) + \gamma \max_{u(t+1)} Q(x(t + 1), u(t + 1)),$$

where $\gamma \in (0, 1)$ is the relative value of delayed vs. immediate rewards. Our aim is to find the action that maximizes Q, which is obviously a recursive process. After a limited number of iterations, we can obtain the optimal action u^* and then the optimal policy μ^*.

The above three steps for solving model (14.1) are carried out at any time t, and influenced by each other. Repeat the three steps from time 0 to T, until the optimal action u^* is obtained ultimately.

14.4 Experimental Evaluation

14.4.1 Data Descriptions

We collected data on field reports and logs for practical search advertising campaigns on an e-commerce website. In sponsored search auctions, a click is an action initiating a visit to a website via a sponsored link, and if a click is an intentional click that has a realistic probability of generating values once the visitor arrives at the website, then it is a *valid click*, otherwise it is *invalid*. In this work, we consider that the generated value will be obtained by some kind of user behavior such as purchase, registration, staying on the landing page for more than 5s, surfing more than two links, bookmarking or downloading relevant pages. We give the concept of effective click-through rate (CTR) as follows.

Definition 14.1 (Effective CTR). Effective CTR is the ratio of valid clicks and total clicks, i.e.

$$\text{Effective CTR} = \frac{\text{valid clicks}}{\text{total clicks}}.$$

Note that the effective CTR is equivalent to the conversion rate if this kind of user behavior is defined as conversion actions by advertisers. Figures 14.1–14.3 illustrate some data characteristics including CPC, effective CTR, and the remaining budget throughout the day,

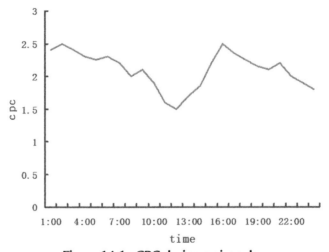

Figure 14.1 CPC during a given day.

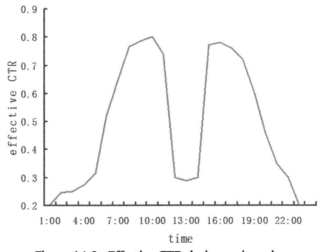

Figure 14.2 Effective CTR during a given day.

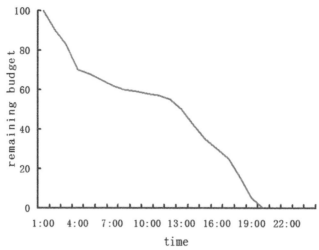

Figure 14.3 **The remaining budget during a given day.**

for instance with a fixed daily budget of $100 and bids of $3.00. These data can be used to initialize and train function f.

14.4.2 Experimental Results

Using experiments, we intend to compare our strategy with two baseline strategies, namely Fixed-Strategy and TwoBid-Strategy. Fixed-strategy is a strategy that considers both the daily budget and bids to be fixed throughout the day. This strategy can be usually seen when the advertisers lack time and knowledge to make advertising decisions. TwoBid-Strategy (Feldman et al., 2007) randomizes bidding between a value q_1 on all keywords, and another value q_2 on all keywords until the budget is exhausted. Note that TwoBid-strategy doesn't consider daily budget adjustment. Our proposed strategy (denoted as DynAdjustment) is capable of both daily budget and bid adjustment.

The comparisons of rewards and policies for these three strategies are shown in Figures 14.4–14.7. From Figure 14.4, we can see our strategy provides the advertiser the highest revenue with 19.681 effective clicks, followed by TwoBid strategy with 16.000 effective clicks. Fixed-strategy has the smaller number of 14.634 effective clicks. Our strategy outperforms these two strategies, with 23.020% and 34.491%, respectively. This can also be explained by the fact that our strategy can avoid wasting the budget on ineffective clicks, as shown in Figure 14.5, through daily budget adjustment (Figure 14.6) and bid adjustment (Figure 14.7).

Both daily budget and bid adjustment can increase advertising revenues for advertisers. We make experiments to validate the effect of these two operations individually, by controlling

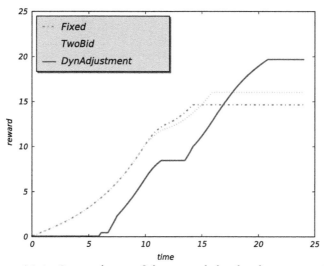

Figure 14.4 Comparisons of the rewards by the three strategies.

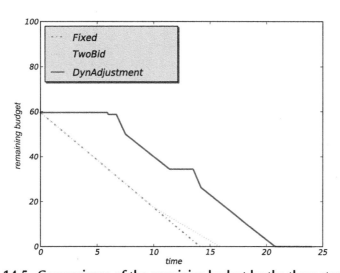

Figure 14.5 Comparisons of the remaining budget by the three strategies.

parameters in our model. Figures 14.8–14.11 depict the comparison results. The revenue in terms of effective clicks from the daily budget and bid adjustment is 17.951 and 16.759, respectively. It is surprising to know that the effect of daily budget adjustment is larger than the effect of bid adjustment in our case. This phenomenon might occur occasionally, which will be interesting to explore empirically in the future.

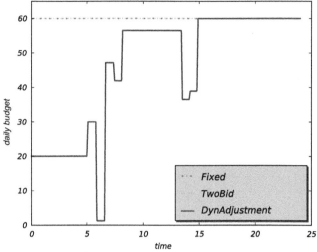

Figure 14.6 Comparisons of the daily budget by the three strategies.

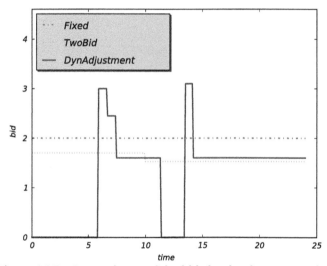

Figure 14.7 Comparisons of the bids by the three strategies.

This chapter provides critical managerial insights for advertisers in sponsored search auctions. On the one hand, advertisers usually take the budget as simple constraints, and put a lot of effort into finding effective operations as defined by various kinds of markets (e.g. sponsored search auctions). This work indicates that a simple strategy for budget adjustment can, to some degree, improve advertising effects in terms of effective clicks. On the other hand, most advertisers pay more attention to bidding strategies in order to either minimize the loss or

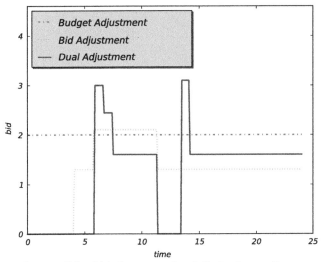

Figure 14.8 Comparisons of the bids between the daily budget adjustment strategy and bid adjustment strategy.

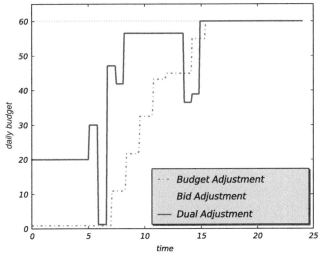

Figure 14.9 Comparisons of the daily budget between the daily budget adjustment strategy and bid adjustment strategy.

maximize advertising performance. In this research, we provide opportunities for advertisers to adjust both the daily budget and bids for keywords of interest. It is proved that dual adjustment of these two factors together could significantly facilitate the journey to advertising goals.

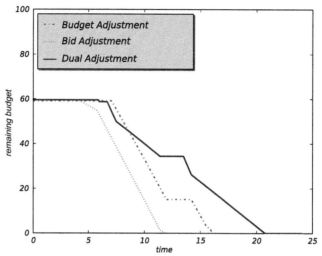

Figure 14.10 Comparisons of the remaining budget between the daily budget adjustment strategy and bid adjustment strategy.

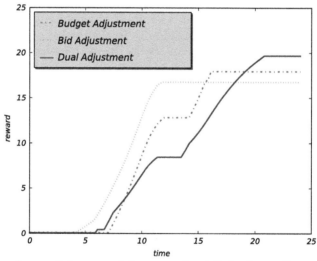

Figure 14.11 Comparisons of the rewards between the daily budget adjustment strategy and bid adjustment strategy.

14.5 Conclusions

In this chapter we propose a CRL-based budget strategy for the daily budget and bid adjustment. By considering the dynamics of search marketing environments, our budget strategy could deal with continuous-time, continuous-state, discrete-real-time-action cases with step functions, where actions can be taken at any time during a given period (e.g. a day). We also provide a numerical solution to our model, and conduct some experiments to validate it with real-world data from practical advertising campaigns. Experimental results illustrate the superiority of our strategy over the two other baseline strategies. This work also reports some preliminary results of dual adjustment of the daily budget and bids.

In ongoing works we intend to explore (a) the theoretical basis and possible empirical evidence for co-optimization of the advertising budget and bids; (b) inter-operation of dynamical budget adjustment across several search markets; and (c) efficient computational algorithms to facilitate online implementations.

References

Abrams, Z. 2006. Revenue maximization when bidders have budgets, In: Proceedings of the 17th Annual ACM-SIAM Symposium on Discrete Algorithm.

Abrams, Z., O. Mendelevitch, J.A. Tomlin. 2007. Optimal delivery of sponsored search advertisements subject to budget constraints, EC'07, June 11–15, 2007, San Diego, California, USA.

Abrams, Z., S.S. Keerthi, O. Mendelevitch, J.A. Tomlin. 2008. Ad delivery with budgeted advertisers: A comprehensive LP approach. Journal of Electronic Commerce Research, 9:16–32.

Andelman, N., Y. Mansour. 2004. Auctions with budget constraints, In: 9th Scandinavian Workshop on Algorithm Theory (SWAT).

Archak, N., V.S. Mirrokni, S. Muthukrishnan. 2010. Budget optimization for online advertising campaigns with carryover effects. In: The 11th ACM SIGECOM International Conference on Electronic Commerce, Harvard.

Benoit, J.P., V. Krishna. 2001. Multiple-object auctions with budget constrained bidders. Review of Economic Studies, 68(1):155–79.

Bhattacharya, S., V. Conitzer, K. Munagala, L.R. Xia. 2010. Incentive compatible budget elicitation in multi-unit auctions, In: Proceedings of SODA 2010, 554–572.

Doya, K. 2000. Reinforcement learning in continuous time and space. Neural Computation, 12(1):215–245.

Du, R., Q. Hu , S. Ai. 2007. Stochastic optimal budget decision for advertising considering uncertain sales responses, European Journal of Operational Research, 183(3):1042–1054.

Feldman J., S. Muthukrishnan, M. Pál, C. Stein. 2007. Budget optimization in search-based advertising auctions. In: Proceedings of the 8th ACM Conference on Electronic Commerce, June 11–15, 2007, San Diego, California, USA.

Jansen, B.J., A. Spink. 2007. Sponsored search: Is money a motivator for providing relevant results? IEEE Computer, 40(8):50–55.

Muthukrishnan, S., M. Pál, Z. Svitkina. 2010. Stochastic models for budget optimization in search-based advertising, Algorithmica, 58(4):1022–1044.

CHAPTER 15

Perspectives: Looking into the Future of Budgeting Strategies in Sponsored Search Auctions

15.1 Research Prospectives

This section is based on empirical discussions about current works and the research vacuum left in the taxonomy of budget optimization, as described in Chapters 2 and 3. It opens a wide scope of interesting and challenging issues on budget constraints and optimization strategies in sponsored search auctions. We will outline some interesting but challenging research perspectives in budget-related issues in sponsored search auctions, covering mechanisms, bidding strategies, keyword strategies, and budget optimization.

15.1.1 With Respect to Auction Mechanism

The limited budget plays a role in the constraints of optimal sponsored search auction mechanisms (Feldman et al., 2008). It leads to the following issues:

- The limited budget is not only a constraint to advertisers, but it also heavily influences the design of optimal mechanisms and possible equilibria in sponsored search auctions. It's valuable to take a dual insight of budget constraints with a balanced consideration of both advertising strategies and optimal mechanism design.
- The Generalized Second Price (GSP) mechanism is widely applied in major search engines. It's still necessary to explore the effect of budget constraints on the GSP mechanism (e.g. whether budget-constrained GSP is optimal and incentive-compatible), properties of budget-constrained equilibriums such as existence, stability, uniqueness, and convergence, and possible adjustments.
- In practical sponsored search auctions, advertisers need to submit bids and their daily budget to the search advertising system, while keeping their evaluation private. It's

Yang and Wang: Budget Constraints and Optimization in Sponsored Search Auctions. http://dx.doi.org/10.1016/B978-0-12-411457-9.00015-X
© 2014 Elsevier Inc. All rights reserved.

valuable to investigate various information structures in sponsored search auctions, and their corresponding equilibria.

15.1.2 With Respect to Advertising Strategy

The budget defines the space for various advertising strategies. In sponsored search auctions, strategies to determine keyword and corresponding bids have attracted considerable attention. However, budget constraints make the existing advertising strategies less effective, and add difficulties in designing optimal strategies for advertisers.

- Current research on the effects of budget constraints on advertising strategies provides some preliminary results, but it's still necessary to consider the design of optimal advertising strategies, properties of equilibria (such as conditions, existence, and uniqueness), and necessary evaluation in terms of efficiency and effectiveness, both theoretically and empirically. These optimal advertising strategies are viewed as the path to achieve the equilibria. It is also interesting to study utility functions open to practical tweaks.
- There are various relationships between keywords such as interaction and overlapping. These can be viewed as markets where different keywords are coupled in the sense that advertising budgets spent in generating clicks for one keyword have an influence on the clicks of other keywords (Shakun, 1965). In the case of a limited budget, more attention should be paid to coupled markets to construct profitable keyword portfolios for search advertisements. After the determination of keyword portfolios, it's necessary to choose appropriate matching options (such as broad matching, exact matching, and phrase matching).
- Some works have appeared on budget-constrained bidding strategies recently, but few consider the effect of the competitors' budgets (Feldman et al., 2007; Zhou et al., 2008; Katona and Sarvary 2010).

15.1.3 With Respect to Budget Optimization

- In traditional optimal advertising models, predatory advertising and informative advertising are distinguished as particular cases that allow an advertisement to have a business-stealing and market size effect (Espinosa and Mariel, 2001). In this sense, sponsored search auctions are not an exception. The two kinds of advertising effects also depend on the lifecycle of the market. In particular, there are a large amount of small (even some emerging) markets in sponsored search auctions. This, together with more players in sponsored search auctions, makes it more difficult to design optimal advertising models.
- The budget is a structural and hierarchical concept in sponsored search auctions, rather than a simple constraint. Thus it's necessary to handle budget decisions in a constructed way, with consideration of the entire lifecycle of search advertisements

(Yang et al., 2012). This implies understanding factors that are related to marketing responses, studying budget decision-making processes and the way to leverage relevant variables (such as the stage in the product lifecycle, market growth rate, and market share), and exploring the underlying theoretical framework and managerial issues for budget optimization in sponsored search auctions.

- There is inherent randomness due to the marketing dynamics (e.g. environmental complexity, turbulence, and uncertainty), heterogeneous responses, and choice of behavior (Prasad and Sethi, 2004). Budget decisions could be influenced by user's perceptions of the marketing environment (Fam and Yang, 2006) and attitudes toward risks and uncertainty (Holthausen and Assmus, 1982; Nguyen, 1985; Yang, 2012a, b). This demands stochastic budget optimization strategies to capture uncertainties of some important factors (e.g. geographic market segments) (Urban, 1975) in sponsored search auctions.

- At the system level, it's crucial to consider advertising competition (Erickson, 1995) to specify and allocate the budget. On the one hand, both consumer attention and the marketing demand are limited (Pruyn and Riezebos, 2001), thus the marginal return of the increased budget never increases (Sasieni, 1971). This implies examining the dynamics of social dilemmas on budget decisions in sponsored search auctions. On the other hand, to search advertisers, the competitors' advertising expenditure will cancel out their own expenditure, and then they will allocate their budget in such a way as to take maximum advantage of each other's mistakes in allocating the advertising budget (Friedman, 1958). Thus, game-theoretical models for advertising budget allocation should be explored to support numerical, analytical, qualitative, and empirical study of budget allocation across several markets, with consideration of different competitive situations (e.g. monopolistic, duopolistic, oligopolistic) (Fruchter and Kalish, 1998) and the customer lifetime value (Venkatesan and Kumar, 2004).

- The advertising budget allocated to search markets should be distributed to maximize the discounted return over a fixed temporal period. On the one hand, it's necessary to consider the trade-off between the short-term benefits of marketing actions such as sales promotions and possible detrimental long-term effects (Sriram and Kalwani, 2007). On the other hand, advertising effects across several markets cannot be neglected in temporal budget allocation and adjustment (Yang et al., 2013). At the campaign level, an effective budget strategy needs to allocate the budget over a series of temporal slots, and adjust according to marketing dynamics. At the keyword level, it is important to adjust the remaining budget adaptively in real time during a temporal slot of advertising campaigns in order to keep valuable expenditure for potential clicks in the future.

15.2 Joint Optimization of Advertising Strategies

For search advertisers, precise and effective advertising strategies are of great challenges for reasons of uncertainty, dynamics, and strong coupling caused by the large amount of search users and search demands. These challenges focus on the following aspects. First, sponsored search auction campaigns have special structures, thus precise strategies should be made at the system level, campaign level, and keyword level according to the advertising objectives and campaign performance. Secondly, advertisers need to make strategies in different time granularities, and the dynamics of sponsored search auctions require self-adapting strategy adjustment and optimization. Thirdly, competitions in sponsored search auction markets require the advertisers to consider the competitors' strategies. Fourthly, sponsored search auction systems have evolved to become complex systems, which means that key factors including budget, bid, keyword portfolio, and target play an influence and tightly connect with one another, but cannot be determined at the same time. Meanwhile, because the sponsored search auctions are real-time, these key factors should be determined dynamically to realize the theoretical optimization. Faced with complicated situations, traditional social science research methods and computational modeling methods cannot satisfy the practical needs of campaign management and decision support across search engines, which brings blindness and risk to advertisers' strategies, and then restricts the development of sponsored search auctions. As a result, it is necessary to undertake joint optimization of advertising strategies to meet the needs of sponsored search auction development and overcome the difficulties faced by advertisers (Yang, 2012b).

In sponsored search auctions, an advertiser has to manipulate a series of interweaving decision-making problems with respect to the budget, keywords, bid values, and targeting. These advertising decisions are dependent on each other, and constrain the strategic space of each other. That means a tiny change in any strategy might influence others' advertising effects and optimality. For example, a good budget allocation strategy cannot lead to optimal advertising effects in a situation with inferior keyword portfolios. Therefore, it demands plenty of research effort in joint optimization, e.g. an integrated framework covering these interweaving strategies forming a closed-loop joint optimal strategy chain.

References

Erickson, Gary M. 1995. Differential game models of advertising competition, European Journal of Operational Research, Elsevier, 83(3):431–438.

Espinosa, M., P. Mariel. 2001. A model of optimal advertising expenditures in a dynamic duopoly, Atlantic Economic Journal, International Atlantic Economic Society, 29(2):135–161.

Fam, K., Z. Yang. 2006. Primary influences of environmental uncertainty on promotions budget allocation and performance: A cross-country study of retail advertisers, Journal of Business Research, 59(2):259–267.

Feldman J., S. Muthukrishnan, M. Pál, C. Stein. 2007. Budget optimization in search-based advertising auctions. Proceedings of the 8th ACM Conference on Electronic Commerce, June 11–15, 2007, San Diego, California, USA.

Feldman, J., S. Muthukrishnan, E. Nikolova, M. Pál. 2008. A truthful mechanism for offline ad slot scheduling, 1st International Symposium on Algorithmic Game Theory, Lecture Notes in Computer Science, 4997:182–193.

Friedman, L. 1958. Game-theory models in the allocation of advertising expenditures, Operations Research, 6(5):699–709.

Fruchter, G. E., S. Kalish. 1998. Dynamic promotional budgeting and media allocation, European Journal of Operational Research, Elsevier, 111(1):15–27.

Holthausen, J., G. Assmus. 1982. Advertising budget allocation under uncertainty, Management Science, 28(5):487–499.

Katona, Z., M. Sarvary. 2010. The race for sponsored links: Bidding patterns for search advertising, Marketing Science, 29(2):199–215.

Dung Nguyen. 1985. An Analysis of optimal advertising under uncertainty, Management Science, 31(5):622–633.

Prasad, A., S. Sethi. 2004. Competitive advertising under uncertainty: A stochastic differential game approach, Journal of Optimization Theory and Applications, 123(1):163–185.

Pruyn, A., R. Riezebos. 2001. Effects of the awareness of social dilemmas on advertising budget-setting: A scenario study, Journal of Economic Psychology, 22(1):43–60.

Sasieni, M. W. 1971. Optimal advertising expenditure. Management Science, Application Series, Part 2, Marketing Management Models, 18(4):64–72.

Shakun, M. F. 1965. Advertising expenditures in coupled markets-a game-theory approach, Management Science, 11(4):42–47.

Sriram, S., M. U. Kalwani. 2007. Optimal advertising and promotion budgets in dynamic markets with brand equity as a mediating variable, Management Science, 53:46–60.

Urban, Glen L. 1975. Allocating Ad Budgets Geographically, Journal of Advertising Research, 15(7):7–19.

Venkatesan, R., V. & Kumar. 2004. A customer lifetime value framework for customer selection and resource allocation strategy, Journal of Marketing, 68:106–125.

Yang, Y., J. Zhang, R. Qin, J. Li, F. Wang, Q. Wei. 2012. A budget optimization framework for search advertisements across markets, IEEE Transactions on Systems, Man, and Cybernetics, Part A, 42(5):1141–1151.

Yang, Y., J. Zhang, R. Qin, J. Li. 2012a. Joint optimization framework of advertising strategies in sponsored search auctions, Working Paper.

Yang, Y., J. Zhang, R. Qin, J. Li. 2012b. A stochastic instantiation of budget optimization framework in sponsored search auctions, Working Paper.

Yang, Y., J. Zhang, R. Qin, J. Li, B. Liu, Z. Liu. 2013. Budget strategy in uncertain environments of search auctions: A preliminary investigation, IEEE Transactions on Services Computing, 6(2):168–176.

Zhou Y., D. Chakrabarty, R. Lukose. 2008. Budget constrained bidding in keyword auctions and online knapsack problems. Proceeding of the 17th International Conference on World Wide Web, Beijing, China, ACM.

Index

Printed and bound by CPI Group (UK) Ltd, Croydon, CR0 4YY

03/10/2024

01040329-0007